Borderless Fashion Practice

Style Discourse: Fashion, Art, and Culture

Series editors: Adam Geczy, University of Sydney, and Vicki Karaminas, Massey University, Wellington, New Zealand

Style Discourse: Fashion, Art, and Culture is a response to the broadening of cultural discourse regarding the crossovers between art, fashion, media, and popular culture. There has been a major shift, noticeable since the new millennium, in which the high-low divide of culture has all but broken down. Instead, we find that the "culture industry," formerly deemed the organ of deception of capitalist consumption, is now a rich haven for discourse and critique. Fashion has a key role to play in this argument. With rare exception, until recently fashion items were relegated to the retail store and the museum, whereas now they are considered valuable components to art collections. While certain fashion has an increasingly critical function once relegated to art, art too is undergoing changes, especially the art that wishes to dissociate from the proclivity toward entertainment that has become the norm for the last thirty years. In short, this series is devoted to documenting the dynamic shifts in aesthetic and material cultures that have developed with extraordinary speed, and which call for new criteria of analysis.

Borderless Fashion Practice

Contemporary Fashion in the Metamodern Age

VANESSA GERRIE

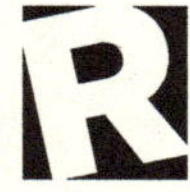

Rutgers University Press

New Brunswick, Camden, and Newark, New Jersey

London and Oxford

Rutgers University Press is a department of Rutgers, The State University of New Jersey, one of the leading public research universities in the nation. By publishing worldwide, it furthers the University's mission of dedication to excellence in teaching, scholarship, research, and clinical care.

Library of Congress Cataloging-in-Publication Data

Names: Gerrie, Vanessa, author.
Title: Borderless fashion practice : contemporary fashion in the metamodern age / Vanessa Gerrie.
Description: New Brunswick : Rutgers University Press, [2023] | Includes bibliographical references and index.
Identifiers: LCCN 2022041200 | ISBN 9781978834361 (paperback) | ISBN 9781978834378 (hardback) | ISBN 9781978834385 (epub) | ISBN 9781978834392 (pdf)
Subjects: LCSH: Fashion design. | Fashion designers.
Classification: LCC TT507 .G465 2023 | DDC 746.9/2—dc23/eng/20221114
LC record available at https://lccn.loc.gov/2022041200

A British Cataloging-in-Publication record for this book is available from the British Library.

References to internet websites (URLs) were accurate at the time of writing. Neither the author nor Rutgers University Press is responsible for URLs that may have expired or changed since the manuscript was prepared.

♾ The paper used in this publication meets the requirements of the American National Standard for Information Sciences—Permanence of Paper for Printed Library Materials, ANSI Z39.48-1992.

rutgersuniversitypress.org

For Mum. My biggest cheerleader, always.

Contents

Illustrations

Borderless Fashion Practice

Introduction

Twenty-first-century fashion practice has become increasingly transdisciplinary, calling into question the very boundaries that define "fashion" in the Western cultural context. In this book I will show, through an analysis of contemporary fashion designers' work, that a practice I have called *borderless fashion* has emerged, which reflects the aesthetics and values of the contemporary zeitgeist. Contemporary fashion practitioners who fall into this category work across disciplines through collaborations and communicate their work in a multitude of ways across various platforms. It is important to note that the borders I refer to are not specifically geographical borders; rather, I use the word to refer to boundaries that have become blurred within the fashion industry in terms of creative methodology; the design principles they stand by; and the way in which "fashion" as an idea is communicated to the consuming audience. Having said this, the designers discussed in this book work globally due to the increasingly democratized access to digital media and information communication technologies.

At the time of writing, the COVID-19 pandemic had begun to take hold globally, affecting every facet of society. In August 2020, Irina Aleksander, a reporter for the *New York Times*, wrote of the death of the fashion industry in the time of a global pandemic that has thrown the systems of how we produce and consume fashion into further microscopic relief.[1] Aleksander mapped the transition of high-profile commercial fashion designer brands away from cyclical production practices and into more, what I would say, project-based *borderless* practices. This includes reducing the amount of yearly seasonal shows they produce as well as a progressive shift further away from creating garments that are situated within the gender binary. Aleksander also analyzed the ways in which designers were presenting and communicating their work to an increasingly scrutinizing and skeptical audience. In the context of people becoming more confined to their homes due to lockdown restrictions globally, consumers and producers of fashion are questioning the mass production of fashion's manufacturing and in turn questioning what fashion is for and how it can be experienced. Borderless fashion manifests in this oscillating space between the physical and digital experience.

On a macro level, this study looks at the ways in which disciplinary boundaries are being ruptured through interdisciplinary practices. Borderless fashion describes practitioners whose work intersects with other creative disciplines and fields, such as art, technology, science, architecture, and graphic design. These designers work collaboratively with practitioners from other disciplines and utilize multidisciplinary design principles themselves. This is in part due to such practitioners often being trained in other creative fields outside of fashion and choosing the field of fashion to present their work. Practitioners are no longer confining themselves to the sole label of "fashion designer"; rather, they are adopting multihyphenated descriptors, or they avoid a label altogether. Their reluctance to label themselves creates a new fertility for fashion practice, one that starts conversations and redefines what fashion practice is and what it can be, expanding its scope as a result. These practices are expanding the definitions of fashion as material object, representation, and experience. As such, this book is driven by the following questions: Why are fashion designers working in this way? And how has the consumer/audience's relationship with fashion, that being the object, representation, and experience, changed?

I chose to use the word "practice" over "design," as I'm not exclusively referring to the specific material design of clothing garments but rather the work that occurs beyond just the physical activity of making products. This refers to the context, ideas, process, communication, and representation of fashion beyond the physical garment, the "total" fashion practice. Thus, the abductive critical textual analysis undertaken in this research is not that of the material garment, block, or silhouette elements of fashion; rather, it is an analysis of the practitioner's overall practice based on the documentation of process, representational output, and communication materials. This implies a shift in the way fashion practitioners are creating, representing, and disseminating their work, which has predominantly been impacted by the use of digital technologies. In other words, this research is concerned with the ways in which fashion practice has ruptured disciplinary borders over the last ten years to move away from the traditional confines of the fixed commercial runway system and into a borderless field of practice. This shift is due to fashion's democratization and its subsequent bleeding across creative disciplines. I have conceptualized the term "borderless fashion" as a way to map and define the rapidly changing phenomena of contemporary fashion.

The fashion practitioners I have used as case studies in this book act as signifiers to a wider community of practitioners disrupting and reinventing the contemporary industry and fashionscape.[2] Virgil Abloh, Aitor Throup, Iris van Herpen, and Eckhaus Latta are established global fashion practitioners who have emerged in this contemporary fashion industry. Although the four practitioners do not look similar in their aesthetic output, they are representative of a plethora of other emerging practitioners who work successfully within the mainstream fashion industry while also occupying a liminal space that spans disciplines. Their output, however, innovates in a way that is visionary, bringing together community, collaborators, mediums, and critical conversations. The late Virgil Abloh's fashion practice converges multiple cultural and disciplinary practices that "trickle across" the fashionscape. Aitor Throup's fashion practice was chosen because of his focus on concept and the primacy of the "idea." Iris van Herpen's practice blurs the boundaries between fashion, science, and technology. Her work is described as wearable art or as "new couture." Van Herpen ruptures the boundaries between body, space, and garment to create work that is conceptual rather than commercial. Eckhaus Latta was chosen because the designers' work is collaborative and spans many commercial outlets. The garments of Eckhaus Latta are genderless, breaking down barriers situated in the gender binary that subverts traditional structures of the fashion system.

As a proposition, fashion is a modernist project that incorporates aspects of the postmodern condition. This book then proposes that fashion in the twenty-first century has evolved into a "metamodern" practice; by this I mean it exhibits a combination of modern and postmodern characteristics, which I extrapolate in the body of this book. This is due to a changed sociocultural consciousness and the democratic development of digital communication technologies. I use the word "democratic" here to describe the action of making something accessible to everyone or a wider group of people through advances in technology. It is important in the context of this book because fashion's democratization has evolved over time because of the invention and dissemination of technologies, both analog and digital, that have progressively given more access to wider audience and consumer groups, therefore influencing the very culture of fashion.

Borderless fashion practice speaks to this democratization, and I argue that this very access has created a conversation between maker and consumer that has changed the way fashion practitioners produce and communicate their work as well as how they define themselves. If this democratization of fashion had not happened, then fashion, rather than filtering down to the masses, could have remained within rarefied spaces and within strict hierarchical structures of class, therefore changing its very cultural production. Along with fashion's democratization, other factors have led to borderless fashion's development, such as the ongoing relationship between fashion and art, fashion's shift into the academy, and the emergence of conceptual fashion. These factors contextualize the development of borderless fashion, and their analysis will make up the first half of this book, which will establish the framework in which to map the four case study chapters.

The fashion industry is a system that generates ideas, content, values, and communication across a global field. Conceptualizing borderless fashion maps the development of fashion practice within the context of this framework. It emphasizes fashion's ability to be situated in the blurry spaces between fiction and reality, transcending and challenging long-held binaries symptomatic of the Western cultural context. As such, the purpose of this book is to propose a new framework in discussing fashion beyond the commodity through the close critical textual analysis of contemporary fashion practices. The application of the theoretical framework of metamodernism is mapped against contemporary developments in the ways in which fashion designers produce and communicate their work and practice, thereby offering an analysis that has not yet been developed beyond the point of speculation.[3] As such, this research offers in-depth analytical case studies of contemporary fashion practitioners' work that reflect the wider sociocultural and economic context, and in doing so supports the conceptualization of borderless fashion. It also highlights the rhizomatic nature of contemporary fashion design practice, which sees its scope and influence go beyond that of just the embodied garment produced within the convoluted commercial fashion system to one of representation. These designers express themselves across disciplines rather than supporting their work through the sole presentation of the main fashion collection event. Borderless fashion practitioners have a more fluid approach to practice without a hierarchy of emphasis on the marketable garment.

The formative moment of this book was a conference called The End of Fashion, held at Massey University, Wellington, in 2016. This conference was based upon the crescendo of contemporary rhetoric surrounding ideas of the so-called end of fashion. This was prompted in part by researcher and forecaster Lidewij Edelkoort's siren call *Anti_Fashion* manifesto, published in 2015, after she spoke on the topic at the Design Indaba conference in Cape Town earlier that year.[4] In this manifesto Edelkoort proclaimed that "the end of fashion as we know it" is here and that the industry has become "a ridiculous and pathetic parody of what it has been."[5] One of her proclamations was that focus on the individual star designer, or the cult of the creator, has become outdated in relation to a creative world that is based on an economy of exchange.[6] She went further, giving a ten-point breakdown on aspects of the industry that need to change, such as education, manufacturing, retail, and marketing. Edelkoort also elaborated on the idea that collaboration between practitioners needs to be more prevalent and that the industry needs to foster altruistic relationships, which she believes contemporary society is hungry for.[7] This would see a move away from the "star designer" system that dominated the 1990s and early 2000s fashionscape, when the likes of John Galliano and Alexander McQueen becoming savant-like figureheads for the industry, even gaining further notoriety beyond fashion into popular culture.

"Fashionscape," as defined by Vicki Karaminas, borrows from the work of Arjun Appadurai by describing and situating the role of digital media in the "global cultural flows" that cross both global and local boundaries.[8] This definition is important to note in the context of this book, as the evolving nature of the contemporary fashionscape is central to the metamodern framework as well as the borderless nature of the designer's practice. A fashionscape is a term for the way that fashion's aesthetic visual imagery makes impressions across the globe, employed by fashion designers in collaboration with image-makers to showcase their collections.[9] A fashionscape can also describe digital media artifacts that are connected with social media technologies such as Instagram and YouTube, which are platforms that have become powerful and accessible formats for "capturing, heightening, and transmitting the energy of collections and ideas around illusion and spectacle."[10]

Building on Karaminas's definition, Patrizia Calefato refers to the idea of fashionscapes as the stratified, hybrid, multiple, and fluid disposition of imageries of the clothed body of our time.[11] Calefato goes on to distinguish these definitions of contemporary fashion from Georg Simmel's classical model of imitation and distinction, from upper to lower classes, and from more recent models of the late twentieth century that were based on the relationship between institutional fashion and subcultures.[12] The mutations of the contemporary fashionscape have also been brought about in the wake of the diffusion of the internet and digital media subsequently blurring boundaries across media.[13] Fashion designers are now multihyphenate practitioners making and communicating their work through various fields. This mutation and blurring of boundaries has also become evident in the dissolution of the idea of identity as it relates to clothing.

The "end of fashion" is a statement that signals finality; however, in Edelkoort's manifesto and in the context of this book it is more of a command for a recontextualization of the meaning of fashion and the way it is produced, communicated, and consumed in this new fashionscape. The "global village," as Marshall McLuhan called it, has seen the blurring of cultural borders because of the effects of electronic media throughout the twentieth century and more progressively (and aggressively) into the digitally dominated culture of today.[14] The proliferation of information and imagery is beamed around the world at an accelerated rate through the widespread use of social media technology such as Instagram. This has enforced the saturation of fashion products, which are ultimately epitomized through "transmedia" celebrities, such as Lady Gaga, who has established a creative collective of stylists, dancers, choreographers, fashion designers, and a business team to manage her public persona and her artistic endeavors.[15] Bloggers and Instagram celebrity "influencers" in the second decade of the twenty-first century have also become the access point of this democratized exposure to fashion. They tell and sell fashion stories across various media, attending exhibitions, "catwalk" shows, and design forums, subsequently sharing these experiences to their vast following.

People all over the world have access to events at the same time they are happening in real life. This means that every six months, when collections from designers are shown on the catwalk at the four main fashion weeks (New York, London, Milan, Paris), the members of the general public are able to see the show from wherever they are behind the flickering blue screen of a smartphone. Due to this, an evolution in the way fashion is communicated has had to occur. Designers have harnessed pluralistic interdisciplinary practices, subsequently becoming both critically and monetarily profitable. One way they have done this is to rethink traditional modes of displaying and presenting fashion by eliminating the body to subsume the garment under the extravagant pageantry of the event (the catwalk).[16]

In turn, the cultural production of fashion has seen a direct alignment with the sociocultural critique of issues relevant to the current zeitgeist. These include diversity, inclusivity, transparent and authentic production, and sustainable design practice, which manifests in what Adam Geczy and Vicki Karaminas have defined as "critical fashion practice."[17] This emphasizes the fact that fashion as a discipline, cultural phenomenon, and basic necessity has great power over how people see each other, the world, and the communities around them. Designers are now creating brands that are experience and concept based, produced to be consumed digitally, which has led to a shift in the fashion system as we know it. Not only is fashion informed by digital technologies, but the very people who create the clothes, the designers, are coming from different fields, such as architecture, industrial design, and fine arts, carrying different sets of creative tools and visions of what defines contemporary fashion. The old guard, with its hierarchies of fashion houses, fashion weeks, editors, and buyers that previously existed in a hermetic space, have become less and less relevant as the consumers of fashion have changed along with their taste and value systems. The end of fashion does not mean that fashion is over; rather, it connotes the beginning of a new era and a necessary acknowledgment of the changing ways in which fashion is created as both a craft and cultural phenomenon, what has instigated this shift, and what it means going forward.[18]

I argue in this book that the decentralization of fashion, the breakdown of disciplinary terrains, and the blurring of Western binaries have directly affected how fashion practitioners work. Chapter 1 maps the theoretical framework of metamodernism and its definition in relation to fashion practice. Chapters 2–5 present the factors that I argue have led up to the development of borderless fashion practice. These include fashion's democratization and entrance into the academy, fashion's disciplinary intersections and predominant relationship with art, and the development of conceptual fashion and its expansion beyond the catwalk. These foundational chapters explore the background and history of borderless fashion practice, looking at the dialogue around fashion's "end," reviewing the nuanced historical narrative of practice that has led fashion practitioners to be working in this specific way, which will then be articulated throughout the case study chapters. The case studies also map the changing way fashion is viewed and communicated with the evolution of the runway catwalk and the emergence of fashion installation that has seen a primacy of the concept and idea occur.

Fashion's entrance into the academy as an important field of practical and philosophical study represents the growing attention given to the field as a rich signifier of sociocultural context. The development of the academic field of fashion studies in the 1990s was a counterreaction to what fashion scholar Elizabeth Wilson calls the "hierarchy of academy" of the previous decades in the twenty-first century.[19] This had deemed fashion a frivolous and shallow commodity because of its association with "feminine" and craft practices, rather than a phenomenon worthy of deeper critical reflection and training within academic systems of education. Chapter 2 maps the entrance of fashion into the academy at the end of the twentieth century and connects fashion to the influence of countercultural movements that emerged in the 1960s and 1970s that instigated contemporary critique of the political and social status quos. We can think of the hippies and punks as the most obvious examples here, and their sartorial choices that connote critical reflections of society at the time of postmodernism. Chapter 2 also describes how fashion became a site of serious study and experimental design practice within the philosophical academy in the form of fashion studies and within practice-based conceptual design schools in the 1990s, represented in spaces such as the Antwerp Royal Academy of Fine Arts.

Beyond fashion's entrance into rarefied spaces of study, it has also become more accessible to a consuming audience economically and culturally by way of digital communication technologies. Chapter 3 examines fashion's democratization as a major factor in contributing toward the development of borderless fashion practice in the twenty-first century. Digital information communication technologies—such as smartphones and the channels of communication used on them, such as Instagram, Facebook, and YouTube—have shifted the way in which people consume fashion. Images of fashion now "trickle across" rather than "trickle down" or "bubble up" from high society to the streets and vice versa. The millennial individual seeks access to the process of making fashion and the ideas that go into its concept, and they are granted such authentic access through a fashion designer's personal social media accounts.

Authenticity has also become a value system, and chapter 3 develops this notion through the mapping of the shift from the service economy to the experience economy for the metamodern individual. This refers to a more holistic system of exchange that focuses on community and the breakdown of societal class barriers of luxury. Audiences can now *experience* fashion, not through buying a garment but through experiential digital engagement. The "end" of fashion is discussed here as a change in cultural consciousness around the consumption of fashion beyond the garment and the opening up of the rigid system by way of digital communication technologies. Borderless fashion's focus on the importance of the conceptual idea and the representational space beyond that of the garment is a direct product of this shift in education and philosophical reflection. No longer is fashion seen as merely a "frivolous" accoutrement to our daily lives: it mirrors the very thoughts of a given society.

Scholarship of this oscillating nature—that is, placing fashion as a medium of its own within an expanded scope—is still growing. Borderless fashion practice sees its earliest manifestations in the collaboration between art and fashion and their experimentations with dress and adornment. Fashion's relationship with art is most notably discussed in Geczy and Karaminas's collaborative body of work. *Fashion and Art* (2012) is an important foundational text on the topic, bringing together scholars who discuss the wide-ranging intersections across disciplines past and present—from conceptual fashion to fashion exhibitions and performance. Similarly, Geczy and Karaminas's *Critical Fashion Practice* (2017) presents in-depth analyses of the work of some of the most important designers from the last three decades. Their work is grounded in criticality: shining a light on fashion by exposing and developing the fact that it has always been more than just clothes. The fashion design practice of Vivienne Westwood, Rick Owens, Rei Kawakubo, and Viktor & Rolf are included in their analyses.

Beyond Geczy and Karaminas, other noted scholarly texts on fashion and art, as stated before, are more centered on the debate as to whether fashion is art or are focused on the collaborations between artists and art movements, and fashion designers and trends, such as Florence Mueller's *Art and Fashion* (2000) and Alice Mackrell's *Art and Fashion* (2005).[20] Peter Wollen's exhibition catalogue *Addressing the Century* (1998) depicts a more theoretical investigation into fashion's and art's similarities and differences and how they have both mutually influenced the culture of the twentieth century in relation to transience and the body.[21] Nancy Troy's *Couture Culture* (2004) is another important text within this context that looks at the fashion designers in the early twentieth century and how they patronized the arts and modeled themselves as artists, with the specific example of Paul Poiret as the first fashion designer to do so.[22] Troy uncovers shared systemic structures between the fashion and art industries of a specific time; this emulates the shared conceptual market structure that the two fields still hold to this day, particularly with regard to the mythology around the sole individual creative genius. Before fashion entered the academy, the field oscillated most prominently with that of art. Chapter 4 discusses how this symbiotic relationship is reflected in the conversations the two creative fields have had over the centuries through collaboration and experimentation.

Fashion has given art access to capital, while art has given fashion cultural cachet. Borderless fashion is a product of this oscillation that has allowed fashion to bleed across multiple creative disciplines. This relationship also represents the ways in which fashion has escaped from the confines of the fixed commercial runway system that has perpetuated fashion as fundamentally a capitalist commodity. Fashion has now entered spaces—such as the art gallery and filmic representations—that subvert this very notion. This not only allows fashion to become more democratically accessible but also offers new methods and channels of creative practice for contemporary fashion practitioners.

The development of fashion as concept is the last factor I have identified as the foundational landscape that has instigated the emergence of borderless fashion practice. *Fashion* as concept refers to the primacy of the idea within contemporary fashion practitioners' work. This stems from the emergence of fashion as a mediator of cultural criticism through its entrance into the academy as well as its increasing presence in curated gallery exhibitions. Chapter 5 reflects on this notion through a discussion of the importance of conceptual frameworks, methods, and stories that connote a connection to cultural context in time and place. Conceptual fashion emerges from the development of conceptual art in the mid-twentieth century; however, it has its own roots in the spectacular fashion shows orchestrated in the 1980s and 1990s by designers such as John Galliano and Alexander McQueen, where the clothes were secondary to the concept of the theatrical performance, affecting audiences' cognitive experience. Designers such as Rei Kawakubo and Issey Miyake are identified here as important agents who subverted the very fundamental purpose of dress. Borderless fashion utilizes concept as a lens for sociocultural critique but also as a process methodology. Fashion has become dislocated from the runway and is now communicated most predominantly through the utilization of installation, changing the very way in which fashion is communicated and consumed.

Throughout these five chapters, metamodernism is used as a theoretical thread that sets the platform and tethers the case studies together to contextualize the hypothetical emergence of borderless fashion practice. Interrogation of the development of metamodernism acts as the theory that motivates the conceptualization of borderless fashion. The "metamodern" is a speculative term, first used by Mas'ud Zavarzadeh in 1975 and then by Timotheus Vermeulen and Robin van den Akker in 2010.[23] Metamodernism takes into consideration globalization and the rise of the internet and digital culture, as well as explaining the breaking of multiple boundaries brought on by these technologies. Described simply, it proposes an oscillation between modern and postmodern principles, breaking down the binary characteristics that used to set them apart throughout the twentieth century.[24] The "meta" alludes to this very in-betweenness, and is a word widely referenced across the fashionscape.

Choosing specific principles that are tracked in definitions of metamodernism, such as collaboration, interdisciplinarity, the collapse of distances (the internet), and multiple subjectivities, I analyzed the practice of each designer to map the designer's work against the theory. This research relied on theory development or theoretical propositions related to the topic of study before the analyses took place.[25] This entailed the establishment of a metamodern toolkit with which to analyze each case study designer. To establish this, I needed to map the metamodern as a viable canonical proposition through tracking fashion's democratization and evolution over the past century and into the millennium.

Through this established theoretical framework toolkit, comparative interpretive case study analyses were conducted to build on the same methods of analysis through alternative examples multiple times.

The four fashion designers who were chosen as case studies for this project each presented a fashion practice that was pluralistic and included projects based around interdisciplinary collaboration that were communicated through exhibitions and installations. These practitioners define this era of the meta through the breakdown of binaries and dissolving of borders. For Virgil Abloh, it was the breakdown of "high" and "low" culture and his training in architecture; for Aitor Throup, it was his process and research-driven practice anchored in the conceptual; for Iris van Herpen, it was her experimentation with materials, form, and space and an intersection with technology and science; and for Eckhaus Latta, it was the designers' community-based practice that dissolves not only disciplinary borders but also gender binaries. Although diverse in creative output, these designers are all successful and prominent within the fashion industry but can also be loosely described as *avant-garde* practitioners. The term "avant-garde" is used here as the practitioners "work both within and outside of mainstream impulses and tastes."[26]

A case study methodology allowed me to track similarities in practices that then highlighted contemporary phenomena in the changing realm of contemporary fashion practice. Unlike an experiment, case study research does not represent a "sample": the goal is to expand and generalize theories (analytical generalizations) rather than extrapolate probabilities. Due to the sustained qualitative analysis of key visual texts, interviews, and articles, the scope of this research allows for only a small number of fashion practitioners to be studied. Because of this, the practitioners are demonstrative of a wider movement toward more sustainable practices that are not solely focused on the commercial fashion system.

Care has been taken since the beginning of this research project to ensure that the chosen practitioners and their creative practices represent the diversity and cross-section of identities practicing in this space. Abductive reasoning was then used to draw patterns and facts from the comparative case study analyses and to explain the similarities that emerged between the four designers. It was chosen due to the qualitative style of analysis, and the process of creative reasoning that was undertaken in this book to construct an argument. Textual analysis was also applied to visual, written, or recorded texts to investigate messages portrayed within media, literature, public press, and personal interviews. Texts included but were not limited to books, photographs, advertisements and campaigns, interviews, films, videos, performances, social media, and historical artifacts—essentially anything that can be *read*. Textual analysis of online profiles, articles, and interviews about and with Virgil Abloh, Aitor Throup, Iris van Herpen, and Eckhaus Latta, which appeared on popular websites, in monographs, and by way of long-form magazine profiles, were important in mapping how the designers talked about and situated their own fashion practices. Alongside these were the multiple online publications on the designers' projects and collections. In building each case study, I collected images from digital archive databases, such as *Vogue Runway*, watched live video presentations and runway performances of collections through online platforms YouTube and Showstudio, and engaged with panel discussions critically analyzing designers' collections and projects, all of which acted as my primary research. Textually, I tracked down press releases for shows and performances, I collected magazines of every profile compiled on the specific designer, and I identified relevant exhibition catalogues.

As such, this project performs an interpretive analysis of the professional work and contextual backgrounds of the four case study subjects. Through the textual analysis of collected data, an interpretation of the given text is produced that is then shaped by the viewer's understanding of the world. Textual analysis involves analyzing a text that exists within a specific context, which also influences how a text is understood. The designers' intentions were also taken into consideration during the course of this research with regard to the specific sociocultural and historical context within which their work was produced. This approach acknowledges that multiple interpretations of the same text may be recognized, understood, and valued when it comes to determining what texts tell us about cultural phenomena occurring within the "sociopolitical, and historical time the text was created."[27]

A poststructuralist worldview was adopted in this research, which acknowledges that different viewpoints exist and interpretation is relative. A poststructuralist worldview expects that multiple variations of understanding from the same text will occur; the point is to find a reasonable interpretation "based on clues found in the text."[28]

Internet-mediated research (IMR) was also central to the methodology and contextual analysis of this book. IMR refers to a range of methods used for the collection of primary and secondary research data.[29] Within the context of this book, primary sources refer to the collection and analysis of "non-reactive" data to "produce novel evidence and research findings."[30] "Secondary data" in the context of IMR refers to information sources like books and journal articles that summarize and back up the existing findings and conclusions.[31] This book assumes a nonreactive approach to IMR, as the research did not include active participants but rather utilized the collection of already existing visual and written texts. This nonreactive or "unobtrusive" method to data collection and textual analysis encompasses two approaches, those of *observation* and *document analysis*.

The first half of this book—chapters 1–5—establishes theoretical framework and context that underpins this study and the factors that have led to the practice of borderless fashion. It lays the groundwork for a critical and contextual analysis of the ways in which fashion designers represent and present their work to consumers. The second half of this book—chapters 6–9—details the four case studies, in which I analyze the history, work, and outputs of each of the four fashion designers: Virgil Abloh, Aitor Throup, Iris van Herpen, and Eckhaus Latta. Each case study is structured through the mapping of metamodern principles against the practitioners' creative or design identity, analyzing first the creative process, then the design methodologies and principles they adhere to in their practice. The chapters then include an analysis of specific projects created by the designers that are mapped against further principles such as interdisciplinary collaboration and hybrid spaces. The main points of analysis within each chapter focus on the contextualization of practice, design process, and communication of their work.

This book identifies a paradigm shift and gives platform to the field of fashion as a creative space that illuminates critical changes in cultural discourse and aesthetics. *Borderless Fashion Practice* concludes with potentially more questions than answers; such is the reality of philosophical enquiry and theoretical reflection as they relate to creative expression. What I hope for this book to do is to highlight the similarities and differences between the diverse practices of fashion designers practicing across the contemporary fashionscape—to propose a conceptual lens through which to view fashion practice as something more, something rich with meaning, beyond that of the commercial fashion system. This lens can be used beyond the pages of this book as means to delocalize definitions of fashion. Fashion practice has become increasingly borderless and pluralistic in this contemporary metamodern era, calling into question the very boundaries that define it. The development of this conceptual framework and analysis of contemporary fashion practices brings us to the understanding that consumers are interacting with the cultural production of fashion beyond that of the physical garment. Digital communities have established, creative methodologies have reconstructed, and the boundaries demarcating disciplinary and material fields have started to dissolve. The consumer and audience value systems have changed, and creative fashion practice has also expanded in tandem to reflect this.

1

On Metamodernism

Establishing the cultural theoretical paradigms that led up to the manifestation of borderless fashion practice maps the emergence of new developments in fashion and highlights new factors that support a contemporary paradigm shift. Following the canons of modernism and postmodernism, we see fashion take on different roles and representations in the twenty-first century, predominantly due to the development of digital technologies and the way in which information is disseminated. What emerges from these uniquely twenty-first-century developments is the divergent concept or theory of "metamodernism," a term that describes the current Western cultural context of current affairs and aesthetics. Timotheus Vermeulen and Robin van den Akker argue that "metamodernism should be situated epistemologically with (post) modernism, ontologically between (post) modernism, and historically beyond (post) modernism."[1] I will contextualize the development of borderless fashion practices using this theoretical framework.

Due to its contemporaneity, however, this framework is more of a rhizomatic theorization than a linear one and will be what threads the case studies of this book together. This speaks to Gilles Deleuze and Félix Guattari's philosophy of the rhizome, theorized in their *Capitalism and Schizophrenia* project (1972 and 1980), which references the botanical rhizome and the multiplicity of its roots.[2] In its opposition to a linear narrative of history and culture in which there is a beginning and an end, rhizomatic theorizing looks at history and culture as a map and uses a fluid approach to research in response to the ever-changing contemporary nature of the topic at hand. This framework helps consider the impact and meaning of fashion beyond its physical utility, discussing fashion as an idea and a concept created in a context. Borderless fashion relates to a school of thought that centers what Geczy and Karaminas call the "metaphysics of clothing."[3] I map the case studies against theorizations of metamodernism, as the practitioners whom I have included in this study have a level of "conceptual functionality" that derives from an intention to expand or disrupt the defining borders of fashion.

The case studies I include, although from practitioners diverse in creative output, are all within the realm of what I define as *borderless fashion practice*: fashion that is at the nexus of interdisciplinary creative practice and is successful both commercially and noncommercially. Concept and collaboration with practitioners from other fields is the cornerstone of borderless fashion practice, not just as a commercial gimmick but also as a fundamental creative process. Fashion installation, interactive performances or immersive presentations, and digital film and editorial are the dominant ways in which these practitioners are communicating their work. Accessible experiences that not only sell an aura and idea of a brand but also create a community around the brand are some of the ways in which these fashion practices manifest. The commercial success of these selected practitioners has most often come after an initial cult following. Their brands have become multiplatform experimental concepts as the practitioner has become a multifaceted creative agent defying singular categorization.

The metamodern, as a theoretical proposition and in line with the theme of blurring borders, can be seen as a collapsing of the polarization of the modern and the postmodern. Critic Stephen Knudsen has recognized that postmodern thought sees utopian ideas of modernism suspicious but believes in our lived experience as "there is much of modernism that the world cannot detach from."[4] He claims that the world he views now is one that does not need the irony and hyperbolic detachment of postmodernism; artistic work can still be meaningful and concrete at the same time it is critical.[5] Rather, there is an oscillation between modernist and postmodernist attributes to the aesthetic culture and practice of our time. Romantic visions of the future now come in the form of sustainable communities, access, and inclusivity through the design of our societies.

As Marcia Morgado states in her 2014 essay on post-postmodernism in fashion, a new body of theoretical work proposes that the postmodern era in culture is waning and that "the conditions that characterized postmodernism are giving way to new circumstances, and that a new cultural ethos is replacing the post-modern condition or is coming to occupy a place within or beside it."[6] New terms that have emerged in the twenty-first century by various theorists to describe this new ethos or paradigm range from "hypermodernism," "altermodernism," "digimodernism," and "metamodernism."[7] What they have in common is a lack of reference to fashion as an important signifier of a changing aesthetic cultural paradigm except for, as Morgado points out, a metaphoric reference by

Modernism	Postmodernism	Metamodernism
Linear historical "progress"	The end of history	After the "end"
Construction	Deconstruction	Reconstruction
Individual creator	Collectives and subcultures	Collaboration
Romanticism	Cynicism	Optimism/Neo-romanticism
Singularity	Plurality	Interdisciplinarity
Utopia	Dystopia	Meta-utopia

TABLE 1.1 Theoretical principal taxonomy. (Created by Vanessa Gerrie, July 2018.)

Lipovetsky where he describes "fashion-like" characteristics such as rapid obsolescence, seduction, and superficiality that he believes comes along with the hyperconsumption of "hypermodern" times.[8]

With the object of study of this book being specific contemporary fashion designers' recent projects and practices and the new ways in which they are redefining the very boundaries of what fashion is, the theory relies on perhaps a more nuanced analysis of the current times that is more applicable to the field and culture of fashion. Although there has been limited discussion of fashion in relation to the theory of metamodernism, the definitions developed offer relevant insight into the changes that are occurring within an increasingly pluralistic commercial fashionscape. Table 1.1 presents a classification I developed through the practice of taxonomy that maps the principal characteristics found in modernism, postmodernism, and metamodernism based on popular readings of the aesthetic theories of the paradigms. The creation of this chart helps in referencing characteristics found through the conceptual and visual output of contemporary fashion practitioners. By framing the work of borderless fashion practitioners within the metamodern philosophical framework, it acknowledges and interrogates the context in which these practices have emerged. In the selection of characteristics, I chose those most popularly discussed in key texts and analyses from the modern and postmodern canons and then collected common characteristics described in theorizations of the metamodern in relation to cultural aesthetics.

Julianne Pederson speaks directly about fashion's "decentralization" beyond its geographic centers as well as beyond the ideologies of the past.[9] Speaking in reference to the rise of digital bloggers and influencers at the end of the first decade of the 2000s, Pederson acknowledges "the culture of participation in style communications and fashion representation has demonstrated that the division between author and consumer has irreversibly blurred."[10] Consumers and audiences have become authors, directly affecting the way in which popular practitioners produce and communicate their work. Fashion centers have become mobile and digitalized, as technology has enabled greater and wider access to information. A breakdown of multiple binaries and power dynamics has occurred due to this democratization through digital media. As Pederson continues, "it situates itself and us between places and pockets in time, geography, states of mind, pretention, reality, hyperreality, and the individual and collective expressions of beliefs."[11] Breakdown in binaries such as those between physical and digital realities, truth and illusion, gendered bodies, and culture and nature all reflect upon this movement to a more fluid and rhizomatic creative output in regard to fashion. The postmodern "meta-narrative has shifted from one of linear organisation to one of multiplicities" and different configurations of understanding or reading of "the same text, images, sounds and feelings built from the foundations of such authored materials."[12]

Pederson also adds that as practitioners in the context of metamodernism, we "have all become poachers, expropriators and repeaters of previously indulged ideation."[13] There is an acknowledgment of the idea that nothing is truly original and that newness within this context may be nonexistent, both materially and contextually. Rather, within the context of the metamodern, creative practice reconstructs the fractures of postmodernism, predominantly through interdisciplinary collaboration and a connection with the consuming audience/viewer that has inverted the power dynamic previously in place in the fashion system. As Pederson confides, "the designer's role in the inversion of power from a trickle-down model into a trickle-up model is more subversive than exploitative at first impression."[14] The fashion design practitioners and authors of fashion product, imagery, text, and code have embraced the changing of the guards and the breakdown of the hierarchical fashion system. The oscillation of power between consumer and author has become a mutually beneficial relationship, as practitioners take on a level of "authenticity" in direct conversation with the consumers. They do so through a connection with authentic and transparent design methodologies in which the process of creation is often unveiled through film, photography, and social media behind-the-scenes brand content. Film, installation, and social media content is utilized as an accessible connection to the audience, allowing fluid meaning making regarding fashion's cultural production. Fashion's material culture, in the form of not just product but imagery and experience, acts as a mirror that helps us better understand the immaterial values in a societal context.

Similarly, Daniel P. Görtz talks about the nomenclature as a marriage between two worlds rather than a cultural war between modernism and postmodernism.[15] He discusses this in relation to the value structures that condition these movements from a societal perspective. Modernism was defined through philosophical thought that valued the progress of scientific discovery and the ideal "rationality of man" or the "dignity of humanity." As it progressed and spread throughout the world, mainly in the West, this progress ultimately led to rapid inequality, alienation, and unsustainable growth linked to colonization and industrialization. Postmodernity was a project of critique of these occurrences in modernity, challenging the idea of universal truths and objective realities.

Skepticism, irony, and a rejection of authoritarian single truths and styles represent the postmodern, collapsing boundaries between mass and high culture.

The prefix "meta" is derived from the Greek *metaxis*, used to describe the condition of "in-betweenness."[16] It is referred to in Plato's ancient text *Symposium*, where metaxy is defined through the representation of the character Diotima as the "in-between" or "middle-ground" or even mediator between the gods and mankind.[17] Metaxis is described as the dynamic space between two separate things "where mediation keeps the universe together."[18] "Meta" therefore refers to that which is with, between, or beyond. Theorists state that while modernism expressed utopic syntaxis (complex) and postmodernism expresses itself by dystopian parataxis (short, snappy), the metamodern is expressed by atopic metaxis (Plato's "in-between"), *atopos* being the Greek word for a place and not a place or "a territory without boundaries, a position without parameters."[19]

In an essay on contemporary atopia and aesthetics, Yves Millet argues that "atopia highlights the fact that rather than viewing current artistic activities as searches for homogenous identity, we need to view them as belonging to plural communities of practices offering modal and qualitative distinctions."[20] Rather than applying this theory of the atopic solely to identity and culture (things that in the current zeitgeist are important to define and uplift and not homogenize, appropriate, or blur), I apply it to the medium and fields in which contemporary practitioners work *in* and *with*. The hybridization of practice within the fashion industry has instigated a shift of foundations and a blurring of the boundaries between them, which can be related to the wider movements of transdisciplinary design within design education and fashion's inclusion in philosophical academic study. Communities and collaborations have become the core of contemporary fashion practice, as well as a search for authenticity in the way that fashion is produced and communicated. Within the context of globalization there is a constant cycle of appropriation, borrowing, and recycling, particularly in the realm of fashion. New technologies have amplified and sped up the circulation of images and information democratizing fashion.[21] With this in mind, we can look at the internet as a metamodern atopia or a meta-utopia. The internet is a sphere without boundaries in which consumers and users are handed agency in driving how we as a society consume and interact and has undeniably changed how fashion practitioners make, what they create, and how they communicate it.

Much like that of Morgado's proposition for a post-postmodern theorization in her paper "Fashion Phenomena and the Post-postmodern Condition," this study is speculative by nature.[22] Through the case study analyses of contemporary designers' creative practice over the last fifteen years and the reactions of industry critics, editors, and buyers as well as consumers, I will theorize how this could reflect a new metamodern condition in fashion, using definitions developed by Vermeulen and van den Akker as well as some definitions offered by Abramson and Morgado. With the centering of fashion as the nexus of multiple other creative disciplines, I will dissect the work of some of the most influential fashion practitioners from within the current zeitgeist who are experimenting with the all-encompassing question: What is fashion?

A metamodern proposition for the borderless state of contemporary fashion practice sees an oscillation or a negotiation of the modern and the postmodern. As Vermeulen and van den Akker state in their manifesto, the metamodern "oscillates between a modern enthusiasm and a postmodern irony, between hope and melancholy, between naïveté and knowingness, empathy and apathy, unity and plurality, totality and fragmentation, purity and ambiguity."[23] The metamodern mentality embraces a multitude of subjectivities, and whereas postmodernism emphasized a compartmentalizing of the self (race, gender, and sexuality), metamodernism embraces the ability to occupy and share these subjectivities, and while these distinctions are important, how they develop, intersect, and interact will in turn help form collective and individual identities.[24] The metamodern "embraces the paradoxical," merging modernism's emphasis on universality and postmodernism's belief in contingency.[25] Although the general consensus is that postmodernism has come to an end as the twenty-first century progresses, metamodernism acknowledges that some tendencies of postmodernity linger on in contemporary culture; hence, the "in-between" and referential nature of the framework.

Under Vermeulen and van den Akker's theorization, the metamodern has neo-romantic tendencies. Vermeulen and van den Akker suggest that artists in the twenty-first century are no longer representing a postmodern world articulated by "illusion, spectacle, simulacrum, and irony."[26] Rather, practitioners defined as metamodern are creating a new desire to embrace forward-thinking hopefulness about the contemporary world, which negates the postmodern characteristic of presenting doubt about reality.[27]

Philosopher Seth Abramson wrote that the main principles of metamodernism are centered on the idea of reconstruction instead of deconstruction.[28] Within the context of a fashion designer or practitioner, this can refer to the idea of not being solely defined by one description or label, as well as the literal construction of garments. More than this, reconstruction as a metamodern principle can encompass Iris van Herpen's new materialism or Virgil Abloh's hybridic design identity. Practitioners come to the field of fashion from many different entry points: in the case of Aitor Throup, it was his interest in product design, functionality, and conceptuality; for Virgil Abloh, it was from the perspectives of architecture, art history, and youth culture; for Iris van Herpen, it was her examination of alternative materials situated her at the intersection of fashion, art, and technology; and for Eckhaus Latta, it was a community-driven art school motivation.

In 2015, Abramson presented ten basic principles of metamodernism as an attempt to define this new paradigmatic lens in which to look at contemporary culture. These principles consist of a negotiation between modernism and postmodernism; dialogue over dialectics; paradox; juxtaposition; the collapse of distances; multiple subjectivities (design identity); collaboration; simultaneity and generative ambiguity; an optimistic response to tragedy by a return to "meta-narratives"; and interdisciplinarity.[29]

Recent developments in the contemporary fashionscape are indicative of this cultural paradigm shift. Zavarzadeh first wrote of the metamodern in 1975 in reference to literary trends and styles that he acknowledged had been emerging at the time in American literary narratives, breaking from what had been defined as postmodern literature.[30] Zavarzadeh says that "metamodernism is a structure of feeling that emerges from, and reacts to, the postmodern as much as it is a cultural logic that corresponds to today's stage of global capitalism."[31] In the context of the 1970s, when Zavarzadeh wrote his paper, the world had become a hypervisible spectacle in which the transgressive side of human existence was finally on display for everyone to see, predominantly in the form of television. The Vietnam War was the first war to have direct footage sent into the living rooms of civilians back home, making it what *New Yorker* staff writer Michael Arlen called in 1966 "the first living room war."[32] This access and visibility jolted people into consciousness of the atrocities happening beyond their realm of existence, while at the same time a process of desensitization occurred through the smaller-than-life television simulacra. Through the latter half of the twentieth century, television shows that covered fashion—such as the Canadian *Fashion File*, hosted by writer and critic Tim Blanks—contributed to fashion's democratization. MTV also played a part in this with its launch in the early 1980s. The creation of the music video manifested a convergence of music, fashion, and art, making subcultural style popular.

The age of television has since morphed into the age of the internet, and with that transformed the way in which we experience the world and how we communicate with one another. Fashion in the twenty-first century is created and communicated specifically for consumption via the internet. The internet has globalized access to fashion, particularly through the social media conglomerate Instagram. Communication and marketing campaigns are now produced specifically for the platform, and authenticity in terms of ethos and output is a top priority. Zavarzadeh commented on the burgeoning technological progress, stating, "We seem to be swallowed by a technetronic reality which defies human moral understanding and obeys machine-generated guidelines."[33] In a twenty-first-century world of "fake news" and "post-truth" politics, this is a relevant sentiment.[34] Like most cultural paradigms, the metamodern can be said to have emerged in response to political, environmental, and economic upheavals of the late twentieth century, just like how the consciousness of postmodernism was intrinsically linked to the social issues of the time, such as the women's and civil rights movements.[35]

Another theorist working in this field, Alexandra Dumitrescu, defines "metamodernism" as "a paradigm whose dominant is the ethical, associated with a search for authenticity and for defining the roots of being in ways that allow the fragmented self to integrate in new configurations of meaning."[36] Her doctoral thesis (completed in 2014) focused on the shift from postmodernism to metamodernism and how that has been reflected in literature with a focus on notions of the self and the ongoing search for authenticity.[37] Authenticity is being sought through the creative practice of fashion practitioners, particularly in the form of collaborative projects, which encourages wider dialogue with communities. Critical and conscious practices also reinforce this idea; fashion with meaning and purpose behind it is an important notion for a business stricken with overproduction and hyperspectacularity. Negotiating this authenticity within this globalized technetronic fashionscape is reflected in borderless fashion practices, which in part can be defined by the framework of metamodernism.

2

Fashion in the Academy

Borderless fashion practice is interdisciplinary by nature and calls for a methodological approach that is also interdisciplinary within its scholarship. Fashion studies as a stand-alone field has absorbed and integrated these other methodological approaches prompted by fashion's relevance and engagement with a range of debates that include identity, the body, gender, and appearance. What has also fed into the development between fields, and what is particularly relevant to my research, is the convergence of practices of fine arts and design academies. In the university domain, this meant the evolution of fashion studies. These developments lay the groundwork for situating fashion's emergence as a form of disciplinary practice in the twenty-first century. Cultural scholars such as Christopher Breward, who wrote *The Culture of Fashion* (1995), a seminal academic text in the field, has dominated discussions around this development. Breward discusses a cultural studies approach to the interpretation of fashion versus the entrenched object-based approach that had dominated studies of dress and fashion until the 1990s.[1] The development of journals, particularly Steele's *Fashion Theory*, which was launched in 1997, has been integral in the theoretical study of fashion, opening up conversations that discuss fashion not just as material history but as an individual field of metaphysical inquiry and cultural phenomenon in and of itself.

I argue that borderless fashion design has developed as a natural progression like that of any creative field. Fashion has hit a point of *pluralism*, much like that identified by Arthur Danto in reference to the art world of the 1980s and 1990s.[2] Pluralism in the context of postmodern art philosophy refers to the multiplicity of reality. Within the context of art practice, this means a field that is "diversified, split, and factionalised," as art historian Rosalind Krauss claimed when discussing the nature of art practice in the 1970s.[3] The art of that time—expressed in video, performance, installation, and abstraction, to name but a few forms that were grounded in conceptual frameworks—reflected on the sociocultural conditions of the moment. Krauss also stated that during this period art's "energy does not seem to flow through a single channel," but rather through a dispersal into "multiple options now open to individual choice or will, whereas before these things were closed off through a restrictive notion of historical style."[4] Pluralism in a wider context is a social construct that allows the ability to maintain individual identity within a broader cultural context, the acknowledgment that society is made up of a multitude of identities and expressions.

Pluralism with regard to borderless fashion reflects upon this philosophy in the same way it was applied to the artist's practice of postmodernism as outlined by Krauss. Designers are now moving beyond the runway and even beyond the "product," working collaboratively across disciplines and mediums to create sustainable project-based practices that reflect upon wider sociocultural conversations. A move away from the strict commercial seasonal runway collections and a move toward project-based fashion production and collaborations are at the heart of this claim.

Situating the Field of Research

The scope of this research is situated within the multimethodological field of fashion studies that has emerged as a valid mode of research since the 1990s. Fashion studies has been an important development for the advancement of fashion research scholarship and indeed fashion practice. Fashion studies as an emerging field is a space that brings together sociologists, anthropologists, and art and cultural historians, as well as scholars and practitioners from disciplines such as design, technology, business, and marketing whose subject of study is fashion. As such, fashion studies is made up of a cross section of methods of inquiry and modes of practice and has become an independent academic field, specifically within the last twenty-five years, gaining more confidence as a field of inquiry with its own disciplinary departments. This is evident in the emergence of the Centre for Fashion Studies at Stockholm University, which was funded by a grant from the Swedish multinational retail giant H&M (Hennes and Mauritz), and the Fashion Studies Master's Program at Parsons, the New School for Design in New York City. From the 1990s onward, in academic institutions such as the Courtauld Institute of Art in London and the Fashion Institute of New York, fashion studies also became its own field of inquiry, instigated by the likes of Lou Taylor, Elizabeth Wilson, Valerie Steele, and Christopher Breward, with their work defining the field fashion studies. As Breward claims, the development of art historical thinking shifted in the 1970s from concerns of "authorship and appreciation of connoisseurly value" to prioritizing social and political contexts by drawing on ideas from "Marxism, feminism, psychoanalysis and structuralism or semiotics."[5] These ideas and contexts led to more prominent debates concerning "social identity, the body, gender and appearance or representation," issues that take center stage in the definition of fashion.[6] This way of thinking was emulated in the shifting attitudes to art practice at the time, what we have come to call postmodernism.

Fashion's shift into academic fields of study has instigated the emergence of borderless fashion as it has opened the scope for fashion to be taken into consideration as a valid area of academic study and has therefore expanded definitions of what fashion is. Fashion studies, as we know it today, is a combination or an intersection of methodologies: "It is an interdisciplinary field where certain concerns and methods have converged. The usefulness of this convergence is that it can enable us to understand cultural phenomena and social relationships that were not accessible through other disciplines, thus enriching our knowledge of an object category (fashion) that has clearly always played a central role in cultural/social processes."[7] In 2015, Lidewij Edelkoort extended this idea of a more borderless education for fashion practitioners with the creation of the hybrid design studies course at the Parsons School of Design. The intention was to break or loosen up disciplinary boundaries between visual arts, performing arts, music, architecture, and design but also to explore how education could better reflect the changing way people think and work. Creative disciplines often have similar methodologies, and the emergence of hybrid design studies breaks down the set boundaries between these disciplines. Edelkoort says that she "believe[s] that the really great things happening in culture today are already a mixture of several visionary and aesthetic movements together with technological knowledge."[8] Creative education is becoming less specialized or fragmented as cross-disciplinary collaborative projects are encouraged. Multidisciplinary designer Thomas Heatherwick, quoted by Marcus Fairs, discussed a similarity in process methodologies between disciplines, stating that whether designing buildings or products, practitioners look at the same problem-solving strategies.[9] As I will go on to argue, this shift in academic attention given to fashion has allowed a cross-disciplinary creative practice to emerge that validates fashion design methodologies and allows processes to become more interdisciplinary and experimental.

Efrat Tseëlon's essay "Outlining a Fashion Studies Project" (2012) critically discusses the emergence of the field of fashion studies. In what she calls the "academizing of vocational schools," Tseëlon states that trends in academic thinking and a "cultural turn" that saw fashion positioned as a cultural phenomenon have validated the development of fashion studies as a field.[10] A shift from quantitative to qualitative methods of research "combined to facilitate the legitimization of this new interdisciplinary field."[11] She goes on to state that there are two levels in the field of fashion studies, the "visible" and the "invisible," in which one focuses on the objects, images, and specific examples by examining them closely and highlighting certain periods and styles.[12] The invisible level involves conceptual layers of meaning, personal and collective, that reflect the wearer's experience and perspective, which can be "metaphorical or allegorical."[13] Within this context, Tseëlon proposes that fashion practice is as much about process as about content; hence, in those instances where the process of representing and displaying fashion through a multitude of terrains can be situated, it is indeed possible to discuss and theorize fashion without conveying the argument with actual clothes.[14] This being particularly prescient in the spaces in which fashion and art converge, clothing might not always be the primary outcome but a vessel or "medium of critical reflection."[15] The interdisciplinary nature of borderless fashion design is due to and reflected by the interdisciplinary nature of fashion studies.

This expanded field of fashion research relates directly to its evolving place within the academy. There has been a continuing interdisciplinary approach to fashion design practice in the 2010s, which is due in part to a more academic approach to the study of fashion. This is a product of fashion practice moving into art and design academies from technical colleges and polytechnics and fashion as a research discipline entering the university domain in the 1980s and early 1990s. Antwerp's Royal Academy of Fine Arts is a specific example, introducing a fashion course in 1963 that was made famous by the "Antwerp Six" set of fashion designers in the 1980s. Walter van Beirendonck, Ann Demuelemeester, Dries Van Noten, Dirk Van Saene, Dirk Bikkembergs, and Marina Yee are known for avant-garde fashion practices that transcended and subverted the status quo of the time, coming to define a niche zeitgeist of 1980s fashion that converged conceptual thought with a deconstructed notion of the garment. In the context of the "Antwerp Six," a convergence of art and design practices manifested in the conceptual clothing designs. This was fostered in what oral histories of the time describe as an intersection of club and café culture, where students would interact, collaborate, and experiment with interdisciplinary projects.[16] The Belgian city's status as one of international merchant trade and a hub of artistic fertility dates back to the sixteenth century, when it acted as a convergence of cultures at the forefront of an expanding colonial world.[17] The city's "abundant warehouses" helped cultivate a thriving underground scene in the 1980s, and the fact that Antwerp as a city is a lot smaller than London or Berlin meant the communities were smaller and more intertwined, breeding collaboration between disciplinary fields creating a new contemporary avant-garde.[18]

Interdisciplinary design subjects thus became core units in design schools, with students from across disciplines working together on design projects much like that which Edelkoort now defines as "hybrid" creative studies. This influenced the cross-pollination with other disciplines such as performance, sculpture, graphics, architecture, and product design. Borderless fashion design can be mapped against these other developing concepts that speak to the evolution and convergence of design, art, and media. The fashion designers of today defy the very name given to them: they are also product designers, material researchers, programmers, sculptors, and architects, who make work that is often more focused on the process of creation and the experience of communication than that of the end physical garment. The meaning of this fashion practice emerges from the collaborative nature of these stages of creation that has been fostered in academic institutions.

In his theory on "convergence culture," Henry Jenkins proposes that media consumption becomes a collective process wherein meaning is made through collaboration.[19] This is in reference to the new media of the twenty-first century and their ability to allow virtual communities to share knowledge on a far grander and quicker scale. This concept of convergence culture as a result of new media can be related to the development of "transdisciplinary" design methodologies. In 2010 Parsons New School of Design launched a Master of Fine Arts in Transdisciplinary Design, the first of its kind. The course description reads,

> The Transdisciplinary Design program was created for designers interested in imagining alternative futures through design-led research tools and methods for addressing pressing social, economic, political, and environmental issues and challenges of local and global dimensions. Students work in cross-disciplinary teams, consider issues from multiple perspectives, learn from community and industry leaders, and emerge with a portfolio that showcases design as a process for transforming social relations and contemporary life.[20]

Transdisciplinary design looks at the transition of focus from stylized aesthetic to process innovation, as James Hunt observes: "Designers must refocus their gaze from the object or artifact of the design process to the complex systems that contextualize it. This shift—from artifacts to systems—mirrors the global shift in industrialized countries from manufacturing and goods based economies to ones built upon services, information, and innovation."[21] With this in mind, Hunt explains that "transdisciplinary design is a connective, collaborative practice," which sees shifts that are allowing designers in all fields to reconsider the boundaries of their own design practice.[22]

Transdisciplinary design as a field of creative academic study has no final or fixed definition; it is speculative and evolving. Focusing less on the single creative practitioner, design is becoming more open source, centering on collaborative relationships between designers, producers, consumers, and users. Because of this, creativity is more of an oscillation between the designer and user, as the audience/user/consumer is given agency in their interaction with the product/experience/service and "puts the agency of design into the user's hands, distributing intelligence, capacity, and creativity away from a monolithic center and toward the heterogeneous edges."[23] Borderless fashion design practices work within this matrix insofar as collaboration and a focus on process are at the heart. Beyond this, a move toward participatory style design methodologies across creative media production due to democratic online platforms has given agency to the consumer/user/wearer and enabled a level of authenticity to emerge across contemporary creative practices: "Indeed, many emerging design practices indicate a mode of design that is closer to facilitation than to craft. They establish decision architectures and situate the user/activator in a role that blends design, curation, sampling, selection, and *bricolage*."[24]

Fashion's move into the academy, and the subsequent collapsing of boundaries between design and art it instigates, is speculated upon by Alex Coles in the book *Design and Art* (2007). In the introduction, Coles proposes that early avant-garde movements of the twentieth century, such as the Soviet constructivists and the Bauhaus group of artists and designers, blurred the boundaries between the two fields.[25] He writes: "In different ways they responded to the technological and political implications of industrialization by fostering new relationships between the autonomous sphere of art and the mass-produced culture of industrial design. . . . The result was a new form of practice wherein traditional boundaries between disciplines were renegotiated."[26] Coles discusses here the collapsing of disciplines, and although speculative, the survey provides a platform for further analysis of these specific developments into the twenty-first century. In this book I propose that there has been a "renegotiation" of disciplinary boundaries in the practice of contemporary fashion designers. In *Design and Art*, Coles maps contemporary art and design practices across three categories: "Paradigms," "Utopia and Collective," and "Coordinates." These three compartments articulate ideas relevant to the development of contemporary fashion practice related to my research. Borderless fashion, which functions within the fashion system, has risen out of paradigm shifts from postmodernism into the metamodern. The idea of utopia is relevant insofar as the designers working in this way rely on a collective of collaborators who are all working toward the same fashion future. The idea of coordinates relates to the speculative space in which fashion is (re)negotiated, or the way practitioners from other fields are negotiating and moving into fashion as a means of expression. Borderless fashion practice is situated within this context.

Critical Fashion Practice

As fashion has moved into the academy, cross-disciplinary studio study and research have developed, giving a critical lens not only to how fashion is viewed but also to how it is represented. *Critical fashion practice* (CFP) is a theoretical framework developed by Adam Geczy and Vicki Karaminas in their 2017 book *Critical Fashion Practice*, a text that offers a contextualization for the contemporary phenomena of fashion practice that acts as a form of societal commentary and reflection. It refers to fashion that has a function beyond just the physical garment, a practice that connotes conceptual meaning and critical reflection. Geczy and Karaminas make note of the fact that CFP "is very much a postmodern phenomenon as a result first of the dissemination of subcultural style, then in the dispersion of fashion itself into the virtual realm."[27] Yet, they acknowledge the fact that this mode of fashion practice has its roots in the modernist development of the fashion system in the mid-eighteenth century in the context of the French Revolution. This saw the formation of the "modern, enlightened subject for whom there were identifiable rights, which also meant agency and freedom," and allowed the space for aspiration and social mobility.[28] As they write, clothing at the point in which it "seeks to perform a social, political, even philosophical role" becomes a "rallying point for agency and belief."[29] CFP validates "any piece, item, or work of fashion that announces a level of conceptual functionality that exceeds the capacity of simple clothing."[20] This fashion practice places criticality as a central concern to challenge precepts and assumptions about the world, therefore destabilizing certain ideologies to "encourage ways of rethinking self and identity."[31] In this way, CFP considers the impact and meaning of fashion beyond its physical utility, and thus CFP can be considered a "metaphysics of clothing."[32]

CFP has its more direct roots in the 1980s and 1990s, when it manifested in the practices of fashion designers Vivienne Westwood and Rei Kawakubo: Westwood using fashion as a platform for political, social, and environmental activism and Kawakubo more directly to the physical garment. Westwood and her partner Malcolm McLaren heralded the *style* of the counterculture punk movement in the 1970s with their interdisciplinary career that encompassed music (McLaren's endorsement and management of the Sex Pistols), politics, and fashion manifesting at their concept boutique on King's Road in London, called in one of its many iterations "SEX."[33] The store acted not just as a commercial fashion endeavor but also as a site for community gathering, theatrical displays, and a treasure trove of objects, which suggests "that the store catered to a lifestyle, primarily an alternative lifestyle."[34]

Today, luxury fashion brands have evolved into entities in which the product often comes in second place to the ideology that underpins it.[35] Modern fashion has always represented and/or sold a lifestyle. The shift to a conscious notion of its own power emerges at the point in which it breaks from a "stable" modernist signifier to an unstable intertextual postmodern practice. Critical fashion practices have emerged since this point in the 1970s alongside the social justice movements predominant in the West, such as the civil rights, gender equality, and LGBTQIA+ rights advocacy movements. Fashion practitioners such as Vivienne Westwood, Issey Miyake, Rei Kawakubo, and Jean-Paul Gaultier are prime examples of designers during this time who critically reflected on both their practices and the world in which they were designing. This mode of fashion declares a "level of conceptual functionality that exceeds the capacity of simple clothing."[36] As Geczy and Karaminas offer, this metaphysical functionality of fashion "helps us to reflect authentically upon our being in the world."[37] Today, this critical lens is integral to borderless fashion practices:

CFP is a mode of contextual practice that fashion designers use to bring attention to the way that clothes participate in critical discourses and political action. It engages with socially discursive dimensions, as well as placing a priority on the articulation of taste and creative innovation. CFP values, like all critical research, a discourse that is speculative and discursive over an aesthetic of resolution and completeness. In other words, it follows an approach to aesthetics that constantly challenges the beautiful and the good.[38]

I would argue that a demand for authenticity in the fashion industry and socially aware critical representations and design methodologies is emulated within the practice of borderless fashion.

This authenticity manifests in the way in which fashion is created and communicated. A universal idealization of the body and of the garment is no longer an important and desirable factor for both the designer and consumer, as it was in the modern era when Dior's sculptured "new look" or Chanel's waifish figures were idealized. I would argue that today a multitude of bodies and identities participate in the cultural production of fashion, predominantly "trickling across" geographical, class, and cultural boundaries, merging through the participatory nature of social media communication technology. This sees a distancing of fashion from the restraints of the commercial market, opening up the mediums in which fashion can be disseminated and expanding the scope of its audience. The critical and the conceptual are more important for these designers and are fundamental to the development of their practice. In turn, the spaces with which fashion is located and positioned are of utmost importance in its communication, whether that is in the museum/gallery, via film or in a constructed performative space, which I will go on to discuss in the following chapters.

This critical aura created by a brand or practitioner changes the way in which people consume the work; rather than act as capitalist "consumers," new audiences present more as a loyal community of followers who invest in this undercurrent of ideology and criticality. Audiences today have agency over what work they consume, which is due to the evolution of fashion's democratization and its shift into academic fields of study as well as the cross-pollination of disciplines indicative of borderless fashion.

End Times

In *Living in the End Times* (2010), Slavoj Žižek claims we are at a point in time in which the late capitalist society that we live in is imploding due to unsustainable changes in the way in which we consume and communicate.[39] Žižek laments that in the twenty-first century we are helpless; we are aware something needs to be done but have no clue as to what that may be.[40] The collapsing of economic hierarchies that dominated the twentieth century directly affected both fashion as a commoditized object and fashion as a cultural product, the physical and the representational. The rhetoric surrounding the "end" of fashion, outlined in Geczy and Karaminas's edited volume on the topic (2019), focuses on subjects as diverse as globalization, time and memory, mediatization and digital retail, and curation and exhibition making. At the end of fashion there is recognition of a need for a change in how fashion is produced and communicated involving new narratives and critical discussion. It is within this changing context that I situate definitions of borderless fashion.

Fashion's entrance into the academy instigated cross-disciplinary collaboration and critical analyses of fashion as a cultural phenomenon in the final decades of the twentieth century. This emergence also coincided with a time in which academic studies were analyzing and mapping postmodern developments in cultural aesthetics and philosophy. Fashion scholar Yuniya Kawamura makes a case for fashion to be analyzed from a postmodern perspective in her book *Doing Research in Fashion and Dress* (2011).[41] She claims that fashion researchers need to be aware of the changes that have occurred in the industry and cultural realm due to fashion's changing sociocultural context. If we are to look at the "postmodern interpretation" on the research and study of fashion, then fashion can be defined by the breakdown of distinctions of clothing, such as those between menswear and womenswear, and the dismantling of hierarchies previously in place, such as that between high fashion and popular culture.[42] I argue that this is due to the democratization of fashion. Kawamura states, "One of the major characteristics of a postmodern phenomenon is the breakdown of boundaries and categories. Whatever used to be classified as a group becomes gradually meaningless."[43] However, I also argue that borderless fashion practice is more than just the breakdown of categories: it is a reconstruction of the idealism that modernists privileged.

In modernism, fashion played a key role in the progress that it championed and became a tangible aesthetic form that represented the technological innovation and social ideas of the time.[44] The postmodern interpretation of fashion is that this connection to "progress" was a façade and that fashion's role was to present the myth of progress.[45] Postmodern theory sees fashion at the center of culture, and thus it is "not only clothing; it is bodies, objects, and lifestyles; it is entertainment, art, morals, politics, economics, and science."[46] The idealism that the modernist narrative worked toward had utopic tendencies, its move away from traditional formalism centered on a Western Christian religious narrative that saw the ability of humans to reshape and improve their environment through knowledge and technology, a continuing sentiment that can be seen during the Enlightenment and the Renaissance. At the heart of modernism, particularly within the realm of art, was an attention to process and material, a self-referential sensibility that saw the decline of realism and the ascension of idealism.

Postmodernity is often associated with the disappearance of cultural and social boundaries and categories.[47] The transformation of reality into representations is one of the great postmodern dilemmas.[48] Although traditionally postmodernism is associated with developments in art and architecture from the mid-twentieth century, an analysis of the way in which fashion responded to the ideals of postmodernism as an aesthetic and cultural zeitgeist is an important precursor to the development of borderless fashion through the lens of the metamodern. Theorist Fredric Jameson championed the idea that through the postmodern there was an erasure of boundaries between high and low culture.[49] Fashion as a field and practice is the physical manifestation of this collision. Fashion's accessibility to everyone in terms of simply wearing clothes day-to-day means fashion is relatable to all humans on varying levels. It is a vessel that carries multiple sociocultural connotations and reflects the attitudes and politics of the wearer and the time in history.

The development of postmodernism was an aesthetic and conceptual break from the aesthetic tradition of modernism, which had dominated the Western art canon from the late nineteenth century to the mid-twentieth. The end of modernism could be said to coincide with the "end of art" rhetoric that started to occur in the 1960s with the emergence of happenings, performative practices, and conceptual art as art moved away from the sterilized white cube of the gallery space. These changes were linked to what was happening socioculturally and politically at the time, as Jameson mentions in his essay on the end of art: "The very deployment of the theory of 'the end of art' was also political, insofar as it was meant to suggest or to register the profound complicity of the cultural institutions and canons, of the museums and the university system, the state prestige of all the high arts, in the Vietnam War as a defence of Western values: something that also presupposes a high level of investment in official culture and an influential status in society of high culture as an extension of state power."[50] Like this era of the end of history and end of art, conversation on the "end of fashion" in the twenty-first century is inherently political insofar as it is a response to the rise of neoliberalism, which, expressed in simple terms, has seen a rise in inequality in the age of globalization and a sharp move away from leftist economic, social, and cultural values. The domino effect from such societal developments manifests in fashion, even if that is in the form of hopeful counteraction with gender neutrality, new materialism, hybrid design methodologies and identities, and research and process-driven methods.

As Fredric Jameson comments in his introduction to *Postmodernism, or the Cultural Logic of Late Capitalism* (1991), the modernist paradigm "thought compulsively about the New and tried to watch its coming into being... but the Postmodern looks for breaks, for events rather than new worlds, for the tell-tale instant after which it is no longer the same."[51] Postmodernism was what he called a "commodity rush," going further to say that within postmodern culture, culture had become a product of its own.[52] He went on to state that "modernism was still minimally and tendentially the critique of the commodity and the effort to make it transcend itself. Postmodernism is the consumption of sheer commodification as a process."[53]

"Re-presentation," "intertextuality," "mimesis," "appropriation," and "deconstruction" are all words associated with the postmodern, particularly within the realm of art and visual culture. French philosopher Jacques Derrida is synonymous with the concept of *deconstruction*, or the process of undoing as a strategy in the close reading of texts—pertaining to something that can be read (the Latin root word *textus* meaning to "weave"). Derrida theorized the deconstruction of modernist design methods that privileged universal symmetry and simplicity that were not reflective of the pluralistic intertextual nature of representational creative expression of the time. Here, the word "deconstruction" as applied to fashion "conflates the philosophical application of the term as destabilising assumed hierarchies with that of a more simplified understanding of destruction."[54]

At the point of postmodernism's solidification in the canon of Western culture, fashion designers such as Rei Kawakubo and Martin Margiela emerged, creating their own break from the modernist fashions of the mid-twentieth century, which were defined by the likes of Christian Dior and Yves Saint-Laurent. They fractured and accentuated the body through the deconstruction of classic garments such as a knitted jumper or crisp cotton shirt. Kawakubo distorted the silhouette of the body with padded "lumps and bumps" in obtuse places in her spring 1997 collection titled *Body Meets Dress, Dress Meets Body*, which threw into question the visual language of the era before it, which was dominated by form-fitting idealized "patriarchal silhouettes" that emphasized the smallness of one's waist and slimness of one's overall physique.[55] Merce Cunningham, a New York–based dance choreographer, went on to use the garments from the collection in a collaborative performance, titled *Scenario*, which premiered in October 1997 at the Brooklyn Academy of Music.[56] The dancer's movements were set against an all-white stage, lit with fluorescent lighting to the "column of repetitive" sounds made by Takehisa Kosugi, the company's musical director.[57] Rather than perpetuating the stereotype of the perfect body, Kawakubo's costumes challenged the vanity of the dancer and the gaze of the spectator, deconstructing the very nature of the relationship between clothing and the body and the politics of the space between.[58] These deconstructive notions of the body, garment, and space have been carried into twenty-first-century fashion practices.

Death and ideas of the end are terms that occur prominently in postmodern rhetoric in relation to art.[59] At the end of art, popular culture became a central focus as boundaries between high and low culture blurred and collided. Within the realm of fashion, we can see this in effect with the appropriation of subcultural styles into the realm of high fashion. This occurred most noticeably from the mid-twentieth century with the dominance of social subcultural movements such as the Beatniks, "mods," hippies, and Punks going on to directly influence the creative output of elite fashion designers such as Yves Saint Laurent, Courreges, and Paco Rabanne. A later example of this is Marc Jacobs's infamous "grunge" collection for Perry Ellis in spring/summer 1993. A decentering happened where fashion, which was previously associated with class distinctions, was focused on everyday people, or fashionable trends that were prevalent in the street. Take, for example, grunge style, which consisted predominantly of the flannel shirt and baggy jeans, a uniform adopted by the Seattle grunge music scene that was co-opted by Marc Jacobs. However, Jacobs made the flannel shirts out of silk material and the polyester thrift store dresses out of chiffon, making a subcultural street style a luxury.

Rather than focusing on ideas of progress, which the modernist paradigm fixated on, designers looked to already existing classic garments and deconstructed them, decontextualizing their functionality and questioning their purpose in relation to the body. This is particularly demonstrative in the work of Rei Kawakubo's Comme des Garçons and Maison Martin Margiela. Today this rhetoric of the end or a death of some sort has fixated on fashion as it has become a more prominent cultural phenomenon in the twenty-first century, and its influence on global culture has been acknowledged and further focused on as an important topic of academic research.[60] For postmodern theorists, the "end times" signified the possibility that multiple histories existed rather than a single one marching toward linear societal progress. The death or end therefore signifies an acknowledgment of a change in how fashion is conceptualized, produced, and communicated.

Francis Fukuyama in his popular 1989 article "The End of History" argued that with the demise of the Soviet Union the struggle between predominant ideologies had largely come to an end, with the world settling on Western liberal democracy.[61] It was a "political meme" that shrewdly described the collapse of communism and "triumph" of the West; however, Fukuyama's article was all too biased in its framing.[62] Fashion is one of the largest and most profitable capitalist industries operating today, with an estimated global industry value sitting at approximately $2.4 trillion (USD), as estimated by McKinsey in late 2016.[63] While this predominantly comes from fast fashion retailers such as conglomerates Zara and H&M, responsibility for change ultimately sits with the "luxury" conglomerates due to the filtered-down influence they have in terms of setting trends, whether that be literal manufacturing trends or conceptual trends such as inclusivity and critical practices. The development of alternative fashion design practices that decenter the product and commercial model are gaining prominence and popularity out of *necessity* due to the changing sociocultural context.

Today, an awareness of sustainability and ethics and an emphasis on a need for a return to "slow fashion" have seen consumers demand more from designers and fashion companies. Criticality, concept, and ethical production are becoming inherent values in design methodologies. Edelkoort is one of the most recent to convey such a great proclamation as "the end of fashion," which was stated in her aforementioned fashion industry callout manifesto, *Anti_Fashion*, of 2015. One of her calls was for more collaboration in the industry and a fostering of altruistic relationships, which she believes contemporary society is hungry for.[64] Focus on the individual star designer or the cult of the creator is outdated in relation to a creative world that is based on an economy of exchange.[65]

Discussions around the globalization and democratization of the fashion industry in terms of its end have also been conveyed in Teri Agins's book *The End of Fashion* (1999).[66] The book takes on an investigative journalistic approach to the ways in which fashion had evolved by the end of the twentieth century. Agins traces the history of couture through to prêt-à-porter and the growth of the fashion market through globalization, democratization, and the mass commodification of the fashion garment. It is a relevant and integral text on the state of the fashion industry in the rich rush of commercial globalization, characteristic of the 1990s. A lot has changed in twenty years and the end of fashion to us in the form of Edelkoort's manifesto sees a need to slow down and foster creativity, collaboration, sustainability, and ingenuity, characteristics that I will argue are happening and are manifested among young designers.

However, Agins's vision of the end of fashion is a lot different to Edelkoort's end of fashion in the second decade of the twenty-first century. Agins focuses on the strain that the consumer-driven mass-marketing of garments had placed on the fashion industry, specifically on the U.S. market, but she does not really come to any set conclusions or any resolution for a way forward. The capitalist boom of the 1990s is over, and the unsustainable model it developed is in need of serious change. Borderless fashion practice is a product of this change. The end of fashion, as a contradiction, does not actually mean the end; it highlights a shift in a constantly evolving industry that has regenerated itself time and time again due to the ingenuity of those avant-garde designers who experiment and push the industry forward.

As discussed, conversations around fashion's end are not necessarily new concepts, particularly in relation to the conceptual and experimental fashion practices of the 1990s, such as those of Alexander McQueen, Martin Margiela, Rei Kawakubo, and Hussein Chalayan. Caroline Evans discusses the concept of death as an artistic theme extensively in her book *Fashion at the Edge* (2003), where she extrapolates on the ideas of death, decay, and melancholy in the fashion aesthetics and shows of the 1990s and turn of the millennium.[67] She relates these motifs and concepts to the sociocultural context at the end of the millennium. She states that in this type of work—that is, fashion "at the edge"—fashion exists at its own margins (or borders) of what had constituted commercial fashion up to that point. She states that "the distressed body of much 1990s fashion exhibited the symptoms of trauma, the fashion show mutated into performance and a new kind of conceptual fashion designer evolved."[68] This type of designer articulated the anxieties of a rapidly changing social, economic, and technological landscape at the end of the twentieth century, through the imagery of disease and dereliction as well as transgressing traditional modes of presentation.[69] It communicated the instability and concern of the collective unconscious at the dawn of the new millennium.

A cynicism arose in fashion through the work of designers such as Chalayan, Kawakubo, Margiela, and McQueen during this time, manifesting in the deconstructed fracturing of the body via the garment. Physical garment attributes included rips and tears on fabric and exaggerated proportions distorting the body, which mirrored the cynicism toward the close of the millennium with a fixation on that which Evans describes as death, decay, alienation, and trauma.[70] The idea of "deconstruction" conceptually relates to the undermining and calling into question the seeming naturalness of relationships between things.[71] Derrida's philosophy of deconstruction as a strategy in the close reading of written word texts has evolved to be popularly used in terms of the "critical dismantling of traditions and modes of thought."[72] Whereas in modernism there was a focus on process and *construction* for a better future, one that representations in art and fashion experimented with, the postmodern sought to *deconstruct* this.

After the end, I argue that a reconstruction is happening in fashion practice and that it is emulated in discussions around the metamodern. At the same time that fashion practice has moved into academic fields of study and has been mapped against philosophical paradigms as a marker of these historical shifts, fashion has also become more democratized. As definitions of what constitutes fashion emerge through postmodern reflections, consuming audiences gain access to the idea and concept of fashion through other communication tactics and digital technologies, thereby becoming more active agents in its production and consumption.

3

Fashion's Democratization

Fashion's democratization describes the way in which fashion as a cultural phenomenon has become more available to a wider range of social groups over time focusing specifically on the way in which it is communicated. This has occurred due to cultural, social, and economic changes such as the Industrial Revolution and rise of modernity in the nineteenth century and the youth revolt of the 1960s. "Democratization" is a developmental term I will use to help historically contextualize borderless fashion. A collapsing of boundaries has occurred since the first democratization of fashion in the second half of the nineteenth century with the advent of the haute couture industry in Paris.[1]

With this in mind, the democratization of fashion can be seen to have happened in waves since the second half of the nineteenth century. Georg Simmel has been associated with the term "trickle down" theory from his 1904 article "Fashion," which took Thorstein Veblen's theory of the class hierarchy of consumer goods and applied it to the analysis of fashion and style of the time.[2] Simmel's application of the *trickle-down theory* can be seen as the first wave of fashion's democratization, or at least an understanding of how it works.[3] This theory claimed that fashion was created by society's elite class in which upward mobility was inherent, and trends tended to trickle down to the lower status groups to be emulated by them in the hopes of climbing the social ladder. By the twentieth century and with the emergence of prêt-à-porter, a *bubbling up* occurred, in which fashion on the runway became more influenced by the street than what those in high society were wearing. Styles associated with subcultures from varying social contexts such as the "bikers," "zooties," hippies, and "mods" were recuperated by the commercial fashion system from the 1970s, subsequently flipping the tide of influence.[4] Fashion anthropologist Ted Polhemus wrote in his seminal 1994 text *Street Style* that the "bubble-up process has made us a fully-fledged creative democracy in which talent isn't thought to be limited by class or race or education or how much money you've got in the bank. For our culture as a whole, it is surely all for the best that the full spectrum of creative energy in our society has been tapped."[5]

Looking back at the history of fashion practice and its cultural production across the modern and postmodern periods of the nineteenth and twentieth centuries, we can see this evolving democratization occur. Fashion's most rapid democratization appears at the advent of the couture industry in Paris in the second half of the nineteenth century with the likes of Charles Frederick Worth and Paul Poiret designing garments for the newly emancipated woman, which was then communicated and reflected in the rapidly developing photographic technology.[6] This form of communication made fashion more visible for those in the lower classes who previously did not have access to the physical spaces in which fashion existed, such as salon presentations. This then led to industrialized mass manufacturing and the collapse of the boundaries between couture and ready-to-wear in the twentieth century, creating greater access for the masses as prices consequently went down.[7] Alongside this, fashion media in the form of magazines such as *Vogue* and representations in film and photography created a greater accessibility to fashion's cultural production. Fashion's most recent democratization has emerged through the globalizing nature and new media of the internet, which has created access to information on a border-transcending global scale.

The internet democratization, brought about through the development of digital media technology, has also created a new site of existence for fashion as personal digital devices have become the predominant way in which fashion is consumed in the twenty-first century. Through these movements we can see a borderless activation in fashion practice has emerged, a contemporary design practice that fuses elements of architecture, fine arts, communication design, technology, and science that is accessible to a wider audience across geographical, class, cultural, ethnic, and societal borders. Clothes are not necessarily the predominant outcome, but a medium of critical reflection.

Developing Simmel's trickle-down and Polhemus's bubble-up concepts, Yuniya Kawamura proposes a *trickle-across theory* in contemporary fashion practice that supports this "collapse of categorical boundaries."[8] This is due to the fact that differences in the way people dress are no longer determined by social class but by a myriad of pluralistic influences that are now open source through the internet. Social identity is no longer necessarily based on political or economic spheres.[9] Fashion today trickles across because consumers and audiences "seek to project and express an imagined identity that is evolving" in a democratic space in which social class is no longer important in one's "self-image and identity."[10] This space where identity is constructed oscillates between the street and digital realm in the metamodern twenty-first century.

The words "democratization" and "fashion" come into contact at points in time in which the connection between fashion (a cultural phenomenon directly connected to human experience and dress) and the wearer has shifted. This is mostly due to the notoriously "exclusive" and hierarchical structure put in place within the fashion system, particularly among the editors, buyers, and celebrities working within that system, which manifests in contexts such as the fashion show. French theorist Pierre Bourdieu acknowledges the value of aesthetic cultural goods such as fashion in the reproduction of social structures and class distinctions.[11] Bourdieu posits that aesthetic experience cannot be explained as an individual expression of the mind but rather as a "socially and historically constituted disposition."[12] He theorizes that an individual agent's position in a field is determined by the agent's capital.[13] In the field of fashion that capital has historically been embodied in the garment (it arguably still is); however, through fashion's democratization a wider group of people have access to this embodied capital through online engagement, and secondary and knock-off markets. Further, as value systems change and agents are able to access the culture of fashion in much more accessible ways, these hierarchies within the field have been disrupted.

Digital access has democratized the fashion show progressively since the beginning of the new millennium. British fashion designer Alexander McQueen's *Plato's Atlantis* spring/summer 2010 show in September 2009 was one of the first attempts to livestream a fashion show via longtime collaborator Nick Knight's online platform Showstudio.[14] This, however, was interrupted by American pop star Lady Gaga's announcement via Twitter that McQueen's show would also be the unveiling of her new single, which instantly flooded Showstudio's site with millions of viewers crashing the livestream before it even went live. This set a precedent however, and by the autumn/winter 2013 season Mercedes-Benz Fashion Week in New York City announced that all fifty-four shows would be livestreamed on their own website as opposed to YouTube, which had sporadically done so for the previous three years.[15] Juliane Pederson touches on this notion in connection with the shift toward a metamodern paradigm: "The meta-modern consumer of fashion goods and services lives more comfortably in the flux of value systems and differences that penetrate life's activities and events."[16] She argues that the emergence of bloggers (independent individuals writing and photographing original content of contemporary fashion to be published on websites and social media platforms) as agents in the filtering of fashion through direct dialogue on digital platforms encourages reader response and engagement; therefore, metamodern fashion consumers have more direct influence over fashion change. Pederson goes on to note that this democratization of fashion communication via the blogger mediator is "more truthful, having the effect that readers identify more closely with the production of fashion, versus merely the consumption of it."[17] I argue this influence of the consumer has gone beyond the mediation of the blogger, as metamodern designers utilize digital platforms to speak to their audiences and consumers directly.

In the twenty-first century, fashion's democratization has enabled the consumer and audience to become more active participants in the experience of fashion. This has been instigated through the development of the internet and digital media technologies propelled forward by online platforms such as Showstudio, which unveils the creative process of making through film. Literal borders have broken down, as information has been able to transcend them, becoming accessible to anyone with a Wi-Fi or data roaming connection. Social media sites such as YouTube (founded in 2005), Tumblr (founded in 2007), and Instagram (founded in 2010) have gone on to shape millennial aesthetic culture, passing agency into the hands of the consumer through the ability to curate one's own page, which conveys image branding and preferences.

However, these platforms have also allowed companies or brands to communicate with their audience on a more direct level. The internet has become the site of the "alternative" fashion system, replacing that of the "conventional" fashion system that was centralized in Paris, New York City, London, and Milan. Anyone can have democratic access to fashion now as designers unveil creative processes through these social media sites. Followers can directly message those creative practitioners they connect with, and in the case of Virgil Abloh they would often even get a reply. This access dismantles the hierarchical systems that previously perpetuated fashion's impenetrable walls. Communities are now built through Facebook groups that facilitate cultural criticism around the fashion system, and because consumption is now quantified through the number of "likes" brands' social media sites get, the agency is now firmly in the consumers' hands, regardless of whether they purchase actual product or not.

A downside to this digital democratization of fashion is the potential homogenization of media information, which disseminates style and creative practice that then filters down to the audience. Although as consumers we have control over what we like, which then turns into data that companies use to resell back ideas, the corporate bodies ultimately end up taking control on a passive level through a process of recuperation. The designers analyzed in this book oscillate between the commercial and noncommercial social sphere. By "noncommercial," I refer to work that may be commissioned for public consumption rather than for the direct purpose of selling. This often relates to fashion that exists beyond that of the embodied garment.

Metamodern Millennial Internet Culture

In the twenty-first-century millennial age, the prefix "meta" has entered the common vernacular as a stand-alone colloquial word that describes anything that is self-referential, a trait common to a generation whose cultural production and direct way of communicating are based upon digital networks such as Instagram and Facebook. Intertextual memes and GIFs have become indicators of intellect and cultural cachet with their layered references and meaning. Borderless designers and brands have taken up the postmodern tactic of intertextuality, defined by poststructural theorist Julia Kristeva as an active dialogue existing in given texts between the text, reader, and context.[18] It is a term that leverages and synthesizes Roland Barthes and Ferdinand de Saussure's theories of semiotics, articulating that the meaning of a given text does not reside within the text itself. Rather, meaning is produced by the reader in the process of consuming the text in question, as well as through an intricate web of cultural signs and traces. Intertextuality renegotiates the relationship between author and reader, relying on symbiotic collaboration and active participation from the reader. Whereas the millennial generation experienced both the pre- and post-internet experience of the late twentieth and early twenty-first centuries, Generation Z has grown up exclusively with an internet connection, their whole experience having been adjacent to the rapidly developed technology sector.[19] The millennial generation anchors itself in the irony and deconstruction of the postmodern zeitgeist. Self-referential, intertextual memes have therefore become a prime signifier of communication, the construction of which often comprises a photographic image or illustration with additional text that often recontextualizes the initial connotations of the image and redefines it with references that humor the viewer in their juxtaposition, or alternatively highlights a social justice issue inherent to the collective critical consciousness of the time. The word "meme" was coined by Richard Dawkins in his 1976 book *The Selfish Gene* and describes something imitated, the detritus of language and culture that has transmitted across time.[20] Memes are metamodern phenomena insofar as they oscillate between irony and sincerity often using text and image to denote ironic signifiers that connote an underlying critical reflection.

This prefix "meta" describes the image or experience referred to and suggests that it may be digested on multiple levels.[21] On a more traditional level and as mentioned previously, "meta" refers to Plato's idea of *metaxis*, which translates to an oscillation between poles, or two binary things. Prefixing it onto another word, "modernism" in this case, "meta" can be defined as "between or beyond" that of the previous cultural paradigms. With this in mind, applying the emerging paradigm of metamodernism to contemporary fashion practitioners, who work between and beyond disciplines, blurring gender, body, and geographical boundaries, feels the most satisfactory in the context of a fashion industry that is self-reflexively commenting on its own end. It also caters to the members of an agentic audience who consume information and products through their screens.

Authenticity as a Value System

Efrat Tseëlon has proposed that authenticity in fashion and art in relation to individual creation is born out of the Renaissance discourse surrounding the "individual creative genius," which has been appropriated by the fashion industry to describe designers who front the large European couture houses.[22]

Looking back to the 1980s and 1990s, we can see this hypothesis in action. John Galliano, Alexander McQueen, and Karl Lagerfeld were all appointed at couture houses as savant creative directors: at Dior, Givenchy, and Chanel, respectively. What became their totem for establishing signature brands, not only for the fashion houses but also most importantly for them as individual creators, was epitomized in the spectacle of the runway fashion show. Tseëlon goes on to discuss the idea of fantasy and desire in relation to fashion that is most certainly on display in the fashion show in her essay on authenticity, a reference that helps convey how fashion's spectacle can be mediated with the authentic.[23]

This democratization throughout the last century or so has laid the foundation for fashion's evolution into other sites of inquiry. The emergence of fashion in the academy and university as a dedicated field of study has resulted in fashion being taken more seriously not only as an art form but as an important independent discipline of inquiry, as outlined in the previous chapter. This is also reflected in fashion's move into the gallery and museum space, which has resulted in the development of conceptual and experimental fashion. Fashion has become a part of our contemporary visual culture and therefore the museum and gallery space, as purveyors of aesthetic culture, become natural partners.[24] I argue that all of these factors lead up to the contemporary development of borderless fashion practice.

Anneke Smelik, in her essay focusing on the performance of authenticity in fashion, states that "authenticity has become the holy grail of today's fashion; and like the holy grail, always sought, never to be found."[25] "Authenticity" is a term that occurs throughout this book in relation to the designer case study analyses and therefore needs some interrogation and defining in terms of its relation to a working consumptive value system in relation to the changing ways in which fashion is consumed in the twenty-first century. The word "authenticity" itself means genuine and real, yet the question is, can this be a label we apply to the current commercial fashion system? Can authenticity be found in an oscillation between commercial and noncommercial fashion practices? I argue that regarding borderless fashion, authenticity in the way designers produce as well as communicate their work is of value. Smelik quotes Gilles Lipovetsky's claim that in the modern age, fashion had a mix of individualism and conformity.[26]

With the rise of digital media technologies and the growing availability of mobile communication devices in the West, consumers have now become producers of cultural content. After the meteoric rise of fashion bloggers and their evolution into digital influencers, fashion's largest brand conglomerates absorbed the cultural capital they were creating. This instigated a mutually beneficial relationship between fashion "influencer" and fashion brand by selling aspirational lifestyles through imagery that consumers are able to access at any time of the day. The influencer identity, constructed through the publishing of branded content online, has become the commodity itself. These images have been disseminated predominantly through image-sharing social media platform Instagram, resulting in influential consumer success for the sponsoring fashion brands. This has contributed to the oscillating nature of fashion communication and advertising, in which we see the consumer become the producer. This contributes to what I describe as fashion's *democratization*, which has provided a unique context for borderless fashion to emerge. The control button has changed hands and the consumer is now the one who influences the culture of fashion rather than the hierarchy of makers and editors behind the scenes.

In an age of post-truth politics and alternative facts, authenticity feels like it has become an elusive aspiration. The authentic or the idea of living authentically feels as though it is constantly out of reach in an age of digitally mediated imagery in which our experience of reality is mere simulation lived through the flickering blue screen of our handheld communication devices. Authenticity within the field of fashion has become somewhat of a commodity in itself. Brands sell the idea of "artisanal" or "heritage" collections to draw customers into buying an idea of authenticity. But can authenticity really exist in a digital culture of exchange where ideas and references are shared freely? Smelik does not believe so, writing that "authenticity is nowadays constructed and performed" and that "it has therefore become an illusion that can no longer be true or genuine. Like the Prada and Louis Vuitton bags on street markets, it is an 'authentic fake.'"[27] Smelik also claims that desire for authenticity is a modern phenomenon and that with the rise of mass production in the modern age, the access to consumer goods and the freedom of choice that it created have led to a loss of tradition.[28] As a consequence, people yearn for what they have lost, which in this instance is the authentic. This is true for both the consumer and the creator. The twenty-first-century consumer of fashion, in all of its manifestations, has become a lot more aware of sociocultural issues due to the fast and accessible proliferation of information that then demands a level of criticality of fashion practices. Fashion brands are unable to get away with products and marketing campaigns that are not diverse, inclusive, and original. Authenticity is a value system that the audience and consumer place upon fashion as a cultural artifact. This democratization has seen fashion become more accessible on multiple levels of experience for consumers and viewers due to the proliferation of information and the mass production of fast fashion. Democratic platforms such as social media sites and YouTube have been utilized as a way to connect not only with the masses but also with the designers and businesses themselves, a connection that had previously been completely out of the realm of accessibility.

In the new millennium, fashion has progressed from a service economy to an experience economy, a term coined by B. Joseph Pine II and James H. Gilmore in a 1998 journal article and subsequent book, *The Experience Economy*.[29] The authors prophesied that the experience economy was the next economy in the historical narrative that comes after the agrarian, the industrial, and the service economies. Pine and Gilmore argue that the memory of an experience in relation to a brand becomes the product. The "experience economy" refers to a move

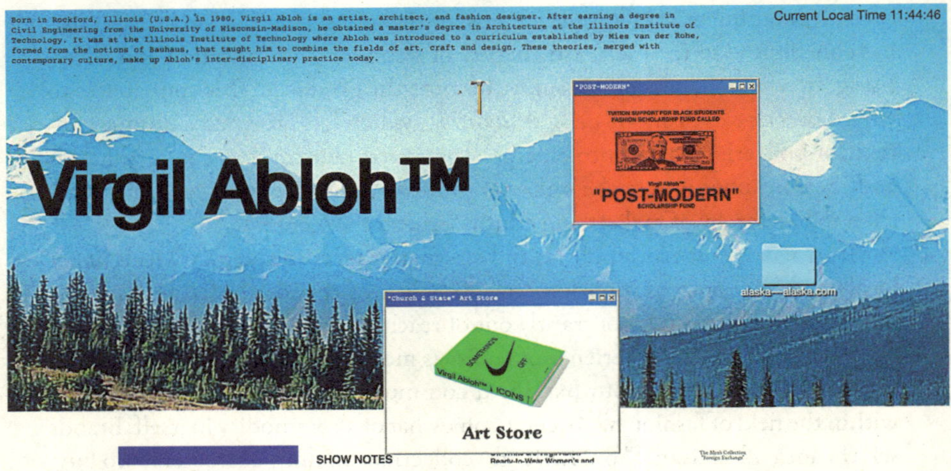

FIGURE 3.1 Screenshot of Virgil Abloh's personal website. Source: canary---yellow.com.

toward a more holistic system of exchange that focuses on community and the breakdown of barriers between "luxury" and "fast" products. As one commentator pronounces in an opinion piece on the experience economy, "The best brand experiences today are not about brands but about life. Life doesn't distinguish between categories. Consumers increasingly expect experiences that are holistic and seamlessly integrate different aspects of their lives."[30]

This idea is linked to the wider themes of authenticity that underscore the metamodern. Borderless fashion practitioners rely on this experience economy to maintain a viable business within the structures of our Western capitalist system. Scholar Elizabeth Moor comments that the shift to experiential marketing has elevated the "spatial and experiential dimensions of marketing," due to the virtually unlimited scope of multichannel business, marketing, and design strategies brought on by developments in technology and media.[31] Art events, commissions, films, retail sites, and digital spaces are all spaces in which this concept arises and is delivered. The democratization that the internet has instigated has given greater scope for digitally immersive experiences. Designer websites have now become spaces in which the brand, community, and individual can express their identity through editorial, memes, GIFs, and virtual reality; they are no longer just service retail centers or portfolios. Virgil Abloh's website, canary---yellow.com, deviates from this service-driven space to one of immersive interaction with the designer's creative oeuvre. On the homepage, visitors can navigate through Abloh's multidisciplinary practice engaging with panel discussions, music, articles, short films, photography, and even the designer's Google calendar, as presented in figure 3.1. This last addition disrupts the inaccessible aura of the designer; the immersive digital space offers transparency, in turn instigating a form of authentic representation.[32] In the analysis of the collaborative multi-disciplinary spaces in which the designers in this book communicate their work, this authenticity based within the idea of the experience economy will become evident. Rather than authenticity, transparency of process and concept has become an apparent development that has dismantled the rarefied aura of fashion designers and brands.

"That which withers in the age of mechanical reproduction is the aura of the work of art," wrote Benjamin of the impact of photography on twentieth-century visual culture.[33] The aura refers to that which situates a work of art or an object within space and time. This sentiment can be equally applied to clothing and fashion. The craft and maker's touch of a garment being the aura, what it has been replaced by over the course of the twentieth century and into the twenty-first is the *brand*.[34] As the cultural critic Alice Hines comments in her essay about fashion and authenticity, "brands are auras of our age, stitching together discrete objects into abstractions of coolness, nostalgia, elegance."[35] She goes on to comment that the life cycle of a garment and its origin have been obscured, particularly in relation to fast fashion and the globalized nature of its supply chain, giving way to the spectacle of the brand. Fashion brands are works of bricolage, to use a classic postmodern term, bringing together fashion designers with a wider collective of makers and creators such as illustrators, spatial designers, sound artists, and hair and makeup artists, as well as a wide-ranging appropriation of themes and narratives to create the aura.[36] In the 1990s this was exemplified in the ultimate spectacle, the fashion show. The fashion show was a site of convergence of high and low culture and the ultimate way of communicating fashion to a consuming audience. It was the ultimate example of Guy Debord's *Society of the Spectacle*, which sees the spectacular commodification and consumption of images, commodities, and staged events.[37] Today, this is no longer the case; designers connect to consumers on a much more immersive level with interactive staged performances and interactive digital marketing symptomatic of the shift to the experience economy. The brand has become much more multifaceted, socially conscious, and democratic as a way of creating authenticity in the eyes of the viewer/consumer.

After the End of Fashion

Art critic and philosopher Arthur Danto wrote *After the End of Art* twenty years ago, in which he proclaimed the end of art's linear narrative and its decline in traditional aesthetics and grand-narrative idealism. What he meant by this was that works of art were so diverse in medium, concept, and presentation that outwardly they contradicted the traditional aesthetic view on what art's— particularly modernism's—agenda had been, especially within his context of postmodernism. Danto wrote, "It became apparent that there were no stylistic or philosophical constraints. There is no special way works of art have to be. And that is the present and, I should say, the final moment in the master narrative. It is the end of the story."[38] Danto proclaimed art's new pluralism because works of art at that point in time, across the board, had outwardly very little in common, hence a less restricted system of creativity.[39] This pluralism marked art's liberation and the end to its need to "understand itself philosophically," or understand itself in reference to an aforementioned master narrative with a set of rules.[40] Art had been freed from the constraints of imitation theory and, admittedly as somewhat of a contradiction, marked the beginning of a new era of contemporary art. Fashion is at a similar junction, and due to its rapid democratization, the same question that previously plagued the art world has now emerged in the fashion world: What is fashion? As it bleeds across different fields of consumption, fashion is coming into contact with a broader audience which does not necessarily have an interest in buying the latest trend-driven garment.

Discussing the development of contemporary art, Danto summed it up articulately, stating, "Part of what defines contemporary art [is] that the art of the past is available for such use as artists care to give it. What is not available to them is the spirit in which the art was made."[41] This spirit refers to the spirit of the time the work was made, the sociocultural and economic context. In the context of contemporary fashion, after its "end" we see new strategies to progress fashion's craft and cultural production in new and progressive ways as a direct response to the spirit of our times. Within the context of this book, this is evident through Iris van Herpen's technological fabrication developments for a new utopic world, Virgil Abloh's democratic haute streetwear, Aitor Throup's immersive fashion installations, and Eckhaus Latta's nonbinary collaborative collective practice.

Like contemporary art, borderless fashion practice has what Danto describes as "no brief against the art of the past, no sense that the past is something from which liberation must be won."[42] It means looking at interpretations of a previous creative ethos and creating for the now in a decentralized, delocalized, digitized global fashion system, notions that are mirrored in the speculations of metamodernism. Abramson refers to this democratization in the era of the metamodern as the "collapsing of distances" in which people socially interact across geographical and cultural borders.[43] We also see the emergence of "multiple subjectivities," by which he means we interact through the "simultaneously anonymous and falsely intimate spaces of the Internet," and because of this "we often find ourselves joining our words and actions with people we know nothing about—except that they agree with us as to the one issue we're discussing in the moment."[44] Fashion trickles across in this way as consumers and audiences group together in online forums to disseminate, share, and critically analyze contemporary projects, trends, and concepts.

Writer Lou Stoppard demystifies the narrative of the sole creative genius by saying that "the fantasy of the designer in an ivory tower, dreaming up wonderful ideas in isolation, has never been accurate."[45] Fashion designers have never worked in isolation. It could be said that the idea of the great fashion creative genius, epitomized by designers from Paul Poiret at the start of the twentieth century to Alexander McQueen and John Galliano at its end, is a myth. The talent and savant creative sensibilities of these star fashion designers are undeniable; however, the nature of creating fashion is based on team collaboration. A cohort of pattern makers, pattern cutters, drapers, seamstresses, illustrators, production managers, graphic designers, and stylists all make it possible for fashion projects and brands to exist. Designers do not work in isolation and never have. They work as part of a team wherein collaboration and dialogue are inherent. Designers today—and those whom I have included within this book, although they are highlighted as the "creative director"—seek to dissolve this myth through highlighting the process and collaborative sensibility of their practice to demystify the aura that has been constructed around the identity of the fashion designer.

For context, Rei Kawakubo never studied fashion; she never sketches her designs and claims that she does not design clothes but that she designs the company, that company being the Tokyo-based global brand Commes des Garçons (Like Some Boys).[46] She is a part of a wider web of collaborators who discuss, conceptualize, and produce fashion together. Kawakubo studied ethics at university before going on to work at a textile factory, where she began styling, and after being unable to find the types of clothes she personally wanted to wear, she started making her own before launching her own company in 1969.[47]

The argument that I make in this book is that contemporary fashion practitioners work across disciplines, creating work that is beyond that of the traditional boundaries of fashion. What is different about the way these designers produce and communicate their work in comparison to those throughout history, who have always been collaborative, is the way in which fashion is produced and communicated, which has also changed. There is less emphasis on the individualized nature of the lone fashion creative genius, because in reality most design teams have a collective of creative practitioners that make up a whole, all with their own strengths and weaknesses, and "multiple subjectivities." Take, for example, Switzerland-based fashion brand Vetements, which started out in 2015 as an anonymous collective of fashion practitioners with ties to Belgian fashion house Maison Margiela. Borderless fashion practices create rhizomatic structures within their design teams that allow for a breakdown of the hierarchical system of creation. The digital democratization of fashion has allowed consumers and audiences access through behind-the-scenes content disseminated via social media platforms as well as immersive experiences that have signified the shift from the service economy to the experience economy.

4

Collaboration and Experimentation between Fashion and Art

The fashion designers whom I have referenced in this book are collaborative by nature, often working with creative practitioners from other fields, such as architects, choreographers, graphic designers, artists, and scientists, as a direct tool in their practice. Abloh, Throup, Van Herpen, and Eckhaus Latta's collaborations with many architects, artists, and scientists are testament to this. Collaboration transforms creativity, which has instigated an experimental or expanded field of fashion practice. Neo-utopian notions of community and collective creativity are reflected in the practice of borderless metamodern fashion that progresses beyond the sole creative designer.

Addressing fashion's experimentations with other fields, in particular art, articulates another factor that has led to the development of what I have conceptualized as borderless fashion practice. Borderless fashion sees its earliest manifestations in the collaboration between art and fashion and their experimentations with dress and adornment. Modern fashion privileged the narrative of the sole fashion genius. This discourse surrounding the individual artist, one with a singular creative vision, stems from early art history—most directly from Giorgio Vasari's biographical accounts *Lives of the Artists* from the sixteenth century—continuing through to the early modern era. In these volumes Vasari emphasized the persona of the individual creative through intimate biographies, ostensibly separating the artists from their artisanal activities and centering them as "idiosyncratic people with a singular artistic vision."[1] Vasari's biographies elevated the status of an artist to that of mythology, in turn separating artists from the binds of quotidian work and commerce.[2] The alignment of modern fashion designers such as Paul Poiret and Charles Frederick Worth with this artist status extends even to the way in which they dressed. Worth often wore a velvet beret and distanced himself from the consumer culture that was evolving during the late 1800s and aligned his work with the rarefied creative capital of art. Today, fashion and art cannot be separated from the commercial market, although fashion's critical discourse still emphasizes the idea of "art" as authentic, separated from the "mediatised, commercial world of mass market culture."[3] I argue that borderless fashion practices push beyond the modern and postmodern fashion designer's alignment with arts. Metamodern borderless fashion designers oscillate between the realms of creativity and commerce, and rather than experimenting with collaboration as a gimmick, collaboration is embedded in the conceptual nature of their practices.

When talking about contemporary fashion's evolution and its expanding borders, the intersections between the field and the art world and system are important to note. Two sources of cultural authority, such as fashion and art and the great influence they have on our collective society and consciousness, have instigated an interdisciplinary polemic that grounds this research. Fashion's relationship with art is as unequivocal as it is complicated. The two fields have progressed in parallel to one another for centuries with what having set them apart historically being fashion's utilitarian necessity versus art's representational nature. As Efrat Tseëlon has mentioned, this "assumption about the permanence of the artwork" in contrast to the "transience of the fashion object is an oversimplification."[4] Art has been legitimized in the aesthetic cultural canon due to what French sociologist Bourdieu calls the "field of cultural production."[5] This legitimization happens beyond the material producer through a process of meaning making by exterior producers such as "critics, publishers, gallery directors and the whole set of agents whose combined efforts produce consumers capable of knowing and recognizing the work of art as such."[6] Fashion's entrance into the academy, which has instigated academic study and interdisciplinary studio experimentation, has started this process of "legitimization" of fashion as an important cultural field and aesthetic. Fashion's democratization has also opened up its scope for a new audience whose members bring their own set of perspectives to its cultural consumption and production.

From the late nineteenth century and into the twentieth century, scholars and artists began testing the parameters of what art was and what it could be. We can think of the likes of the early conceptual artist Marcel Duchamp, who first placed found objects, most famously a urinal, within the gallery setting in 1915 calling them "readymades" and consequently throwing into question the very notion of what art is. The question as to whether fashion is art or a form of art is irrelevant in the context of this book, as they have coexisted in tandem for centuries. However, it is important to note that according to Bourdieu, a work of art only exists as such due to the collective belief "which knows and acknowl-edges it as a work of art."[7] Art then is socially and culturally constructed. For fashion to be legitimized within cultural aesthetics, Valerie Steele states that "for fashion to be art, it needs to be legitimated, or symbolically produced, by critics, curators, editors, and other agents with the power to consecrate fashion as art and capable of convincing the public that a dress is to be regarded as a work of art."[8] Borderless fashion is the process of fashion's "legitimization," and a focus on criticality and concept as well as its oscillation of design methods and material output allows for "meaning-making" to take place, in turn creating fashion's cultural production.

The designers outlined in this book oscillate between the avant-garde and the commercial, in turn validating fashion's ability to instigate philosophical conversations as their practices can sit outside of commerce. Robert Radford notes in his essay "Dangerous Liaisons" (1998) that when it comes to fashion ver-sus art, "'Fashion' is inescapably a more slippery term: for the most part it refers here to the conventional understanding of the field associated with the produc-tion and usage of clothing and personal appearance; but, on occasions, the use of the term 'fashion' intentionally slips into a broader category of design and information that is definitively shaped by seduction and ephemerality."[9] Radford goes on to say that through fashion's expanded field, which encompasses social commentary, aesthetics, and human expression, "we are encountering different scales of comparative topography, in that, by this definition, the entire field of art would be subsumed within the territory of fashion."[10]

Beyond this, fashion has had a close relationship with, or even subsumed, sci-ence and technology in relation to new materialism and the field of architecture in terms of the relationship between body, garment, and space. With the con-stantly evolving nature of contemporary fashion practice, the question that arises is how the different fields inform one another and how the parameters of both have been redefined over time due to exterior sociocultural forces in their con-tinued fields of cultural production. Rosalind Krauss developed the concept of an expanded field, theorizing a shift to postmodern art aesthetics and theory in a 1979 article, "Sculpture in the Expanded Field."[11] Other fields picked up this rhetoric to identify a paradigm shift in visual aesthetic movements too, such as "Photography's Expanded Field" and "Design in the Expanded Field."[12] Krauss identifies this expanded field of sculpture by stating that by the 1970s, sculpture had entered "the space of what could be called its negative condition—a kind of sitelessness, or homelessness, an absolute loss of place."[13] By this she means that sculpture had become abstracted and the space it exists within, that being the landscape or architecture beyond the plinth, is where the expanded concept of the sculpture should be read; thus, she wrote that "sculpture is rather only one term on the periphery of a field in which there are other, differently structured possibilities."[14] The same can be said for fashion: the plinth can be aligned with the runway catwalk, and fashion as an expanded notion can be read and experienced beyond its traditional confines. Fashion has become abstracted and liberated from the runway catwalk, as it is now being experienced or "read" across multiple spaces and fields.

Anne Hollander, in *Seeing through Clothes* (1978), discusses the way in which clothing captures the eye and "comes to be mediated by current visual assumptions made in pictures of dressed people." She goes on to state that "changes of style in clothing are consequently inextricable from changes in the medium of art."[15] This mediation of fashion via art perhaps explains why art has been seen to validate fashion, whereas fashion has been seen to give art commercial cachet. This synergy between the two has continued to develop in different ways over the decades because there has been a need to validate the creative process of a designer by anchoring it in the revered art world. We can think of Paul Poiret's alignment and patronage of fine art or Elsa Schiaparelli's relationship with the Surrealists in the 1920s and 1930s as prime examples. However, writer and scholar Marco Pecorari contends that contemporary fashion collaborations are no longer "perceived as attempts to elevate the social recognition of fashion designers," but are joint collaborations that actually modify fashion practices.[16] This is a key characteristic for borderless fashion practitioners. Collaborations are not solely for advertising or accoutrement to the production of garments; they are ingrained in borderless practice, once again central to metamodernism's shift away from the focus on an individual creative genius.

Collaboration between artists, architects, and fashion designers has occurred throughout time, particularly since the onset of modernity and the industrial and technological revolutions of the late nineteenth and early twentieth centuries. Fashion designers have always relied on the technical and creative ability of artisans to enable their vision to manifest materially, and in turn designers have been inspired by this technical mastery. Throughout the twentieth century, creative collaborations became what Andrew Bolton calls "synergistic partnerships based on shared creative visions that speak of collusion, complicity, and conspiracy," rather than an act of service, the collaboration was symbiotic.[17] This "synergy" has its origins in Poiret's modern fashion industry defining collaborations with the most famed artists of the day, such as those with illustrator and graphic artist Paul Iribe. As previously mentioned, Schiaparelli's collaborative projects with the Surrealists are an important example, particularly the output of her relationship with Salvador Dalí, as was Coco Chanel's work with Jean Cocteau. Fashion was opened up to a new art audience whose members brought with them a new refinement of taste and value systems.

The start of the twenty-first century saw collaborations between artists and fashion labels became more frequent and mainly acting as a marketing tool to create a broader field of consumers. Marc Jacobs's tenure at Louis Vuitton womenswear (1997–2014) saw multiple collaborations with the likes of graffiti artist Stephen Sprouse, Japanese artists Yayoi Kusama and Takashi Murakami, and American artist Richard Prince. The fashion house banked on the distinguishable nature of these artists' iconography to gain cultural cachet, while the artists gained commercial gravitas creating a new audience and of course further capital to continue with their practice. These collaborations created a heightened visibility for the luxury house, contributing to the democratization of fashion into the twenty-first century.

Italian fashion designer Miuccia Prada is a prolific patron of and collaborator with avant-garde artists and architects, such as Scandinavian artists Michael Elmgreen and Ingar Dragset and Dutch architect Rem Koolhaas. In 2005, Prada collaborated with Elmgreen and Dragset to produce *Prada Marfa*, a conceptual installation piece situated just outside of the city of Marfa, Texas, in the United States. It is a nonfunctioning sculptural work with large windows, through which visitors can look and see a curated selection of Prada handbags and shoes chosen by Miuccia herself. Prada and her husband, Patrizio Bertelli, also own and manage Fondazione Prada in Milan, a nonprofit contemporary arts foundation. As Nicky Ryan writes in "Prada and the Art of Patronage," "the 'cultural capital' of artists such as . . . Elmgreen & Dragset, and architects such as Rem Koolhaas is appropriated to produce symbolic capital for the Prada brand."[18]

The concept of *cultural capital* derives from the Bourdieu's research in the 1970s that analyzed the field of French high fashion, arguing that the rarity of the producer, as in the fashion designer, establishes the rarity of the product.[19] An "artistic identity" was constructed in regard to Prada that "contributed to an obfuscation of commercial operations as the 'spectacle' of fashion was privileged above manufacturing and production processes."[20] The collaboration that produced *Prada Marfa* is evidence of this. The cultivation of fashion designer identities throughout the early 2000s, evidenced through the cultural capital built around Miuccia Prada and her extracurricular collaborations, is still apparent today. The difference, however, is this desire for transparent authenticity required of designers through the access of different social media channels. Rather than gaining this cultural capital through tangential projects that enhance cultural cachet, contemporary borderless fashion practitioners are interdisciplinary and pluralistic in the way they produce work, oscillating between and within creative spheres.

Beyond the necessity to acquire collaborators for the construction of fashion shows and presentations (producers, set designers, sound, and lighting), contemporary fashion practitioners collaborate with practitioners from other fields in projects that reach beyond seasonal collections. They act more as experimental incubators for ideas and stretch beyond collaborations with highly esteemed fine artists; fashion practitioners today are creating collaborative projects with mainstream companies. What is significant about collaborative relationships in the twenty-first century is their prevalence across different creative disciplines and fields.[21] In her book *Fashion Together* (2017), Lou Stoppard compiles interviews by some of the greatest fashion collaborative partnerships to occur in the twenty-first century. In choosing the partnership collaborators to include, she stated, "I was drawn to the less tangible, more unexpected partnerships that operate outside of the usual structures of the industry."[22] Among others, Iris van Herpen and architect Philip Beesely, Rick Owens and Michele Lamy, and Gareth Pugh and filmmaker Ruth Hogben were included. The specific ways in which contemporary fashion designers create in the twenty-first century has developed into a multidimensional, pluralistic practice.

The democratization and convergence of digital communication technologies with diverse design methodologies have changed the way fashion designers produce work and how consumers consume fashion "products." As Jessica Bugg notes in her article "Fashion at the Interface," "fashion is now serving new roles, functioning in both commercial and non-commercial arenas and across creative disciplines."[23] This is due to the changing way audiences/consumers interact with fashion, which has moved into a more active rather than passive role in the experience economy. Fashion is also connected to the changing value system of the audience/consumer, which is now based around a desire for authenticity in regard to production and communication. The designers examined in the second part of this book are used as case studies and sit at the nexus between "commercial and non-commercial" creative practice. The close analysis of their oeuvre, which includes details of their specific projects, explains how audiences and consumers connect with fashion today.

Fashion's Mediation

The rise of the fashion exhibition is another example of fashion's cultural "legitimization," coinciding with its entrance into the academy. The blockbuster fashion exhibition, made infamous by Diana Vreeland's phantasmagoric exhibitions curated for the Metropolitan Museum of Art's Costume Institute from the 1970s, was the seminal moment in which fashion gained accessible critical attraction. The now infamous Alexander McQueen *Savage Beauty* exhibition first held at the Victoria & Albert Museum in London in 2011 just a year after his death was one of the most visited exhibitions in the museum's history. A seminal moment in which the fields collided was the Florence Biennale in 1996. Modeled after the Venice Biennale, the Florence Biennale was to be focused on fashion, the first of which centered on the connection between fashion and art, appropriately named *Il tempo e le moda* (Looking at fashion).[24] It centered on the analysis of fashion, placing meaning into the field under the artistic direction of Germano Celant, Luigi Settembrini, and Ingrid Sischy. At the turn of the twenty-first century, the Florence Biennale acted as another validation of fashion as a field of cultural production. To quote the introduction of the catalogue, "Like art, fashion can be looked at anthropologically, sociologically, and even philosophically. It is an expression of individual and collective desire. It is a barometer of change. It involves issues of identity and sexuality. It engages with, and even stimulates, technology, science and business, just to name a few of the elements that are a part of fashion."[25] Collaborative installations between Jenny Holzer and Helmut Lang, Tony Cragg and Karl Lagerfeld, Roy Lichtenstein and Gianni Versace, and Damien Hirst and Miuccia Prada instigated a conversation that demanded fashion to no longer be presented and analyzed from just a news perspective "but from a cultural and scholarly one."[26] Celant states further that "fashion is an aesthetic object that implies projections and arguments that are at once sociological and anthropological, psychological and technical, economic and creative. Realizing a Florence Biennale devoted to Fashion means creating an exhibitional and critical space that will periodically confront this phenomenon in all its complexity and richness of communication and philosophy."[27] The biennale acted as somewhat of a rejection of the runway show. Rather than focusing on the commodity spectacle, the directors sought to unveil fashion's layers of meaning within global culture and society. It spoke to the more complex concept and processes that go into the production of fashion by aligning it with the language of the art space. It mapped fashion's relation to creativity and intelligence, subverting the hierarchies that have existed in the fashion system in which audiences were passive consumers of the ultimate fashion commodity.

Fashion is fundamentally a commodity, and because of this, more often than not, it is seen on a lower tier than that of fine art. Paradoxically, due to the hierarchy of the fashion system, people often feel excluded from it. As stated by Geczy and Karaminas in *Fashion and Art*, as soon as the fashion object is placed within the context and space of the museum or gallery, "its value as a commercially driven mass-market product transitions from consumable merchandise to art installation."[28] Fashion's role as a "fast" commodity slows down and is aligned with a new value system as a commodity to be collected.[29] This subverts the long-held opinion that fashion is a frivolous and shallow commodity. Fashion has been dismissed by individuals under this premise. Elizabeth Wilson describes this as the "hierarchy of academic study," as fashion was, in her words, "associated with the body and therefore assessed as low and degraded; it was associated with women and therefore dismissed as frivolous; it was associated with capitalism and therefore denounced as exploitative; it was associated, especially in utopian socialist thought, with inequality, ugliness and unhealthiness and therefore rejected on all three grounds."[30] Borderless design practices subvert these long-held opinions by centering collaboration, concept, and innovation with an emphasis on criticality, process, and design methodology. Fashion's entrance into the museum and gallery spaces, such as the 1996 Florence Biennale, presents factors that have led to fashion's ability to articulate and oscillate across many cultural fields today. Fashion mediated through an exhibition gives space to map fashion's linguistic, symbolic, and conceptual relationship with other fields of creativity, such as art, photography, music, and architecture.

In 1982, a decade and a half before the Florence Biennale, *Artforum* magazine released a cover featuring a model adorned in an Issey Miyake–designed nylon-and-polyester bodice and skirt. That issue of *Artforum* posed the question of why fashion was not considered as art, but it also asked the same question of other pop culture phenomena such as comics and record and magazine covers. Ingrid Sischy, *Artforum*'s editor at the time, stated in an interview with fashion critic Amy Spindler for the *New York Times* in 1996 that "it had nothing to do with being on a mission to say fashion is art, I don't think fashion is art, but why is that definition for artistic creativity so narrow that it's just a painting in a frame?"[31] The cover emerged within a context in which postmodernism was in full swing within the art realm, championing conceptual multidisciplinary works of art and design that challenged the viewer to pose these same questions. It was also an era in which high culture diverged with low culture in the form of art works from the likes of Jeff Koons, whose *Inflatables* series appropriated imagery from pop culture and remixed them for the context of the gallery space. Of course, Andy Warhol and his Factory had initiated this more than a decade earlier and Marcel Duchamp and the Dadaists fifty years before them. However, there is a trajectory here in which we see a questioning of the status quo or a conceptual functioning and primacy of the idea. As Bourdieu claims, culture is both material and symbolic; "belief in the value of work" is produced by both the direct artist of the *material* and then the producers of *meaning* who are the writers, critics, and curators.[32] These producers of meaning then in turn create consumers that are in the know and recognize the produced value of the work of art.

Throughout the postmodern period of the 1980s and 1990s, fashion designers embedded symbolic meaning in their work. Alexander McQueen used to sew a lock of his own hair into the seams of his garments as a physical offering of devotion to his creations, while Martin Margiela's signature was in fact no label at all, just four white stitches on the interior of his garments.[33] Both acted as a token of esoteric cultural cachet for those lucky enough to possess a garment. A niche field of conceptual fashion practice was developed as a consequence that acted as an alternative voice to mainstream fashion. These more experimental designers provided a resistance to homogenized mass manufacturing through conceptual critique using themes such as death, trauma, and deconstruction to speak to contemporary anxieties; any commerciality was veiled with alluring theatrical dream worlds in the form of runway performances, expanding the very notions of the definitions of "fashion."[34]

Performance and Performative Space

Beyond the art and fashion collaborations and their legitimization in the gallery space, fashion's critical consideration of the body and performance contribute to the breakdown of gendered binaries of fashion and question what a fashionable garment is and in turn what it means. Fashion's direct connection with the body and creative expression has invited artist's experimentation with dress and fashion to speak to ideas regarding gender, identity, and body politics, as well as the environment, religion, and socioeconomic politics. Performance artists Cindy Sherman, Jana Sterbak, and Marina Abramovic are obvious examples. Postmodern artists from the United States, Canada, and Serbia, respectively, they experimented with the boundaries of the body, space, and viewer through the utilization of dress during the 1960s and 1970s—a time in which sociocultural politics were breaking down suffocating Western social structures and perceptions of gender, sexuality, class, and race. These artists used their body, dress, and movement in the form of photography, installations, and transient performances to challenge these boundaries and to push back against modernism's conservatism.

Australian multidisciplinary practitioner Leigh Bowery is another important performance artist to emerge from the 1980s who has had a major influence on experimental and critical fashion practice in relation to dress and the body. Bowery was an important figure in postmodern queer politics that were emerging at the time in the London club scene in the 1980s, which saw a convergence of fashion, music, dance, and performance. Bowery transgressed gender and body politics by distorting his body shape and changing its contour with garments that he created. These were presented at club nights—such as Taboo in London—which were heterotopic spaces that acted as subversive, experimental runways for designers who did not fit into the commercial fashion system. Bowery questioned the traditional body (one that is bound by expectations of gender and size) and its representation, subsequently influencing creative practitioners of all fields.[35]

What these performance artists have in common is the use of costume and fashion as a means of activating their performances, or in the case of Jana Sterbak's *Meat Dress* (1987), they use the adorned body as the performative focus. In this, to quote Barbara Vinken, in the "post fashion" era, fashion designers have begun to work interdisciplinarily taking on a borderless design practice by creating fashion that is grounded in concept and escapes the typical or traditional modes of presentation, such as the runway catwalk in favor of performances (in real life and virtual), installations, and curated exhibitions, and referring to the fashion items themselves as products, objects, or even simulations.[36] I argue that borderless fashion designers would not be creating in the ways they do without the experimentations of postmodern performance artists such as Bowery, who practiced at the boundaries of fields.

The important factor is the communication of the concept and the space that is represented, which ends in a different relationship to the finished project. The focus has shifted away from fashion's relationship to the lived body and onto the space in which it is situated. What has become more important is the body in relation to a spatial fantasy; the space adds meaning and narrative to the clothing and the clothing activates the space. This concept is derived from performance studies—in particular, performance design—which itself is related to architecture, an interesting notation when many contemporary "fashion designers" have in fact been trained in other fields.[37]

Fashion film cannot be ignored in reference to fashion and performative space. Robin Healy in her essay "Immateriality" from *The Handbook of Fashion Studies* (2011) states that "the device of image-making or cinematic/video media has given fashion designers and curators the possibility to construct atmospheric environments and has facilitated interdisciplinary practices. In this context clothes are presented as part of a larger composition or image signifying the fashion idea."[38] In a time in which people are consuming more online than in real life, fashion film offers the experience of constructing a "fashion idea" as well as envisioning fashion in movement as it was intended. This is linked to a wider history of fashion film dating back to the moving images of modern dancer Loïe Fuller produced around the turn of the twentieth century. Fuller was and is famous for her Serpentine Dance produced in tandem with voluminous fabric swept into the air. This was immortalized on film in the late nineteenth and early twentieth centuries.

What makes borderless fashion practice different from those practicing in the 1990s, such as Galliano, McQueen, and Chalayan, is the accessibility of the fantasy, the accessibility of the immersive experience of fashion. This is also what makes the fashion exhibitions that museums hold so successful: the accessibility to the fashion fantasy that is so often made untouchable by the many hierarchies put in place by the fashion system manifested in the fashion runway show. Today, borderless fashion practitioners disrupt disciplinary borders by utilizing conceptual frameworks and methodologies from other disciplines, occupying new performative spaces such as installation, and rupturing boundaries of the body and the dynamic of body, wearer, and viewer. The experimentations of postmodern designers and postmodern artists like Bowery act as foundational practitioners for this contemporary development in twenty-first-century fashion practice that has emerged at a transitional "end" point to the twentieth-century model of fashion practice.

5

Fashion as a Concept

The twenty-first century has seen a *delocalization* of fashion as it has progressively moved beyond the runway and even beyond the body while still remaining in the commercial fashion sphere. Fashion no longer exists just on the catwalk, in magazine editorials, and in department stores, but in museums and art galleries, conceptual retail spaces, ephemeral performative and installation sites, and of course digital media. A delocalization has also happened in fashion's relationship with the body: what constitutes fashion is no longer contingent on the lived body or the body at all. Cultural theorist Paul Virilio talks about the delocalization of art in conversation with designer and artist Lucy Orta, commenting that art is no longer found exclusively in galleries or in museums but "where mutating social situations condense."[1] Virilio was speaking in the context of Orta's work in 1995, the defining project being her *Body Architecture* (1992–1998), which consisted of portable architecture that could be worn on the body, representing issues of autonomous survival and blurring the lines between art object and designed object. At the same time, Orta created *Nexus Architecture* (1994–2002), which was a participatory performance work that saw people wear suits connected to one another, thereby creating a physical collective structure that spoke to ideas surrounding the concept of social connectivity. Virilio made the observation that in Orta's work there is "a reflection on packaging, on the garment no longer considered as body covering, as a second skin, but as packaging, somewhere midway between architecture and clothing."[2] Orta's work presents a specific development of fashion practice that is grounded in a similar way to that of postmodern conceptual art. Through work such as Orta's, fashion at the turn of the twenty-first century started to be considered as something that can be read and experienced through acts of performance and installation rather than just within the commercial trappings of the runway catwalk show and the commercially mediated pages of fashion magazines.

Speaking on contemporary art's relationship with the gallery and museum space, Arthur Danto writes that "Artists today treat museums as filled not with dead art, but with living artistic options. The museum is a field available for constant rearrangement, and indeed there is an art form emerging, which uses the museum as a repository of materials for a collage of objects arranged to suggest or support a book."[3] This speaks to fashion's entrance into the space of the gallery, as it did most prominently with the Florence Biennale in 1996. Danto's claim was that by the mid- to late twentieth century, art had become self-conscious of its own history, speaking directly to the creation and exhibition of Andy Warhol's Pop Art Brillo box works. "All there is at the end," he wrote, "is theory, art having finally become vaporized in a dazzle of pure thought about itself, and remaining, as it were, solely as the object of its own theoretical consciousness."[4] Art had become much more than just that of physical representation, or an abstraction of reality; it was a concept or an idea that relied less heavily upon the physical material and more upon the metaphysical, hence its delocalization. Borderless fashion, I argue, has become "self-conscious" of its own history and its intricate relationship with commerce, craft, and art, which has in turn manifested in more than "just" its physical representation. Analyzing developments in fashion design practice against the evolution of art practice is helpful as I claim that like art, fashion has come to take up space across the borders of disciplines, continuing a process of rearticulating what the designed fashion object is, much like there has been a rearticulation over time of what classifies an art object. The spaces that fashion now occupies in relation to how it is presented and the practice itself have expanded as a field.

The development of experimental, interdisciplinary fashion practice has added to discussion around the importance and consequential relevance of the runway catwalk as the most important step in revealing the latest ideas in fashion, which is tightly bound up in the cyclical expectations of the fashion system. The fashion runway has been, and still is, a capitalist spectacle. Only the most famous and influential people are seated in the front row. Hierarchies are established through these seating arrangements: the closer to the models and the garments, the more cultural capital one has; the farther away, the less. Borderless fashion practitioners have become critical of these constructs and democratized the way in which people view their work due to technology such as social media, immersive and interactive presentations, and an ability to utilize fashion as a vehicle for a wider conversation as an expanded borderless field. The primacy of the idea in fashion, which stems from fashion's entrance into the academy and gallery spaces, has allowed fashion to open up into new creative spaces.

Conceptual Fashion

What stands out at these boundaries of fashion practice and what has become a central focus with regard to what I define as borderless fashion practice is the primacy of concept. As Hazel Clark states, "any reference to conceptual fashion immediately draws us toward the conceptual in art."[5] The conceptual in art developed in tandem with installation and performative mediums from the 1960s onward. Subject matter, authorship, aesthetic nature and physical existence of the art object were all called into question during this time, and by the middle of the century the gallery and the permanence of a work of art were being eschewed by experimental art practice.[6] Challenges to the idea of what defined art were brought about even earlier in the twentieth century with the European and American Dada movement and most notably Duchamp and his "readymade" artworks that called into question the very definition of what art is and can be.

The Dadaists emerged in response to the outbreak of World War I, in protest of the bourgeois nationalism and colonialism they believed started the war.[7] The art movement combined poetry and spoken word poetry, collage, sculpture, paintings, and illustrative design. Meetings between founding artists of the movement converged at the Cabaret Voltaire, an artistic nightclub started by writer Hugo Ball in 1916 in Zurich, Switzerland, which was a neutral state in which many artists emigrated at the outset of the war in 1914. Dada is said to be at the roots of abstract art, performance art, and a prelude to or influence on pop art and postmodernism.[8] The movement was an "anti-art" convergence of sound, music, poetry, and visual arts that emerged at a time of great social, economic, political, and cultural upheaval, and it has gone on to influence a multitude of creative fields into the twenty-first century, including laying a foundation for conceptual art and fashion.

Duchamp's most infamous work was a urinal signed "R Mutt" and titled *Fountain* (1917).[9] The work was submitted to the American Society of Independent Artists in 1917 and was subsequently rejected; Duchamp, a member of the society's board, resigned.[10] The famous photographer Alfred Stieglitz then photographed *Fountain*, the photograph becoming the actual work of art itself after the urinal vanished; however, conceptual art as we historically know it was born.[11] *Fountain* questioned the definition of the material and conceptual nature of art, particularly the formalism of modernism. Through decontextualizing a readymade, mass-produced, everyday item with crass connotations, the action acted as a critical and conceptual challenge to the art world. Questions of temporality and the state of existence in space and time were conceptual art's fundamental hypotheses, factors that we see inherently in fashion. Fashion fundamentally is, with its performative nature and relationship with time, what Clark labels "a silent reflector of culture and society."[12]

Concept sits at the center of borderless fashion practice, and each designer that I have chosen as a case study in this book creates a conceptual framework that acts as a foundation or a starting point for the creative process of a project or seasonal collection. Their design methodologies are subsequently fluid in the way in which they conceptualize projects, not just through focusing on the structure of a garment but also how the garment interacts with space, with the viewer, with the wearer, and with all of the intersectional dynamics in between and beyond the garment. This includes how this work is experienced through the democratized mediated digital realm. Film, photographs, interactive virtual reality, 3D animations, and livestreams do not just act as communication tools for a fashion product. I argue that they have become the fashion "object" themselves.

The conceptual in fashion came to prominence in the 1980s with the emergence of Japanese designers into the Western market. Rei Kawakubo's label Comme des Garçons (Like the Boys) and Issey Miyake's namesake brand were at the forefront of the industry, challenging audiences with transseasonal, androgynous, and sculptural garments that subverted the fashion system's trend cycle and the formal binary conventions of dress. They also challenged the very fundamental purpose of dress, working at the nexus of art, architecture, and fashion by using new technologies and challenging traditional tropes and spaces. This fashion exemplifies Clark's "silent reflector," and as Geczy and Karaminas have pointed out, introduced the idea of fashion as sociocultural critique.[13] Working at this nexus, these designers conceptually and critically challenged traditional tropes, particularly in terms of what was in vogue at the time, such as the "power dressing" made popular in America, through not only what fashion looked like but also how it felt on the body and how it was displayed and sold.[14] Retail spaces resembled the "white cube" of the gallery space, and garments were monochrome and asked for the creative intervention of the wearer over how to drape and wrap a garment around their own body.[15]

Japanese fashion designer Issey Miyake opened his design studio in the early 1970s and immediately went about conceptualizing new ways of approaching clothing and fashion design. The designer's first encounter with the idea of design was the two bridges in his hometown of Hiroshima that were named "To Live" and "To Die." The bridges were built in 1952 to commemorate the one hundred thousand civilian lives lost when the atomic bomb was dropped on the city at the end of World War II.[16] This interaction instigated in Miyake an awareness of "design's ability to inspire powerful emotional responses; and hope."[17] From the beginning Miyake's creative process was based upon his trademarked concept of *one piece of cloth* (A-POC), a process that explored the relationship between the body, cloth, and the space in between, which he claims divests itself of the labels of "East" and "West."[18] The concept was developed further in 1978 with a book titled *Issey Miyake*. This was the first monograph of a living fashion designer to be published, which included photographs and essays by practitioners from different mediums who explored Miyake's concept of "a piece of cloth."[19]

This development of Miyake as a conceptual fashion designer rather than a creative director of a brand was fostered through his connection to other creative mediums. Miyake's work was put on the cover of *Artforum* in 1982, as mentioned in the previous chapter, the first image of fashion, and throughout the 1970s and beyond he exhibited his work in spaces across Japan, Europe, and America, presenting his work more like that of an artist than a commercial fashion designer.[20] It may now be common practice for fashion practitioners to present their work within a gallery or museum setting. However, within the context of the 1970s, this was new and considered groundbreaking and avant-garde. To quote a 1998 *New York Times* review of a ten-year retrospective of Miyake's work exhibited at the Cartier Foundation in New York, "he is, perhaps, to be regarded as a visual philosopher of modern movement, an architect of traveling light."[21]

A modern philosopher and subversive architect he may be, but it is important to remember that one of the most iconic items of clothing within pop culture of the new millennium, the infamous black turtleneck worn by Steve Jobs, was made by Issey Miyake.[22] This dichotomy between practical designer and conceptual philosopher and the success and impact it has had on fashion culture and beyond sets the foundation for contemporary designers' ability to dislocate fashion from its formal boundaries both materially and representationally. After living and studying in Paris at the Chambre Syndicale de la Couture Parisienne during the spring riots of 1968, Miyake stated in 2006 that he "witnessed first-hand the beginning of a new era: the era of the common man."[23]

Beyond this moment in history, Miyake was interested in new and innovative fabrications for the non-elite, which is how his concept of A-POC occurred. The concept was further defined in 1998 with collaborator and engineering designer Dai Fujiwara.[24] To quote Miyake's design manifesto:

> A-POC was not only able to create clothing with a high degree of variation, but was also able to control the amount created through the process of casting, where each thread receives computerized instructions. A-POC was revolutionary in that it began with a single thread and resulted in fabric, texture and a fully finished set of clothing in a single process. It led the way, along with the concept of engineering design, to a new methodology of clothing design.[25]

The work had models walking along a runway connected by one long piece of vibrant red fabric. The concept utilizes a manufacturing method that uses computer technology to create clothing out of a single piece of thread in a single process. The presentation of such on the runway was a way of theatrically representing a process not usually made visible. Through this conceptual process as well as others such as the studio's Pleats project from 1988, we can see that Miyake's practice is project based and collaborative, which has created conceptual longevity for the brand. Similarly, Aitor Throup works within this legacy of global conceptual design practice with his conceptually anchored design projects. Whether the concept is within the specific design of a garment, such as perfecting the simple buttonhole, or in the overall conceptual framework of a project and collection, Throup makes meaningful work that is situated outside of trend forecasts and seasonal runway shows, much like that of Miyake's design-manifesto-led, project-based practice.

Conceptual fashion, as defined through this lens, has concurrently been developed by designers Rei Kawakubo, Martin Margiela, Hussein Chalayan, and even Alexander McQueen, whose runway presentations always told a story through concept and subversive design and acted as either social commentary or critique. In the 1990s the runway became a stage, a gallery, and a set for the immersive creation of fashion theater heavily utilizing concept. Chalayan's collection from autumn/winter 2000 was presented on a staged living room with white walls and floor emulating more of a pseudo gallery space than theatrical platform. A Turkish choir sang live in the background, creating a mesmeric atmosphere as the models walked out and around the mundane lounge chairs and coffee table situated in the middle of the stage. As the presentation neared its end, four models walked out in gray shift dresses and began to disassemble the lounge chairs, taking the upholstery and transforming them into utilitarian layered gowns. Assistants then came out to fold the frames of the chairs into suitcases. One last model came from the back of the stage for the finale: she lifted a panel out of the middle of the coffee table and stood in the middle, pulling at the table until it transformed into a tiered skirt. In the recording of the performance, you can hear the ecstatic surprise and elation of the audience clapping and gasping in response to the conceptual transformation happening in front of them.

Rather than offering mere spectacle, Chalayan was commenting on the experience of refugees of war, people forced to flee their homes, carrying their worldly possessions on their backs.[26] Chalayan is a Turkish Cypriot who emigrated to England as a child in the 1970s when tensions between Turkish Cypriots and Greek Cypriots on the island nation were at their highest after the Turkish invasion of 1974. New geographic and cultural perspectives are made visible as designers such as Chalayan and Kawakubo—both from non-Western backgrounds—have developed practices in Western fashion capitals, particularly since the 1970s, creating a somewhat borderless fashion praxis that has brought diverse conceptual frameworks as well as new design techniques into fashion's global industry. As Herbert Muschamp writes of Miyake's practice, "Miyake grew up in a nation whose traditions had been substantially obliterated by nuclear holocaust and foreign occupation. Artists of Miyake's generation started from ground zero. Their work has been shaped as much by Western as by Japanese influence."[27] This grounding in cultural and historical context evident in Miyake's practice shows an embodiment of a global perspective that is mirrored in the borderless fashion of today.

As Geczy and Karaminas point out in *Critical Fashion Practice* (2017), conceptual fashion practice introduced the idea of fashion as sociocultural critique with designers such as Vivienne Westwood, Kawakubo, and Miyake in the 1970s and 1980s.[28] This type of conceptual fashion falls in line with the wider movement toward social justice activism that has occurred in the past ten years. Fashion is an accessible medium for people to access social commentary and critique due to its democratic and highly visible nature. Rather than solely reflecting on sociocultural climates, fashion can indeed be a part of social change, which is a point Geczy and Karaminas make in *Critical Fashion Practice* and one that I will illustrate in the case study section of this book. Contemporary fashion brand Vetements reflected this sentiment in its Saks Fifth Avenue department store window display from 2017. To comment on the immense waste of clothing production and the growing rhetoric about sustainability in fashion, the brand installed a large pile of clothes donated by the store's employees that increasingly filled the window space over time. At the end of the installation, the clothes were then donated to RewearAble, a social justice charity that recycles clothing.[29] This installation is demonstrative of the ways in which contemporary brands are disrupting the fixed fashion system to be a part of the critical conversation and change.

Hazel Clark claims in her essay on conceptual fashion that "sustaining marketable and conceptual activities [that run] in parallel is characteristic of the work of many younger fashion designers."[30] This symbiotic practice occurs for practical and ideological reasons—the commercial work often provides an income to support and develop the conceptual practice of a designer while giving access to the fashion system's networks of publicity and visibility.[31] This is of particular importance when it comes to commercial collaborations. Fashion is becoming conceptually self-reflexive as it is presented in more diverse public spaces, such as the museum and gallery, and even digitally through film and social media galleries, which are becoming more popular spaces than that of the fashion runway. What these spaces do is allow for a more immersive experience for the viewer and audience to interact with the work that in turn allows a concept to have a greater impact—whether it's a reflection on identity, ethics, the body, or aesthetics.[32]

The End of the Runway

Designers are changing the way their work is created and presented, and in turn they are subverting the traditional runway seasonal model. The development of borderless fashion practices emphasizes the fact that fashion is entering a new phase. Some designers are moving away from the traditional performance of the catwalk show and into the realms of installation, changing the way that fashion is viewed, presented, and in turn, bought.

After the democratization of fashion, due to the development of ready-to-wear in the 1960s, fashion lost its distinctions of class and became less bound to other social categories such as gender, race, and age.[33] Drawing on Guy Debord's theory of "the society of the spectacle" of the 1960s, the spectacle of fashion has been discussed in regard to the fashion runway by scholars Caroline Evans, Ginger Gregg Duggan, and Natalie Khan as the ultimate marketing device for large fashion houses, predominantly from the 1980s onward.[34] Debord's theory was a condemnation of mass media, critiquing society's consumption of images, commodities, and staged events.[35] Evans analyzed the fashion runway of the 1990s, describing the catwalks produced by John Galliano and Alexander McQueen as having a "transgressive spectacularity," and stating that the temporal immersive dreamscapes these designers created to communicate their work echoed a "seduction of the commodity in the nineteenth-century department store and world fair."[36] Evans has dominated scholarship about the fashion show, predominantly through her books *Fashion at the Edge* (2003) and *The Mechanical Smile* (2013) as well as her article "The Enchanted Spectacle" (2001), which all take a critical and theoretical methodology in their analyses of the catwalk's development in relation to memory, gender, and identity.[37] This scholarship emphasizes an era in which designers took advantage of multiple media and design practices in the communication of their collections, introducing music along with spatial, set, and industrial designers into the creation of the fashion shows. Borderless design goes beyond this notion, acknowledging the importance of collaboration and process but mapping the concept through spaces beyond the body and beyond the runway. This has emerged due to fashion's evolution as a field of cultural production and legitimization as previously outlined.

Anneke Smelik believes that the spectacle had previously been relegated to the realm of fiction, but in the last two decades it has entered media, blurring the lines between spectacle and reality.[38] Sensationalist coverage of news events and the manipulation of "reality TV" are prime examples of this in action; however, in the context of the fashion system we can see the fantasy of the runway spectacle, from the likes of Galliano and McQueen, lead into the spectacularization of other aspects of fashion and how it is communicated, from advertising campaigns and editorial, through to contemporary Instagram influencers. Ginger Gregg Duggan's article "The Greatest Show on Earth" (2001), which accompanied an exhibition on the topic, is a comprehensive survey of spectacular fashion shows predominantly of the 1990s and discusses their significance at the juncture between fashion and art aligning the catwalk show directly with the practice of performance art. To quote: "The late 1990s marked a significant point in this development of a heightened art/fashion phenomenon that is more far-reaching in its effect, as it results in fashion show productions that communicate through the medium of performance art."[39] The "end" of the runway as it traditionally was—that is, mannequins presenting garments to clients—sees the emergence of an intersectional field of fashion that focuses on more than just that of the garment.

In addition, Natalie Khan discusses the representation of the fashion catwalk by focusing on digital media and photography, two important technological developments that have pushed the runway show via multimedia platforms into the expanded field it is today. In her chapters "Catwalk Politics" (2000) and "Fashion as Mythology" (2013), she writes about myth and aura via digital technologies, looking specifically at the use of McQueen's early and progressive use of holograms and virtual reality in his runway shows.[40] She emphasizes the importance of the image in the representation and display of fashion in relation to the evolution of 2D fashion photography to fashion film and the livestreaming of catwalk events.[41] The development of these technologies has been crucial to the expansion of the fashion show beyond the catwalk. They have become not just mediated representations but fashion objects in themselves. These digital developments have opened up opportunities for designers to experiment, in turn becoming inherently interdisciplinary. To use the vernacular of the metamodern, fashion now oscillates between different platforms and spaces that instigate a critical reflection of the field beyond its commercial confines.

These developments align with a general desire for what Hazel Clark describes as "slow fashion" (a term attributed by Clark to fashion writer Angela Murills in 2006) in the industry.[42] Slow fashion implies an approach to fashion design and production that is both sustainable and ethical, which will in turn have implications for its creation, communication, consumption, and use. Clark states one key element of the slow fashion movement is the idea of there being "less intermediation between producer and consumer," which makes the idea of the traditional catwalk immediately redundant.[43] One of the designer case studies I will present emphasizes this need for transparency in relation to how fashion is presented. Aitor Throup, in conversation with Lou Stoppard, stated, "With luxury products there is a growing public demand for proof of authenticity and integrity, showing the process can prove that something is expensive for a valid reason, not just because it has a logo on it. It is about transparency."[44] He goes on to discuss how he likes to create experiences that are more accessible in terms of allowing a better connection between the viewer and his work.[45] This notion of connecting the viewer and the work of fashion aligns with a focus on the search for authenticity in cultural media. The statement by Throup quoted above also mentions this need for authenticity from an audience that has attempted to find it, albeit ironically, through the constructed simulacra of image platforms such as Instagram.

The demise of the catwalk, or the evolving nature of it, has been discussed extensively in recent cultural fashion criticism—to name a few prominent articles: "The Catwalk, Darling? It's So Last Year" (2003); "Fashion Week, Reinvented" (2015); "How Smartphones Are Killing Off the Fashion Show" (2016); and "Is Fashion Week Becoming Outdated?" (2016).[46] I argue that such articles evidence a desire within the industry for change, even at the level of how fashion is presented, as well as the wider growth of dissatisfaction with the politics of fashion, referring specifically to the total lack of diversity communicated in the fashion industry across gender, race, size, and age. Although words such as "diversity" and "empowerment" are integrated into magazine editorials and campaigns, rather than actively practicing and engaging with what these words connote, designer companies are instead capitalizing on them for marketing purposes, perpetuating an industry of spectacle and smoke and mirrors. For example, Dior's slogan T-shirts from spring/summer 2017 proclaimed, "We Should All Be Feminists." However, the models walking the runway were young, thin, and white, not diverse or inclusive at all. Rick Owens subverted these engrained paradoxes in his spring/summer 2014 show *Vicious*. Rather than predominantly using young, white, tall, and thin models, Owens cast a diverse roster of models and had them stomp, dance, and beat their chests in a tightly choreographed procession, which saw them scowl and howl in a now iconic warrior-like performance.

While some designers practice what they preach, predominantly very few follow through. They instead fall prey to the traditional trappings of the runway catwalk with regard to models, concept, and spectacle. Borderless fashion practice has emerged at this "end" of fashion, not as an antidote to the shortcomings of the modernist fashion system or even that of the experimental postmodern one, but as an evolution that mirrors the sociocultural ways in which we act socially, how we consume information, and how we create in the technologically democratic twenty-first century. In a similar manner to the way in which art exited the white cube of the gallery space, fashion is exiting the confining space of the runway catwalk, or rather it is expanding and evolving the medium as it is traditionally known and is engaging with space in new ways to satiate the audience's desire for authenticity.

Hybrid Spaces: Installing Fashion

The term "installation" encompasses static presentations, interactive presentations and performances, film, and the curated exhibition as well as digital developments such as virtual reality. This changes the structure of the fashion system itself and opens up a plethora of other creative possibilities. Borderless fashion connects the viewer on an immersive level, in turn transcending the hierarchical and out-of-date catwalk system. As stated in Geczy and Karaminas's interrogative book *Fashion Installation* (2019), "'installation' is an elastic term for the ways in which art, and now fashion, objects are provided conceptual settings by which to expose and provoke meanings that are open-ended, critical, and inimical to accepted opinion."[47] Fashion beyond the catwalk, or what Geczy and Karaminas call the "negative" space of fashion, or that "which exists around the garment," has become a realm in which designers invite viewers or consumers to sit alongside them, to become active participants in the cultural production of fashion.[48] Fashion installation is this hybrid space in which "fashion is primarily mobilised," which can be in the design of retail stores and spaces that fashion occupies, and in the "manifold types of images that give fashion its broader 'image.'"[49] Fashion installation "places the viewer in an interrogative relation," and in turn the consumer is empowered to feel like a participant in "an active speculation" with regard to where the consumer fits in a specific fashion scenario.[50]

Fashion installation also suggests "a new way of thinking about fashion that moves away from the materiality of the garment to its simultaneous situatedness in imaginary and constructed realms."[51] In their definition of fashion installation, Geczy and Karaminas structure the analysis into three parts: "Body," "Space," and "Body in Space."[52] The last definition refers to the contemporary fashion show and the "open" and "closed" nature of the experience with regard to the dynamic between performance and viewer. Borderless fashion practice— that is, disruption of disciplinary boundaries that converge on fashion—is most suitably communicated through this definition of fashion installation, a hybridic space itself. In an age where global fashion counterfeit industries are prolific, the search for authenticity sees brands search for new ways to connect with their audience and consumer.[53] Fashion installations and exhibitions have become a dynamic and immersive space in which this authenticity can be experienced.

Fashion installation works in some respects as an evolution from ideas developed by the Bauhaus movement. The Bauhaus, which translates to "building house" in English, was an influential art and design school, active during the interwar years of the twentieth century. It was founded by architect Walter Gropius and operated roughly between 1919 and 1933, when it closed due to pressure from the Fascist Nazi regime. Gropius opened the school in the German city of Weimar directly after World War I, which saw the first use of industrial warfare, changing the very nature of modernity at the beginning of the twentieth century. In spite of its name and the profession of its founder, Bauhaus did not have an architecture studio department in its foundational years.[54] Instead of focusing on separate studio departments, the school focused on the research and development of a "total" work of art, or *Gesamtkunstwerk*, a concept coined in 1827 by German Romantic theologian Karl F. E. Trahndorff in his general study of aesthetics. It was then made popular by Richard Wagner in two essays—"Art and Revolution" in 1849 and "The Artwork of the Future" in 1852—in which he discussed the power of operatic theater, which he believed manifested a synthesis of the arts that when combined would result in a heightened sensorial experience for the audience.[55] Installation art has what Faye Ran states as a "totalising impulse" that is both "sensorial and dramatic."[56] This, Ran concedes, owes much to Wagner's "creative synthesis"—a totalizing aesthetic shared with the futurists, Dadaists, constructivists, and others, which conveyed a desire to "ally artistic endeavour with design, science, technology, and architecture" manifested in different ways.[57] Bauhaus sought a harmony of function and design and sought to break down old artistic hierarchies both culturally and socially.[58] Borderless fashion designers create this synthesis insofar as their practices encompass design, science, technology, and architecture communicated through a multitude of platforms. Fashion installation has developed as the experience economy has taken over from the service economy. Audiences desire experiential memories over a material garment in their consumption of fashion.

Fashion is also becoming more pluralistic due to this as advances in technology, such as social media, 3D printing, film and virtual reality, push forward progression in not only how designers create their garments but also how they represent and display them. Creative design principles from art, architecture, and product and spatial design have converged subsequently. Alexander McQueen's utilization of technologies in the early part of the twenty-first century, championed by Nick Knight's Showstudio, was groundbreaking in how fashion can be communicated; his ghostly hologram of Kate Moss for his fall 2006 *Widows of Culloden* ready-to-wear collection presentation is a prime example. He was also the first designer to livestream a fashion show for *Plato's Atlantis* in spring/summer 2010; by doing so he expanded the scope of his audience and fashion became mediated by the digitized image of fashion.

Although this relationship between fashion, art, and technology is nothing new, the mediation between the fields is becoming more aligned, and fashion installation has emerged as an integral part in the communication of contemporary fashion. The runway catwalk is no longer the primary, or most effective, means of communicating fashion, and designers are now utilizing techniques taken directly from other creative practices to create immersive fashion installations that are made for experiencing fashion in real life and digitally, for example, through social media platforms such as Instagram and livestream events and online galleries. The dissolving of the runway and the emergence of fashion installation have enabled fashion to take on other forms beyond just that of the garment.

The fashion retail space has also become a site of experimentation in the twenty-first century. The growing e-commerce industry threatened brick-and-mortar retail stores, which were at risk of becoming redundant, throwing customer experience into virtual reality. Although virtual platforms have become the dominant means in which consumers come into contact with fashion, online retail has plateaued to a point at which the mere saturation of fashion e-commerce stores has come to feel algorithmic and inauthentic.

Looking back at the history of the fashion retail space, we can see its roots in the emergence of the department store, particularly in nineteenth-century Paris. Walter Benjamin's *Arcades Project* discussed the city life of modern Paris, focusing specifically on the physical structure of the arcade and its relation to modernity and the immersive experience of the city dweller, the flâneur.[59] It was a commentary on the enchantment of the aesthetic capitalist development of the department store, which is tied up with what Geczy and Karaminas described as the first wave of fashion's democratization.[60] At this time, department stores like the Bon Marché became sites of fashion spectacle where society's most fashionable bourgeois promenaded as they window-shopped, which was considered a new phenomenon of the time.[61] The radical new techniques of fashion display in these department stores, such as creating elaborate tableaux vivant that borrowed from conventions of the theater, transformed the way in which fashion was consumed in the modern age. Customers, of different classes, were able to consume the dream and fantasy of fashion in these displays, whether they were able to afford the product or not.[62] This phenomenon can be seen as a precursor to the concept stores of today that have become hybridic installed spaces that blur the boundaries of art and commerce as well as the elaborate performative fashion shows that hit their crescendo in the 1990s.

Concept stores such as Dover Street Market (London), 10 Corso Como (Milan), Collette (Paris), and Opening Ceremony (New York) have become embedded in the fabric of the world's fashion capitals over the past two decades, becoming "local hubs of cultural significance, loyal communities and global influence."[63] As globalization pushes ahead, fueling new wealth and growing consumer sophistication in areas outside of London, New York, Milan, and Paris, a new breed of fashion retailers has emerged, establishing similar hubs in broader international markets such as Hanoi, Rio de Janeiro, Moscow, and Copenhagen.[64] Flagship stores, particularly for conceptual designers, have become a place of experimental spatial design in which designers collaborate across disciplines to create elaborate in-house installations.

Within the context of borderless fashion, this represents fashion's expanded field of significance, where consumers come to the concept store for the aura that is constructed in the space, which is much like that of a gallery or community center where fashion subcultures converge to create meaning beyond the commodified garment. In 2020, Virgil Abloh collaborated with AMO (architect Rem Koolhaas's research organization) director Samir Bantal to create a multipurpose concept store in Miami, which is adjustable and transformable based on the needs of the space at any given time, for the designer's label Off White.[65] These changes could allow for events, panel discussions, and other cultural happenings, while the fulfillment side of the brand is stored away. The main focus is not the garments but the culture that fills the space around it that activates the fashion. The store's function is to "rethink how physical shops should operate amid the growing popularity of digital shopping."[66]

Fashion has broken away from the runway catwalk as its primary initial means of communication, like sculpture broke away from the plinth. The development of borderless fashion practice has added to discussion around the importance and consequential relevance of the runway catwalk as the most important step in revealing the latest ideas in fashion, which is tightly bound up in the cyclical expectations of the fashion system. The hierarchies perpetuated surrounding the runway spectacle, not only between the fashion object and the viewer but also among the viewers themselves with a code of the front row in which only the most famous and influential are to be seen, have become a spectacle in and of itself. Borderless fashion practitioners have democratized the way in which people view their work due to technology such as social media and immersive and interactive presentations, as well as an ability to utilize fashion as a vehicle for a wider sociocultural conversation, fashion in the expanded field. Fashion as concept, manifesting in installation practices, concept stores, and digital platforms prioritizes the idea and research process over the material garment, infusing it with layers of meaning.

Fashion as a field of cultural production has evolved throughout the twentieth century, most predominantly, however, at the century's very end in which the field started to be taken more seriously as a site of academic study and critical philosophical consideration. Fashion's interventions, collaborations, and experimentations with the field of art present the earliest manifestations of borderless fashion practices. Its millennial digital democratization and expansion beyond the physical space of the runway have changed the way in which people engage with fashion, but they have also expanded its audience. In the subsequent four chapters I will analyze four designer case studies that I argue demonstrate the manifestation of these contextual factors. They take into consideration the changing contextual paradigm based on these illustrated factors that have seen cultural aesthetics shift to an oscillation of the modern trajectory with the postmodern fracturing of history and narratives. I posit this here as the metamodern. The mapping of practices illustrated in these case studies supports the conceptualization of a new borderless fashion practice.

6

Virgil Abloh's Democratic Fashion Practice

Cultural relevance is more important
than fashion relevance.
—Lou Stoppard, *Fashion Together*

In November 2017, *System* magazine asked the question "What is Virgil Abloh?" The editors asked leading fashion insiders "what they really think" about the American designer. Edward Enninful, editor-in-chief of *British Vogue*, mused, "Virgil's the perfect Renaissance man. He's stimulated by the world and the world is stimulated by him."[1] On the other hand, fashion writer and critic Angelo Flaccavento commented, "Mr Abloh represents to me everything that is wrong about the fashion system right now."[2]

Virgil Abloh was a practitioner working in the realm of fashion who was both celebrated and reviled, mainly because of the fashion media's inability to categorize him. The designer passed away in November of 2021 at the age of forty-one, leaving behind an immense canon of multidisciplinary work, and in turn an enduring aesthetic and conceptual fingerprint on the fields of art and design. As a creative, Abloh embodied this new metamodern borderless fashion practice through the design identity he inhabited, as well as the way he communicated his practice. Labeled a "Renaissance man" by many writers and critics, he was a multihyphenate practitioner who worked across the disciplines of fashion, fine art, architecture, graphic design, product design, and music to break the boundaries between "high" and "low" culture.[3] To quote Abloh, "When it comes to discipline, I early on gave myself a pass to think without boundaries and that in a way is my own private renaissance . . . across disciplines."[4]

In this chapter I articulate Abloh's design practice in the context of a changing fashionscape that reflects upon the crumbling of disciplinary borders in the practice of contemporary fashion designers. Taking characteristics from aesthetic and conceptual elements of metamodernism, explained in the theoretical framework chapter of this book, I analyze Abloh's practice through specific case study projects he worked on. Those metamodern characteristics include design identity, interdisciplinary collaborations, and hybrid spaces. These ideas are directly reflected in how Abloh produces, creates, and communicates his projects; therefore, critical textual analysis of recorded fashion presentations, exhibitions, and media campaigns as well as interview profiles are the primary data sources for this chapter.

In terms of interrogating Abloh's design identity, I will first analyze the loaded aesthetic concept of *streetwear* through which his early career gained traction. If we conflate streetwear with a certain style that emerges from urban city spaces and communities, Brent Luvaas interrogates the proliferation of such a street style from a DIY ("do it yourself") aesthetic culture of the twenty-first century, the images of which having been circulated via the global mediascape.[5] Luvaas reflects on the notion that this digital circulation of images regarding fashion has fostered a culture in which the "remixing and reworking" of other people's "cultural labours" is more accessible than ever before.[6] In the context of the global use of social media that has effectively democratized fashion, a saturation of street style images has occurred across the mediascape. Due to this, a "critical appropriation" has emerged in which there is a "defiant assertion of the social nature of production over the individual rights of 'the author.'"[7] The context of Abloh's practice is driven from the culture of global "streetwear," which is the lens through which I interrogate his practice regarding this "cut paste" aesthetic logic.

Ted Polhemus's "bubble-up" theory from 1994 is also relevant here, as subcultural styles make their way into the work of Abloh, particularly that of skate and hip-hop aesthetic cultures. Fashion "bubbles up," according to Polhemus, from the "streetcorner" to the "backs of top models on the world's most prestigious fashion catwalks," through the postmodern act of appropriation.[8] In Abloh's practice this was not represented through the act of appropriation of subcultures because Abloh himself embodied a lived experience of the skate and hip-hop communities. Growing up in Rockford, Illinois, and later moving to Chicago to study for his master's degree in architecture, Abloh DJ'ed, skated, and made screen-printed T-shirts, converging the different communities of music, skating, art, and fashion together. Viewing Abloh's work through this contextual lens speaks to wider discussions of transparency and authenticity that have emerged in the contemporary fashion industry. This emergence has consequently given agency to the audience and consumer and has brought up further critical conversations around authorship and appropriation.

Out of this context, I discuss the ways in which Abloh has redefined a contemporary fashion identity through transparency, reconstruction, irony, pluralism, collaboration, and the breakdown between "high" and "low" culture that has in turn uprooted traditional definitions of "luxury" and disciplinary borders. This fluidity in design identity has become an overarching theme in the way practitioners in the realm of fashion are positioning themselves. Abloh represents a shift beyond the postmodern and into the new developing paradigm of the metamodern, through such design-based principles. He epitomizes the "in-betweenness" of Plato's metaxis, as a mediator between creative disciplines and cultures.

However, rather than sitting between binaries, Abloh takes up a space between multiple disciplines and cultural signifiers contextualized within metamodernism's oscillating, fluid notion of fashion. Thus, through this lens, Abloh was a cultural influencer who fluidly worked across disciplines rather than in the sole position of "fashion designer." In the twenty-first-century millennial age, "meta" has entered the common vernacular as a colloquial word that describes anything that is self-referential, a trait common to a generation whose cultural production and direct way of communicating are based upon digital networks such as Instagram and Facebook. In the contemporary cultural climate that is lived and experienced predominantly online, image-makers such as Abloh—who have millions of online followers—are the ones dominating the cultural production of fashion.

After building on Abloh's contextual framework I will discuss the design codes he uses across all of his creative outputs. These codes relate to the appropriation of corporate branding and the emphasis on logos, which have become apparent in the way in which some contemporary fashion designers are producing a brand identity. This aesthetic identity is then expanded on in relation to Abloh's plundering of art historical motifs that he then juxtaposes with his own luxury streetwear garments. This design identity expressed through specific aesthetic design codes is then discussed in relation to the multitude of ways in which Abloh communicated his work through interdisciplinary collaborations with both corporate and cultural collaborators.

Abloh was welcomed into the high-fashion European luxury system with his intersection of luxury and streetwear garments included in his own label Off White, but he was also a trained architect and former creative director for musical auteur Kanye West. His collaborations with conglomerates such as utility sportswear brand Nike and Swedish furniture conglomerate IKEA, as well as those with artists such as Takashi Murakami, gave Abloh street credibility and cultural cachet both on and off the internet. Abloh's practice broke hierarchies and barriers that were once prevalent in the fashion system. He created a new fashion identity for both fashion maker and consumer through the newest digital democratization of fashion that he instigated through the collision of luxury products and streetwear aesthetic language. A consistent design language enabled

Abloh to work across disciplinary platforms and media from music, graphic design, and product design to fashion and art. Communicating this language through technology, predominantly social media, also allowed the designer to transcend geographical boundaries, making his brand, or the aura of it, accessible to millions of people worldwide, with a particular focus on youth culture and the millennial and Generation Z audiences.

"Streetwear" and Its Definitions

Abloh was the head of a new guard of fashion designers who within the last decade have elevated the style of "streetwear", heralding its entrance into the world of high fashion with Off White and his recent rise to Louis Vuitton menswear's artistic director. For Abloh, streetwear is a sentiment, a way of thinking about the physical world that for him "started from skateboarding, graffiti, street culture" and has now grown in popularity to a point that it has risen into a global movement among youth culture.[9] Abloh believed that streetwear as a culture and design concept can also be applied to objects, architecture, and art, stating that "My position as an artist is to exemplify that philosophy, that cross-disciplinary way of working, within fields that largely aren't seen as streetwear—within high fashion, within art. That's the whole scope of my practice."[10]

Abloh practiced alongside other fashion designers such as Shane Oliver of Hood By Air, Heron Preston, Martine Rose, Demna Gvasalia, and even Eckhaus Latta, whose work could be said to use streetwear fashion codes that speak to a generation of "hypebeasts." Hypebeast is a name given to someone who follows trends to gain cultural cachet; it is referred to mostly in relation to streetwear brands in which cult limited-edition fashion items gain iconic status. More than this, hypebeasts are devoted to fashion, finding a sense of community through the attainment and adornment of clothes. There's an earnestness and romanticism to this devotion that designers like Abloh have picked up on, elevated, and centered in their creative ethos. In the past five years, Abloh gained the same popularity (or infamy) as other designers such as Gvasalia, creative director of Vetements and Balenciaga, and Alessandro Michele, creative director of Gucci. This is due predominantly to Abloh's ability to transcend fields, which subsequently opened his work to a wider audience with differing interests to that of the typical fashion consumer. With his brand Off White, which has shown at Paris Fashion Week every season since 2016, Abloh converged high- and low-cultural signifiers integrating codes such as sneakers, jeans, and screen-printed T-shirts. With his references to art history, architecture, and contemporary design practices, Abloh's work is also conceptually rich, rupturing the boundaries between disciplines that converge on fashion such as art, architecture, music, scenography, and graphic design.

Since 2002, Abloh worked as creative consultant to Kanye West's creative think tank Donda.[11] Some may attribute Abloh's success in the cultural consciousness as a direct consequence of this relationship. However, in interviews, Abloh spoke very little about the relationship, seemingly not as avoidance but rather as more of an abstraction.[12] Abloh instead reflects on their collective of creative collaborators and the left-of-field entrance point they paved into fashion, this entrance point being from a completely different creative field—that of architecture, music, graphic, and product design.

Like West, Abloh has created a cult of personality around his brand not unlike the infamy surrounding other "creative directors" of the past two decades such as the American fashion designer Rick Owens, Alexander McQueen, and even on a different level Martin Margiela, who is often referenced by Abloh and West as a design influence. The difference is that Abloh is situated more prominently within popular culture and transcends the boundaries between the more esoteric cultures of fashion and the more mainstream. Rather than gaining this "cult of personality" through technical and creative excellence as Owens, McQueen, and Margiela have done previously (which is not to say Abloh and West do not have these attributes in other fields), Abloh has gained it through collaborations with other big brands, artists, and architects and has banked on the cultural cachet of the covetable fashion item. Previously designers like Abloh who had no formal training in the field of fashion would not have been accepted into the upper echelons of high fashion due to the nature of his design aesthetic and the hierarchical and homogenous associations placed upon the streetwear aesthetic. And although Jean-Paul Gaultier gained success in the late 1980s with his collections inspired by the street, his access point was fashion, and his work was more appropriative. Today, streetwear designers are authoring and driving the culture of fashion forward. Abloh's relationships with famous musicians and models can undoubtedly add to the hype around his brand; however, in this era of borderless and concept- and consumer-driven fashion, the designers who dominate youth culture are those who easily oscillate between creativity and commerce.

To discuss Abloh's fashion practice, a mapping of what defines the complex notion of streetwear is necessary. Within the realm of fashion, streetwear has emerged out of the in-between spaces of modern life—those quotidian urban spaces such as a skate park or a subway station—that were previously relegated to the realm of subculture. Streetwear has now entered the realm of luxury fashion thanks to the adoption of product drops in commercial brand models and the trend-based drive for the need for sartorial comfort. The bubbling up of fashion from the street means that luxury becomes influenced by the everyday, and social classes intertwine where before they were demarcated and based around hierarchical layers of conspicuous consumption—as Thorstein Veblen outlined in his 1899 book *The Theory of the Leisure Class*.

In the late twentieth century, "high culture" as defined by Veblen had "given way to popular culture," and as Polhemus theorized, "street credibility" regarding style and culture became crucial.[13] Polhemus went on to write that "street-style garments radiate the power of their associations. Every age uses dress and body decorations to signal what is most important at that historical moment."[14] Furthermore, Polhemus argues that in postmodern times aesthetic messaging was all about authenticity "in an age which seems to so many to be one of simulation and hype."[15] The same could be said of today; however, the popularity of streetwear is bound by the value system of authenticity. As the authors of such cultural production, like Abloh, are coming from these very same subcultures, does this mean authenticity has been found? Or is authenticity "sought, but never found," as Smelik contends?[16] Regardless, in the metamodern era consumers seek at least the aura of the authentic and the "street credibility" of the identity that is associated with engaging in the design world of designers such as Abloh.

Situating Abloh within the context of streetwear also includes him in the longer lineage of designers influenced by the everyday. In 1966, couturier Yves Saint Laurent heralded the age of the ready-to-wear, with collections that included mix-and-match separates in practical and comfortable knit and synthetic fabrics designed for the modern woman. The "casualization" of fashion has only accelerated since then, but it also belongs to a longer history of "casualwear" that designers such as Jean Patou and Coco Chanel advanced in the early twentieth century.[17] Coined by designer Willi Smith in the 1970s to describe the idea of an oversized casual silhouette, streetwear developed out of sportswear, workwear, and combat-wear.[18] Hoodies, sneakers, combat boots, cargo pants, and bomber jackets are all common streetwear references. The recontextualization of such utilitarian styles of clothing "freed the garments from their original intended use," as hip-hop and skater subcultures appropriated them in the late twentieth century on the streets of cities like New York, Los Angeles, and Chicago.[19] Streetwear is about remixing and adapting these elements and reconstructing something completely new. Labels rely on logos emblazoned on garments to broadcast what brand someone is wearing, and the logos themselves have become just as recognizable as Gucci or Louis Vuitton monograms. New York–based Supreme, created by James Jebbia, has become one of the most famous skate streetwear brands, mastering the game of limited-edition "drops" of product that have created the culture of customer queues outside storefronts—with customers waiting for stores to open so that they can get their hands on the products that inevitably sell out in minutes. The concept of streetwear is born out of what Adz and Stone call a "a human reaction to the wounds of growing up in the sub/urban environment."[20] It is a reaction that expresses a physical manifestation of a post-traumatic response triggered by racist and classist structures of oppression, particularly palpable for African American communities.[21]

By combining the "authentic" subcultural style of streetwear and luxury fashion, Abloh acknowledged the barriers between the two: that is, namely, the "social, cultural, and even racial stereotypes that separate them."[22] "Street culture was born out of feelings of powerlessness and alienation," Adz and Stone state, and therefore they become "about communal solidarities connecting across lines that normally polarize, separate, and divide."[23] Abloh's synthesis of streetwear aesthetics with fashion, art, and commerce creates a total practice that goes between and communes cultural and aesthetic barriers. The difference between Abloh and other designers who have appropriated streetwear aesthetics into their designs, such as Marc Jacobs's "grunge" collection from 1992, is that Abloh *arrives from* the subculture of streetwear rather than *appropriates* the culture. To quote writer Lou Stoppard in discussion about Abloh's contribution to streetwear: "Rather than starting with a hypothetical woman or man in mind . . . as so many fashion brands do, these 'streetwear' brands begin with a physical space or geographic meeting point. Real people, rather than the imagined."[24] If streetwear bubbled up to the realm of high fashion in the time of the postmodern, then its democratic and widespread proliferation in the second decade of the twenty-first century emerges from the metamodern ability to transcend hierarchies through the digital fashionscape. Instead, streetwear cultural aesthetics and identities "trickle across" the multiple creative fields they occupy due to the contemporary engagement of the internet and the subsequent earnest community building that follows.

Curating a Design Identity

In 2013 Abloh created Off White, a democratized luxury fashion brand that speaks to the youth culture of today, which covets ephemeral fashion objects, as well as older consumers who want the prestige of a luxury item. The brand is a convergence of streetwear, luxury, art, music, and travel. He defined the brand simply as "the grey area between black and white as the colour Off-White," a suitably metamodern name for the technetronic globalized era.[25] The quotation marks that adorn the label were from the outset a part of the brand's graphics and design codes, implying a certain postmodern irony that signifies something that has come before. This design feature appears across his other projects, solidifying a consistent design identity from his first collection as artistic director for Louis Vuitton menswear in June 2018, a position he was given at the end of 2017.

Abloh took over as creative director at Louis Vuitton following Kim Jones, the designer infamous for the Supreme × Louis Vuitton collaboration that saw the phenomenon of streetwear hype and couture come together. The coveted product, which saw the classic Vuitton monogram merge with the Supreme graphic, is undeniably recognizable with its vibrant red-and-white Futura typography. It was, and still is, one of the most coveted fashion signifiers of the past decade, speaking to signifiers of corporate branding that oscillate between art and commerce. The graphic holds the connotation of coolness, intelligence, and street credibility.

Supreme's label design was appropriated from American postmodern artist Barbara Kruger's collages, adding an extra layer of significance. The use of this typography in this context is cast in a new light, oscillating between the realms of art, subculture, and fashion. The unlicensed appropriation of the box Futura Supreme logo by the label's founder James Jebbia is the foundation of the streetwear label's aesthetic success and can be seen plastered on T-shirts and billboards around the world. The logo is as recognizable as that of high-fashion luxury logos such as that of Louis Vuitton or Gucci and has become a commodity in itself. Postmodern artists relied on appropriation of style and imagery to activate their critical concepts. The references to Kruger's collages go back to iconic graphics such as the Coca-Cola Company's logo and to the Russian Constructivist posters made in the first half of the twentieth century by artists such as Alexander Rodchenko and Vladimir Mayakovsky that were used to mobilize social movements before and after Russia's Communist revolution. Abloh worked within this retrospective context to curate a design identity that plunders semiotic imagery from various historical movements.

Kruger herself retaliated against Supreme with her 2017 project series for Performa Biennale in New York City, which comprised five installation works, a billboard in Chelsea, a roving yellow school bus, a limited-edition MetroCard, and an installation at the skatepark in Coleman Square Playground.[26] She reappropriated her iconic Futura bold typography and applied quotes such as "Who owns What?" on red vinyl decals that lined the skate ramps. That very question was one of Abloh's core design values, which, mixed with an earnest approach to the accessibility of fashion, has made his design identity so popular in the contemporary context, now pushing his streetwear brand beyond that of the mere appropriation of postmodernism and into the more fluid borderless sphere of metamodernism.

The ability of Abloh to move fluidly between creative disciplines mirrored the context of his technical and academic training. At the Illinois Institute, where he completed a master's degree in architecture, Abloh was introduced to a curriculum originally established by key modernist architect Mies van der Rohe, which in turn was formed by the framework of the Bauhaus.[27] Abloh combined the modernist Bauhaus aesthetic ethos that primes functionality and cohesive aesthetics with postmodern self-referential intertextuality. The oscillation of these two principles represents a metamodern framework for Abloh's practice. On the front page of Abloh's personal website—which showcases projects and initiatives that form his total practice—there is an opening statement, which acts as a manifesto and reads, "Abloh was introduced to a curriculum established by Mies van der Rohe, formed from the notions of Bauhaus that taught him to combine the fields of art, craft and design. These theories, merged with contemporary culture, make up Abloh's inter-disciplinary practice today."[28] A modern minimal design principle reduces the sum of a design's parts to a succinct final product that can communicate the process of creation to the viewer, as Abloh stated, "whether they are a tourist (a newcomer to art elitism) or a purist (seasoned elitist)."[29] Abloh's fashion practice fits into this lineage of a synthesis of the arts, or a total work of art that breaks down traditional hierarchical boundaries. He

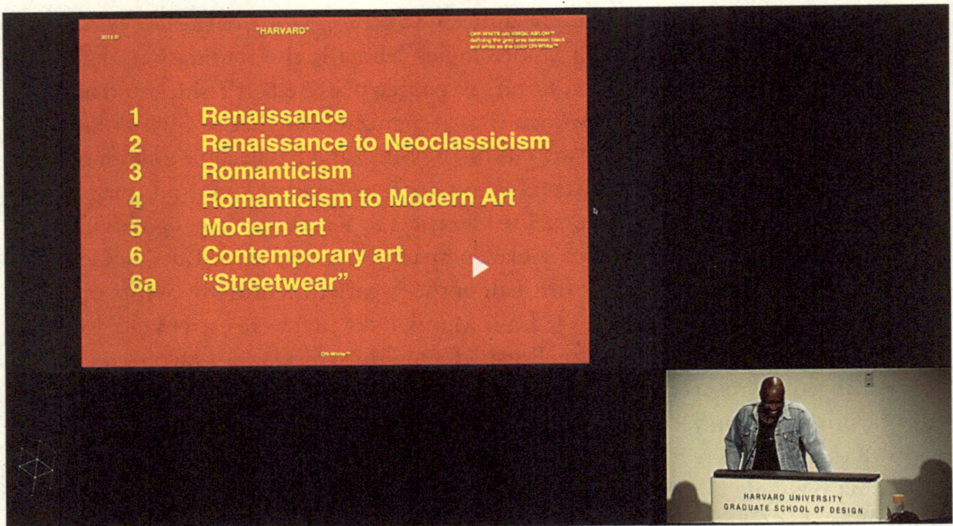

FIGURE 6.1 Screenshot of Virgil Abloh's livestream lecture at Harvard Graduate School of Design, "Core Studio Lecture: Virgil Abloh, 'Insert Complicated Title Here.'" Harvard University Graduate School of Design, https://www.gsd.harvard.edu/event/virgil-abloh/, 26 October 2017.

disrupted the abrupt terrains between different territories such as fashion, music, art, architecture, scenography, and industrial and graphic design. They all come together in the way that he created fashion objects in terms of his identity as a designer as well as how he communicated his work, which was predominantly in the form of an installation, whether that be film, exhibition, immersive presentation, or through digital media platforms.

Design Principles

Abloh curated a creative identity through a number of design principles that trickled across all of his creative outputs, creating this harmony of function and design. An oscillation between modern and postmodern principles can be identified within the specific design codes that he used. In October 2017 Abloh gave a guest lecture at Harvard Graduate School of Design, which was livestreamed online for people to watch remotely. At this Harvard lecture Abloh deconstructed his creative methodologies to an open arena, making process a collaborative endeavor. He stated that his practice is cross-disciplinary and inclusive, emphasizing the importance of looking back at and recognizing where one stands in the lineage of previous designers, artists, and movements.[30] He outlined his place within an art history narrative, claiming that a subgroup of the current contemporary art paradigm is streetwear, as depicted in figure 6.1. By placing streetwear within this art history narrative, Abloh took ownership over the validity

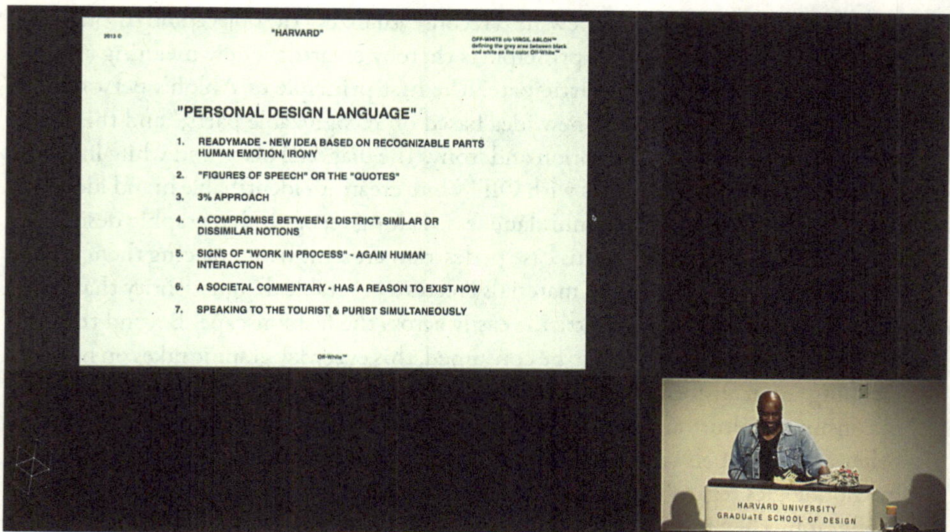

FIGURE 6.2   Screenshot of Virgil Abloh's livestream lecture at Harvard Graduate School of Design, "Core Studio Lecture: Virgil Abloh, 'Insert Complicated Title Here.'" Harvard University Graduate School of Design, https://www.gsd.harvard.edu/event/virgil-abloh/, 26 October 2017.

of his fashion practice, which at its heart is based around everyday product design, but more importantly the brand aura or the cultural production of his ethos and consistent design principles.

Abloh adhered to what he called design "cheat codes," one of which is the "3% approach," an idea that one might create a new design by changing an original by 3 percent.[31] The visual language of Abloh manifests across all his chosen projects. Diagonal black and white lines, quotation marks, and Helvetica typography have all been instrumental in developing a consistent and recognizable design language that has been cemented into the aesthetic zeitgeist, the characteristics of which he outlined during his Harvard lecture illustrated in figure 6.2. Here he presents his "Personal Design Language" that reads as manifesto-like in its simple but impassioned tone. The logo Abloh created for Off-White is indicative of his canny marketing intuition. It consists of a monochromatic Helvetica type with quotation marks bracketing the name, along with a small "TM" copyrighting the logo. Another signifier of Abloh's personal brand is the "c/o" (meaning "care of") he includes in all collaborative projects.

Abloh has referenced conceptual practitioner Marcel Duchamp as an artist model for his creative practice, particularly in reference to the artist's infamous readymades. The reference is relevant to the copy-paste logic of the internet era and in the ironic undertones of Abloh's practice.[32] By taking a classic shoe like the Nike Air Force 1 and writing "shoelaces" on its shoelaces, Abloh is changing the perception of an existent object, much like that of Duchamp's urinal;

rather than creating anything new, he is recontextualizing the object, and through his "three percent approach" principle is thereby creating a new meaning and inviting a new audience to participate. The first principle of Abloh's personal design language states that a "new idea based on recognizable parts," and this is leveraged to evoke human emotion and irony. The diagonal black and white lines that have become synonymous with Off White create an identifiable brand identity through their quotidian mundaneness. Taking recognizable graphic design elements from the street (in this case pedestrian crossings) and placing them on garments and communication materials creates a covetable design identity that is broadly recognizable and can trickle easily across the fashionscape. Beyond this, when placed on a luxury item to be consumed, this everyday graphic takes on new meaning as it transforms into corporate branding and comments on "the frivolity of consumer culture and the perceived value of clothing."[33] This act sits alongside other fashion labels such as Vetements, which practice similar brand identity methodologies regarding the appropriation of corporate branding directly in the typography they use. Unlike Duchamp, Abloh used branding as a way of distinguishing his practice across multiple mediums in an increasingly competitive market in which graphic branding rules. Aligning himself with artists such as Duchamp, who hold great cultural cachet, in turn allowed Abloh to tap into some of that cultural capital.

In a 2016 advertising campaign for Off White, the audience watches a group of models in a streetscape acting as everyday people buying fake luxury knockoffs. The photography is covert, with a blurred foreground connoting a voyeuristic point of view. Focusing on the action of antifashion and recuperating the street culture of fake designer items ironically tells the audience and consumer that Abloh is very much aware of the capitalistic space in which he is occupying. Abloh ironically winks at the consumer and audience here to let them know that he is just like them.

Abloh wanted streetwear to become a point of reference in a creative vernacular, like that of the Bauhaus modernist design movement, and claims that the resistance he has had from critics only means that it is working.[34] Fashion critics, such as the duo behind Instagram account Diet Prada and fashion lawyer and blogger Julie Zerbo of The Fashion Law, have been critical of Abloh's seemingly appropriative practice, claiming his work is derivative of more established and esteemed fashion designers such as Raf Simons and Miuccia Prada.[35] The difference for Abloh is that he did not claim to be a fashion designer. He was a transdisciplinary creative director, and the design codes that he applies to his own label as well as to his collaborative projects speak to this: there is a cohesiveness, covetability, and hype that he created through the intersecting nature of his practice. To quote the designer:

Why can't something super commercial be artful? Why can't something popular be artful? And why do garments that don't have words on them deserve higher esteem? This is the new clash between commerce and art. And it's happening in fashion, because fashion is the industrial arm of the art world. And all the kids who studied art are working in fashion now.[36]

Through specific and effective principles that travel across his own brands and his collaborations, Abloh negotiates between modern aesthetic design principles and postmodern recontextualization and deconstruction to create a new fashion identity that is entirely of the current global digital zeitgeist.

Designer as "Merchant": Questions of Authenticity and Originality

Fashion has been a discipline to benefit the most from the popularity of Instagram, an important platform that supports fashion's proliferation of images. The emergence of the "fashion influencer" has seen the rise of independent agents who drive sales for big brands through sponsorship and advertising on their personal social media sites.[37] This breaks down the linear hierarchy and timeline of the fashion system developed throughout the twentieth century. The fashion system previously relied on a hierarchy that presented garments in a seasonal runway show. These shows were then watched and translated through fashion editors, who put their favorite pieces in magazines, subsequently allowing some select garments to be chosen by buyers to go into department stores for commercial sale six months later. This is still very much a part of the system today; however, consumers are becoming skeptical. With the instantaneous accessibility of Instagram, the general public does not have to wait months for garments to be shown in magazines and then sold in the stores; rather, images of the show are placed online straight away. Fashion influencers have ostensibly replaced the editors and buyers, and in turn, as an insurance that fast fashion retailers will not copy the designs before the designer can get them in the stores for sale, a lot of designers are now adhering to a "see now, buy now" process. The consequence of this is the increasing pace of fashion output, which is unsustainable for the creative agents as well as the environment. Martin Margiela famously left the industry in 2008 before the onset of social media as a response to the unsustainable speed of the fashion industry.[38]

What has replaced the coveting and the waiting of the previous system in the contemporary context is hype. The "commodity rush" outlined by Jameson in *Postmodernism, or the Cultural Logic of Late Capitalism* (1989) saw "culture" become its own product in the era of postmodernism. This is still in action today, albeit on a different level, where we see the branding and image of fashion labels become more important than the product itself. Consumers and audiences invest in an authentic identity, or at least the illusion of one. The identity of a brand that is communicated in democratic online spaces is bought into rather than specific garments. This transaction is not monetary but manifests in "likes" and "follows" and general online engagement that then proliferates across the fashionscape.

Abloh's first point of success in the designing and making of clothing came in the form of his first label, Pyrex Vision, launched in 2012. The brand also acted as societal commentary and as a reflection of the growing popularity of rap artists such as A$AP Rocky, whose style was a mash-up of high and low fashion, such as mixing Rick Owens with streetwear brands such as Palace or Supreme.[39] The label consisted of hoodies, T-shirts, basketball shorts, and flannel shirts with varsity lettering and Renaissance art reproductions from the likes of Caravaggio, a tactic later seen in the Louis Vuitton × Jeff Koons collection of luxury bags that contained prints of paintings by Manet, Gaugin, and Titian. An intertextual tactic gives cultural cachet to the fashion object while democratizing access to some of art history's great artists. Despite the luxury pricing for an unknown streetwear label, the collection was instantly picked up by Paris-based concept store Collette, a longtime supporter of Abloh's work. This intertextual strategy of referencing historical and contemporary architects and artists is an important element to Abloh's practice: "I don't come from where I'm supposed to come from, so I have to prove that this is design, that this is art, that this is valid."[40] By referencing Caravaggio and Mies van der Rohe in his work, Abloh was able to gain credibility and cachet in a notoriously hermetic fashion industry, while at the same time introducing consumers to work they would not usually have access to.

In 2012 Abloh took flannel shirts from Ralph Lauren and blank Champion T-shirts and hoodies and screen-printed his own logo onto them for Pyrex Vision, charging $550.00 per shirt. The garments sold out after being retailed alongside collections by luxury brands such as Givenchy and Celine at Collette.[41] This was the first instance in which Abloh appropriated imagery from art history—here in the form of Renaissance painter Caravaggio's dramatic *The Entombment of Christ* from 1603–1604 (figure 6.3). The hoodie was worn by Kanye West on stage at 12-12-12: The Concert for Sandy Relief, the benefit concert at Madison Square Garden, New York City, in December 2012. However, the inclusion of a famous painting on a clothing item is not a new tactic. Issey Miyake exhibited his signature seamless pleats garments with Renaissance paintings printed on the fabric for the 1996 Florence Biennale. Similarly, Vivienne Westwood appropriated the paintings of French Rococo artist François Boucher and placed them on corsets in 1990. This historical revivalism in fashion incorporates Abloh into a lineage of fashion designers who invoke Walter Benjamin's *Tigersprung* (Tiger's Leap), the concept of fashion that leaps into the past to create an ever-evolving future. The difference here in Abloh's work is the placement of a classical Renaissance image on an everyday streetwear item of clothing. The recontextualization of the painting within this contemporary framework works to claim Abloh as somewhat of a millennial Renaissance man, through appropriation and association.

In 1981, Jean Baudrillard brought to attention Plato's concept of the simulacrum, with the publication of *Simulations*. Baudrillard argued that reality was

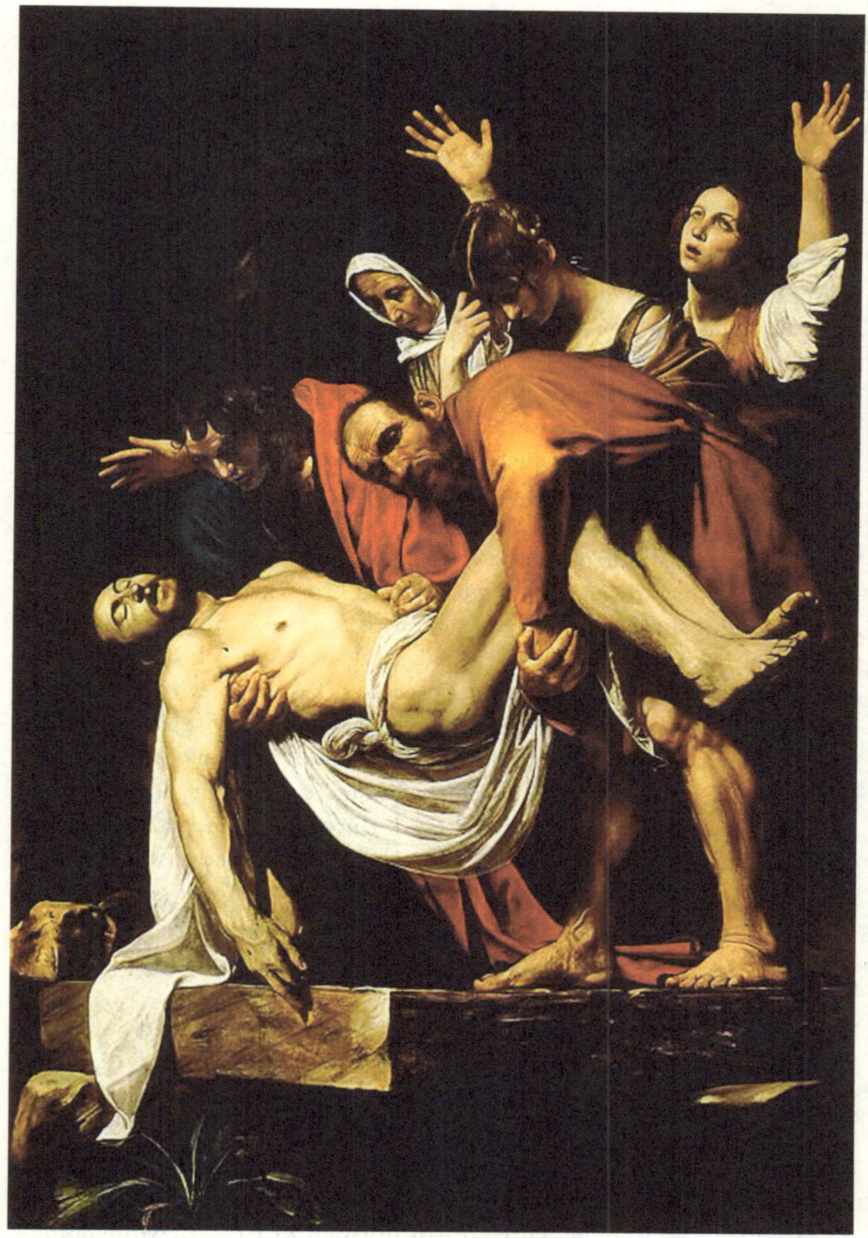

FIGURE 6.3 Caravaggio's *The Entombment of Christ* (1603–1604), oil on canvas, Pinacoteca Vaticana, Vatican City. Source: Wikipedia Commons.

reduced to signs and symbols and the "original" is a copy—in fact, the idea of the "original" does not exist at all.[42] This is apparent in Abloh's practice through the use of intertextual sampling. The word "sampling" is derived from the world of music, or specifically DJing, Abloh's first creative pursuit, in which beats and melodies, often from multiple songs, are stripped and merged to create a new composition. As Jameson noted, "the culture of the simulacrum comes to life in a society where exchange value has been generalized to the point at which the very memory of use value is effaced."[43]

Appropriation and mimesis, however, have had a more notable tradition in art rather than in fashion. Creative and progressive design originality has always been a nonnegotiable prerequisite in the practice of fashion creation. Reconciling the two, that is, appropriation and originality, is where Abloh's practice sits. This is demonstrably true with Abloh appropriating signifying codes in his designs; however, the way in which Abloh has constructed his identity and community is with an earnest romantic optimism for the future that negates the very nature of the postmodern era. Duchamp was an artist who moved objects from one place to another; as opposed to creating an "original," he transformed the notion of what art can be through an object's contextual dislocation. Abloh does something similar with streetwear and his design principles that have been moved and dislocated from their original setting; he becomes a "designer as merchant," moving away from traditional processes that had previously identified fashion designers. The metamodern embraces a multitude of subjectivities, and whereas postmodernism emphasized a compartmentalizing of the self (race, gender, and sexuality), metamodernism embraces the ability to occupy and share these subjectivities, and while these distinctions are important, how they develop, intersect, and interact will in turn help form collective and individual identities.[44]

Fashion "Hype" in the Digital Age

"Hype" is what could be said to have catapulted Abloh's career in fashion. By "hype" I refer to the aura that is created around a person, product, or experience through image saturation and meaning making. In the twenty-first century, this meaning making is achieved through digital social networks. Abloh's multiple collaborations with commercial conglomerate companies such as Nike and IKEA sit alongside collaborations such as his exhibition installation with artist Takashi Murakami. He was prolific across creative disciplines that converge on fashion.

Hype is created through what Paul Virilio describes as the delocalization of the fashion idea and is created when design practitioners do not adhere to the strict seasonal presentations and social hierarchies that confined the modern fashion system.[45] An online presence contributes to the creation of the hype of a brand, and collaborations with limited-edition drops of product and merchandise tap into the human desire for coveting something. Social communities are then created in online spaces where people come together to share their love or passion for a specific designer or object.

In the case of streetwear, this is particularly evident in the sneakerhead communities. Kawamura states in her book on the topic that sneakers "can be identified as a subculture, a status symbol, a fashion item, and a modern and a postmodern social/cultural object that binds a people together."[46] If a sneaker is a limited-edition release, it can sell out quickly and then go on the secondary resell market at a much higher price than the price at which it originally retailed. Abloh's ongoing reimagining of the Nike Air Jordans through his creative collaboration with the sports brand incorporated the design principles he has come to be known for, most prominently the quotation marks.[47] The hype around the product is created around the cultural history of the brand and the aura of the sneaker as well as the branding identity of Abloh himself. Demand creates desire, which in turn creates hype around a brand. The design codes, typography, and intertextual references that Abloh used and makes his own all feed into this hype.

Abloh was a designer who banked considerably on this idea of hype, particularly due to his personal connections with celebrity influencers and models such as Bella Hadid and Kendall Jenner. As stated in one of many profiles written about Abloh, "while the inspiration in creation might come from the disenfranchised, only the fortunate can make it popular."[48] This statement brings to light questions of appropriation and commodification that attend the collapsing of high and low cultural boundaries. In Abloh's case, this would be the skateboard street culture he frequently cites as inspiration. This rhetoric, however, does not do justice to Abloh's creative output and practice. Whether his product is affordable or not is irrelevant; people still buy into his brand and the image that he creates. Because Abloh operated in multiple other fields, he connected with the youth culture that consumes his design identity and ideology just as well as he did with young celebrity consumers of luxury products. He inhabited many of these spheres seamlessly because he used the same design codes across all of his projects.

It is important when discussing Abloh's design identity and his subsequent popularity, particularly with his position as artistic director for Louis Vuitton menswear, to note that he is one of only a few Black designers, alongside Oliver Rousting of Balmain and Ozwald Boateng formerly of Givenchy Homme, to be appointed to such a position in the hierarchical realm of European fashion houses. In the paradigm of the contemporary metamodern, these conversations about race are important in the reconstruction of an industry whose very foundations are shifting. For his first Louis Vuitton menswear show in Paris in June of 2018, Abloh presented a design vocabulary that centered on diversity, including catwalk models from every continent in the world (except Antarctica). Guests at the show in real life got a map of the world that pinpointed the birthplace of each of the models, as well as the birthplace of their parents. In an Instagram post the designer shared with an image of the map, he stated that the map represented "a global view on diversity linked to the travel DNA of the brand." Stuart Hall discusses cultural identity specifically regarding African diaspora communities and offers two proposed definitions of such. The first is the idea of a shared collective identity that represents a common history and ancestry.[49] The second definition recognizes and reflects the fact that cultural identities are under constant transformation, which is to say cultural identity is not a "fixed essence rooted in the past"; it is "subject to the continuous 'play' of history, culture, and power."[50] Abloh was brought up in America but born in Accra, Ghana, and identified as "African" rather than as "African American."[51] Recognizing the hybrid nature of his cultural identity, which is reflected in his hybrid global fashion practice, his identity sits in the in-between metaxis, negotiating between not only cultural identities but also creative disciplines.

Out of this oscillation Abloh has produced a total practice that is highly referential and intertextual. The designer claimed that there are no new ideas but an unconscious collective of creativity progressively working together toward the future, a rather modern utopian outlook.[52] He has stated that his design process is part of a wider creative historical context: "I'm sure that you're trying to challenge yourself to invent something new, trying to be avant-garde. Basically, that's impossible. These are things that I've figured out through working. As designers and artists we exist as a result of the many iterations before us, and we're collectively trekking in the same direction."[53] Joerg Koch, the editor of independent fashion magazine *032c*, claimed in the *Financial Times* that "It doesn't matter if it is art or fashion or design. Everything is digital. Everything is accessible. There's no future, there's no past, there's just the Big Flat Now."[54] Koch went on to discuss the idea that traditional ways of thinking about fashion and retail are irrelevant and that brand borders are blurring. They are more multifaceted and not solely centered around the spectacle of the seasonal runway show. In relation to the metamodern, this is reflected in van den Akker and Vermeulen's concept of the atopic metaxis: fashion is taking a position of no parameters and expanding territories in terms of how it is created and expressed.

Interdisciplinary Projects and Collaborations

Abloh's alignment with streetwear culture saw him collaborate consistently with Nike. His vested interest in art and the progression of art history has seen him collaborate with Jenny Holzer and Takashi Murakami. Other commercial collaborations include those with IKEA, perfume company Byredo and even French water company Evian—speaking to an interest in fashion's cultural production beyond that of the garment. Abloh has said of his collaborations with such a diverse range of people, brands, and companies that "the amount of collaborations should near the amount of relationships that I have with either brands or people."[55] Speaking to journalist Chantal Fernandez, Abloh went on further to state that all of the project collaborations he works on allow him to tell smaller stories that would not necessarily fit into a traditional seasonal fashion collection.[56] Borderless fashion practice is about more than materiality; it is fashion as a representation situated within a specific sociocultural and historical context in which critical conversations can be had. Collaboration was at the heart of Abloh's practice, driving it forward through conversation; on this topic he has stated, "I have a distinct set of rationales that make up my practice that are deeply personal to me, however, in practice this set of rationales works in collaboration with a brand or an artist in some way."[57] Through collaboration—that is, starting the creative process together rather than bringing someone into a project halfway through—the process of design is made transparent. Abloh posted process images on his Instagram daily, demystifying the very nature of what it means to be a fashion designer in the twenty-first century. One image sees him deconstructing a Nike sneaker with a craft knife, another behind the decks of a DJ booth, and another in conversation with figures such a curator Hans Ulrich Obrist or contemporary artist Arthur Jafa.

Abloh highlighted societal commentary as an important part of his design language and the ability to say something with the work produced or a reason for it to exist.[58] This manifests most explicitly with his collaborative projects, such as Abloh's Off White collection presented at Pitti Uomo in Florence 2017, with artist Jenny Holzer. This collaboration manifested in the runway presentation for the collection. A return to the strategy of postmodern artists and designers to convey social commentary is being used by some contemporary fashion designers in an increasingly oversaturated market that is being criticized for its ecological damage. The invite to the show was a bright orange T-shirt with life-jacket instructions screen-printed on the front—on the back there was text that read, "I will never forgive the ocean," a quote taken from UK-based Iranian refugee writer Omid Shams.[59] Holzer's contribution came in the form of two films projected onto the side of the Palazzo Pitti with her signature walls of text as the content; the projections shifted through various texts over the duration of the show while models walked on the runway. One of the films contained the poetry of Polish World War II resistance fighter Anna Świrszczyńska. The other film consisted of a compilation of poems related to conflicts in Syria, Iraq, and Palestine by seven poets from the region living in exile overseas. The disruptive installation was a way for Abloh to add to the political conversation about the global refugee crisis, using his platform as a way to start further conversation.[60] Regarding the installation, Abloh commented that his intention was progress: "I'm using my platform to nudge things along in a direction that is, I guess, a little more utopian."[61] Metamodern collaboration proves that fashion no longer has to be just clothes; it can also be the metaphysical cultural production of fashion and the utilization of its platform to progress critical conversations as well as advance product design.

International design and art fairs have become platforms, which validate the work of fashion designers such as Abloh with his frequent booths at events such as Art Basel and Frieze Art. These have become sites of communication for fashion practitioners who are moving away from the hierarchical infrastructure of the runway show. Abloh and Murakami had an ongoing relationship that manifested in multiple collaborative projects, which ruptured disciplinary boundaries. Most recently they created an installation at the Gagosian Gallery in London called *Future History*, which coincided with London Fashion Week in 2018. The installation consisted of a confluence of both practitioners' aesthetic signifiers. For Murakami that comes in the form of maximalist pop imagery derived from references spanning from Japanese painting and *otaku* subculture to Western art history and American hip-hop culture. To quote the press release for the show, "The duo's ironic and insouciant artistic gestures are designed to disrupt the divisions and tiers of stratified cultural production. The sculpture *Life Itself* (2018) is a kind of architectural carapace designed by Abloh to house one of Murakami's brightly sinister flower sculptures."[62] The installation incorporated Abloh's signature quotation marks and arrow icons juxtaposed with Murakami's smiling flower motif, which for the artist has become an icon of his brand identity. Collaboration has allowed fashion practitioners to occupy space between disciplinary boundaries. As someone not trained in fashion, Abloh escaped the confines of specific labels and was able to move about these different terrains with ease through developing a specific, cohesive design language that was not only recognizable as his own but also took references from everyday iconography.

The volume of collaborations and projects Abloh participated in added to the insistence of his brand in the cultural consciousness. An ongoing partnership with Nike saw Abloh's design features adorn the side of limited-edition sneakers that were released through "drops," for example, his collection "The Ten," which was released in October 2017. Like that of West's "Yeezy" sneakers in collaboration with Adidas, the covetable nature of these releases with their signature design principles pushed their resell prices up to four-figure numbers. In figure 6.4 you can see the design codes explicitly cited on the products exhibited in Abloh's 2019 retrospective show at the Museum of Contemporary Art in Chicago aptly titled *Figures of Speech*. In a pdf "textbook" that accompanied the collection's release, Abloh and Nike exposed the process of the collaboration and the "reconstruction" that the designer used to re-create ten classic Nike sneaker silhouettes, or "Ten Icons Reconstructed."[63] This idea of reconstruction plays on postmodern concepts of deconstruction. By deconstructing the iconic sneakers and reconstructing them with his personal design principles, Abloh created a meta fashion object that revealed the product's past, present, and future, "leaping" back to bring forth a new context in the present. The multifaceted ways in which he communicated this collection—through the online "Textbook," through in-store retail launches, and through live videos via Instagram—created an authenticity in his design persona that relied on the

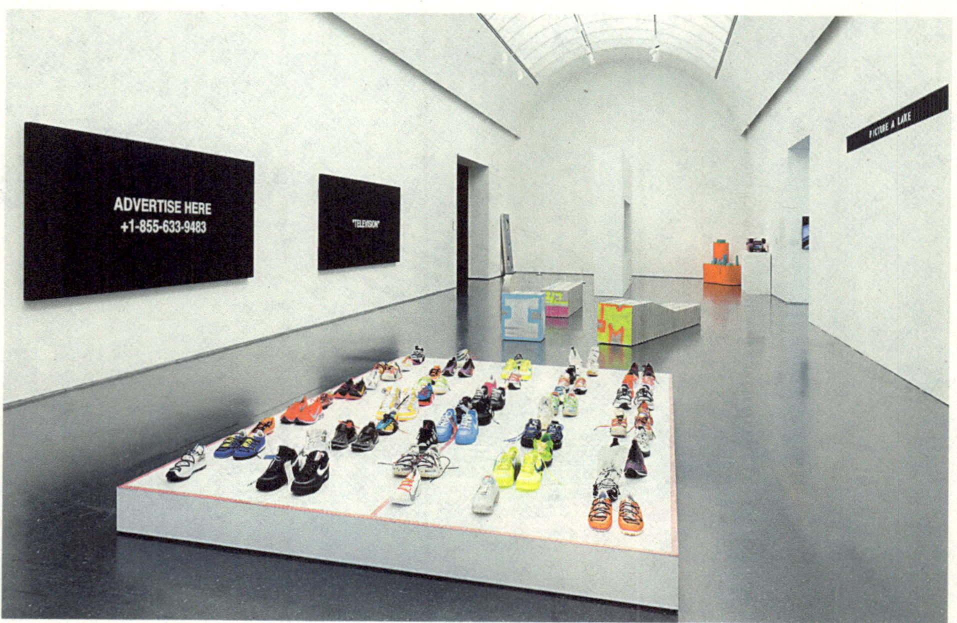

FIGURE 6.4 Installation view, Virgil Abloh, *Figures of Speech*, MCA Chicago, 10 June–22 September 2019. (Photo: Nathan Keay, © MCA Chicago. Permission granted to reproduce image of work by estate of Virgil Abloh.)

accessibility of Abloh as a practitioner, that has only been made available in the technetronic era.[64]

Abloh's work with Nike also reflected upon the streetwear context of his practice. Streetwear was born in the early 1980s in New York and Chicago and from the beginning represented a lifestyle that grew from the "constant alienation and frustration felt mainly by inner city youth. . . . A community was formed that was influenced by skateboarding, punk, hardcore, reggae, hip hop . . . graffiti, travel, and the art scene."[65] Sneaker culture arises from the context of like-minded people who have put value into a style that represents their everyday life. As Kawamura contends, even one who does not wear sneakers "will learn much from this mundane object because they are filled with multiple as well as complex layers and levels of ideas, attitudes, and beliefs. They are much more than mere footwear."[66] Not only does Abloh bank upon this sentiment with his Nike collaborations; more than that, he *embodies* these complex layers of meaning due to who he is and where he has come from.

Not only did Abloh design garments and accessories, but he designed furniture as well. Other designers such as Rick Owens have delved into the practice of furniture making as a sideline venture to their predominant fashion practice but none have been so ostentatious and meta as Abloh's collaboration with IKEA.

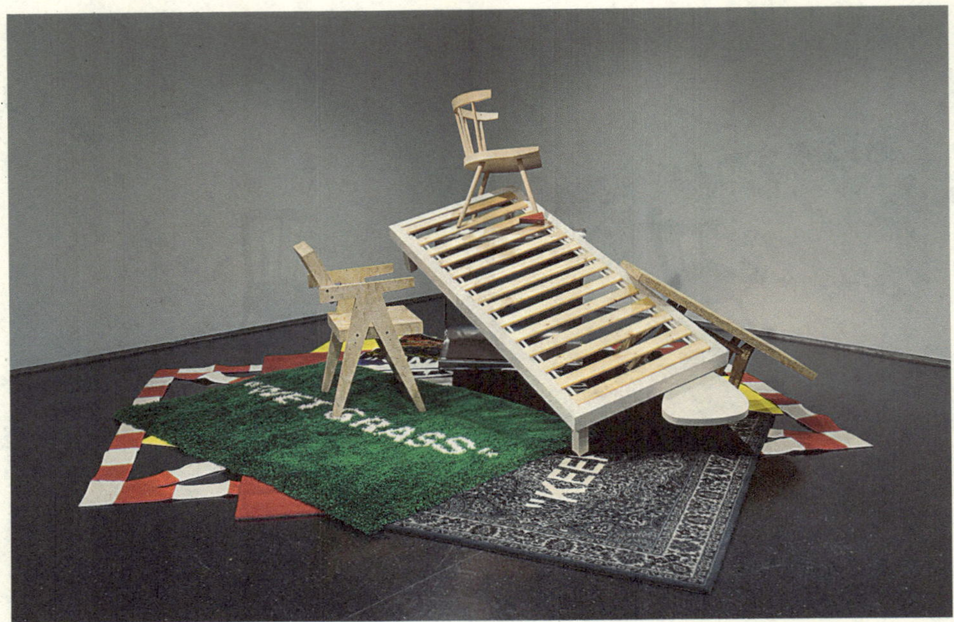

FIGURE 6.5 Installation view, Virgil Abloh, *Figures of Speech*, MCA Chicago, 10 June–22 September 2019. (Photo: Nathan Keay, © MCA Chicago. Permission granted to reproduce image of work by estate of Virgil Abloh.)

Unveiled at IKEA's Democratic Design Day in Älmhult, Sweden, in June 2018, Abloh's furniture capsule collection for the Swedish company paid homage to the millennial lifestyle. The collection consisted of classic utilitarian Persian rugs, daybeds, and Paul McCobb–style chairs, all with the added twist of Abloh's design codes and language.[67] This can be seen with the use of inverted commas bracketing words as evidenced in figure 6.5, in which a doormat in green is inscribed with "WET GRASS." The juxtaposition of the visual language becomes a meme and easily recognizable to the vast and diverse consumer audience of Abloh's work. This collaboration also embodied Abloh's design principle of offering access to the consumer "tourist" and "purist." Speaking with architect Rem Koolhaas on the research he undertook for the collaboration, Abloh said that "it started out as an aesthetic, but has become more of a survey. It's turned into travelling the world, interviewing millennials, and finding out how they understand the objects they live with. Where they place importance. How they live with their roommates."[68]

An object that speaks to the current climate of "reduce and reuse" was a glass cabinet with wooden framing that is used to display shoes or objects. The purpose of the cabinet is to make visible purchases that are so often hidden away in wardrobes and drawers. Through displaying them in a glass cabinet and plinth, Abloh hopes to discourage overconsumption.[69] With tactics such as these, this collaboration is the most democratic for the designer. The quantitative research he undertook to understand the needs of the millennial young professional consumers speaks to Abloh's wider design ethos and to the democratization of luxury. IKEA's price points are achievable for the targeted younger consumer, and therefore, IKEA obtains cultural cachet through Abloh's popular reputation across creative disciplines. Abloh's fans and consumers of his brand are able to gain access to his product, joining "Virgil's gang"—not that buying actual product is necessary to do so, due to the fact that more than anything, it is about the exchange of ideas rather than product.

As an accompaniment to the IKEA collaboration that trickled across popular mass culture, Abloh designed furniture for the 2019 Venice Biennale. Titled *Acqua Alta*, the collection of furniture was inspired by the city of Venice and its precarious ecosystem. *Acqua Alta* is a phrase used for the natural phenomenon whereby high tides periodically occur over the Adriatic Sea and coincide with the warm Mediterranean winds that push water into Venice, thereby creating floods. Sirens go off around the city, followed by warning whistles. Abloh's design project speaks to this idea of submergence through uncontrollable natural phenomena. "This land is not our land," says Abloh; "we're part of an ecosystem. With growing concerns about climate change, design is a powerful vehicle to explain that message to a broader public. Anyone can understand a chair."[70] Chairs, benches, and floor lamps make up the collection, which is cast in bronze and designed at uncanny angles to appear as though parts of the structures are submerged under water. For Abloh, these pieces sit within the context of a more Duchampian readymade, as functionality gives way to a conceptual recontextualization of the designed object and turns it into fine art.

The amalgamation of collaborative projects solidifies Abloh's design identity as a borderless fashion practitioner. The prolific nature of these collaborations creates a democratic access that allows many different access points to Abloh's design identity. His fashion practice is dislocated into many spheres, creating a rhizomatic map of work that oscillates and trickles across cultural terrain, communicated through physical and digital spaces.

Hybrid Spaces

In 2019, the Museum of Contemporary Art in Chicago held a retrospective of Abloh's multidisciplinary practice. It reflected not only on the multifaceted nature of Abloh as a creative agent but also on how his practice reflected millennial culture and the contemporary zeitgeist. Exhibiting work from his eponymous labels Pyrex Vision and Off White, it also incorporated objects from his DJing career as well as objects from his collaborations with Nike and IKEA. To catalogue this exhibition, the curator Michael Darling employed a specifically designed taxonomy that included two information classification systems: "discipline" and "topic." The "disciplines" include album packaging, architecture, engineering, fashion, furniture, graphic design, music, painting, photography/video, product design, sculpture, and set design, while the "topics" consisted of advertising/branding, language, race, readymade, social commentary, subverting the norm, transparency, and tourist/purist. This taxonomy was created to "make the conventions of museum cataloguing fit the practice and output of an artist working in a wide range of disciplines and roles."[71] Speaking about Abloh's work, Koolhaas stated that Abloh's cumulative practice emerged at a moment in time in which "the break-up of borders around professions that were once isolated" is occurring and that these professions, populated by industry veterans, "are now protecting their invasion by a generation of self-declared wunderkinds amplified by self-organised social media."[72] A young population of empowered and driven creative practitioners who are undoubtably influenced by Abloh's legacy.

Abloh's ability to occupy multiple spheres speaks to the wider context of dissolving creative disciplinary boundaries and the democratic accessibility this allows for consuming audiences. Having a public institution exhibit a catalogue exhibition of a living fashion designer's work tells us a lot about the cultural value we as a society place on fashion as a cultural phenomenon. It also confirms the idea that fashion is something beyond that of the embodied physical garment when the fashion concept is placed within a context beyond that of the runway catwalk and retail space. The ways that it is consumed by an audience take on a completely different value system. This value system is one based on communal interaction, immersion, and meaning making through the activation of fashion installation.

Abloh's practice was about process just as much as it was about product, which is a tether that binds the designers that I examine in this book together. The earnest postmillennium internet age, or the metamodern, demands full disclosure on what happens behind the scenes for creative practitioners of all fields to a point in which that becomes marketable itself. For Abloh, nothing existed in isolation; he claimed no responsibility for preconceived notions of fashion or art. Not only did he oscillate across the terrains of many disciplines, but he also broke the barriers right down. In a time when fashion designers move between fashion houses as creative directors so frequently, it is important that an authentic brand identity and its clear communication is evident. The audience and consumer experience fashion today predominantly through the internet, and therefore their value system has changed to prioritizing authenticity and aspirational identity. Being part of a community is the commodity in borderless fashion practices. This is true whether it is through participating in the critical and conceptual conversations that happen beyond the garment through engagement with fashion installation, or whether it's owning a piece of branded fashion to construct a version °of self. The nature of Abloh's practice and "hype" that surrounds his name (even more so posthumously) and the output of product and content that he produced is unmatched by any other designer working within the realm of fashion today.

Over the past five years Abloh cultivated an identity that seeks to hold on to his roots in art and architecture and streetwear culture, while successfully existing in the realm of high-luxury fashion. Michael Darling, who has previously curated an exhibition about choreographer Merce Cunningham and pop artist David Bowie, comments that "Virgil feels like the next Merce Cunningham, in that he is working with all these different collaborators in all these different artistic fields, and is unbridled by different categories and genres. It's a very contemporary model."[73] To quote an essay on the designer, "YEEZY is Kanye and Kanye is YEEZY. Similarly, Virgil is Off-White™ and Off-White™ is Virgil, creating all-encompassing super brands."[74] Abloh remained neutral about his success, stating in a recent Instagram post about his first Louis Vuitton presentation, "You can do it too." In the age of Virgil Abloh and millennial internet culture, where everything is a representation, the culture and experience of fashion has certainly become the product and commodity.

The metamodern as a proposition for interrogating the aesthetic and cultural expressions of contemporary fashion beyond postmodernism is defined by the globalized, borderless, and technetronic nature of contemporary society. What we can see of it in the practice of Abloh is the way in which he moved seamlessly between disciplines, centralizing fashion while blurring the boundaries of what can be defined as fashion, predominantly through multiple collaborations with practitioners from other fields and the "delocalization" of fashion's spatial existence. Vermeulen and van den Akker's use of atopic metaxis is epitomized in Abloh's work as he moves between modernist design principles and postmodern ironic deconstruction tactics for the products he created. His connection to youth culture and luxury fashion audiences gave him leverage to address important sociocultural and political issues such as racial diversity, environmental impact, and global politics and makes them known to new audiences. Abloh built upon the history of modern and postmodern cultural aesthetics to center fashion as both a physical and metaphysical driver of criticality and progress, which is a utopic thought for an industry that is so frequently self-reflexively commenting on its own end.

7

Aitor Throup's Divergent Design

On the edge of discourse of "civilization,"
of speech itself, experimental fashion can
act out what is hidden culturally.
—Caroline Evans, *Fashion at the Edge*

Aitor Throup is a fashion designer who does not adhere to the cyclical seasonal nature of the mainstream fashion system. However, this has not deterred critical interest in his work. Unlike Abloh, branding is not important to Throup, but he has developed a design practice that is recognizable in the formal elements that make up the product he produces and how he communicates his ideas. He has produced work across creative disciplines as a product designer utilizing the medium of clothing, as a creative consultant for the band Kasabian and Dutch denim company G Star Raw as well as his own studio. Throup's work is an amalgam of different practices, and the label that probably describes his oeuvre the least is "fashion designer." This chapter will be an exploration into Throup's practice, analyzing his design process, codes, and techniques as well as how he communicates his work, which is predominantly through the utilization of fashion installation. Like Abloh, Throup represents and signifies a group of young millennial designers redefining the way in which their clothes are created, communicated, and received through an expanded field of fashion. This multidisciplinary practice is becoming more prevalent, specifically in the way in which new graduates are working. There is more space in the industry to be taken seriously as a cross-disciplinary practitioner, particularly at the intersection between fashion and other creative disciplines. This is a product of fashion's entrance into art academies and the nurtured collaboration that is fostered within educational institutions. Journalist Maisie Skidmore describes Throup as an "anomalous designer," as he deviates from what is expected from fashion designers and from what is considered the "norm" in mainstream understandings of fashion.[1] Although Throup studied fashion design at Manchester Metropolitan University and London's Royal College of Art, he identifies as a "product designer" first and foremost.[2] Throup's work sits at the edge of the fashion system not adhering to its unwritten but specific rules that are strictly based around time and commerce. He has found success through process-driven and project-based fashion that is grounded in collaboration and an intricate conceptual framework. What this chapter will affirm is the blurring of boundaries of what fashion design has become and how it functions in the contemporary metamodern paradigm in which fashion has become a *practice*.

In this chapter I argue that Throup has a practice in which he designs products and objects based around intricate research and concept development, much like how architects or product designers conceptualize and test their work. His practice is project driven and does not adhere to the same traditional commercial confines of the modern fashion system. Throup has continued to garner praise despite the difficulty of categorizing his output, and he has stayed prominent within mainstream fashion media such as the online platforms for publications *Vogue* and *Highsnobiety*, which have championed his more esoteric process. Throup's practice oscillates not only between the conceptual and the performative but between modern and postmodern sensibilities, making him a metamodern borderless fashion designer that instigates a rethinking about how fashion is consumed in the twenty-first century. If not through traditional modes of consumption like purchasing a garment, then how is Throup's work experienced? What does this tell us about the changing notions of the way fashion is communicated and consumed, and in turn how it is valued? Taking characteristics from aesthetic and conceptual elements of metamodernism, I will analyze Throup's practice through specific case study projects he has conceptualized and realized. The metamodern characteristics I will focus on will mirror those that I used in the previous chapter to analyze Abloh's fashion practice. These include design identity, interdisciplinarity, collaboration, and hybrid spaces. These ideas are directly reflected in how Throup produces, creates, and communicates his projects. Therefore, critical analysis of fashion presentations, exhibitions, and editorial imagery as well as profile interviews with the designer will be the primary data for this chapter.

Speaking to the wider hypothetical questions of this book, I contextualize Throup's work by first analyzing his personal design manifesto, which has been developed over the past fifteen years. This manifesto serves as a reference point underlying Throup's design methodology. Developing a manifesto is situated within a wider lineage of art manifestos and fashion designers who have developed manifestos for their conceptual practices such as Kawakubo and Westwood. I then look at how Throup has curated a design identity based around specific design principles and a slow creative practice that values research into a designed product and a core conceptual narrative. I then analyze specific ongoing projects grounded in the research of human anatomy and design "archetypes" based on Throup's dedicated illustration practice that directly informs all of his creative outputs.

Like Abloh's practice, I describe Throup's as a "total" creative practice, or the *Gesamtkunstwerk*, a synthesis of the arts that when combined result in a heightened sensorial experience for the audience. This manifests in Throup's fashion presentations and performances, which I describe here as installations and "hybrid spaces." I then go on to discuss the multiple collaborations Throup undertakes, ranging from designing combat costumes for the Hollywood film *The Hunger Games: Mockingjay Part 1* (2014) to ongoing creative collaborations with the rock band Kasabian since 2011 and multiple creative consultation and designer collaboration roles for companies such as Umbro, C. P. Company, and Stone Island. This amalgamation of projects displays a convergence of disciplines that manifest in borderless fashion and underscores the changing of paradigms into the metamodern.

Fashion's Expanded Field

As scholar José Teunissen states, fashion in the twenty-first century has become a discipline in which designers can "comment on the fashion system itself, bringing fashion to a more conceptual plane."[3] Due to this new approach to the practice of fashion, "the concept itself, and its aesthetic dimension, has become more important than presenting an ideal" person in clothes.[4] Fashion's democratization over the twentieth century, as outlined in chapter 3, plays a part in this, as well as a shift toward critical fashion practices in which fashion becomes socioculturally and politically conscious and self-aware. Concept, narrative, and experience have become authentic markers in how fashion is valued by the consuming audience. Teunissen goes on to state that fashion aesthetics have shifted from an "object centred discourse to one driven by concepts and ideas, the creative process, and multi-dimensional product experiences."[5]

As scholar Lara Torres states in her article "Fashion in the Expanded Field," "Fashion today seems to consist of a vast array of complex and elusive phenomena where the boundaries have become harder to map."[6] Expanding on from the work of Krauss, she goes on to elaborate that the development of interdisciplinary fashion practices allows designers and creative practitioners to engage in critical discussion of the fashion system.[7] It also allows them to be situated outside of a market-led fashion framework that leads to a focus on ideas rather than a manufactured object, prioritizing concept and experimentation over a final product.[8] Torres labels this phenomenon "post-product logic," meaning fashion that is not created for mass production and mass consumption but rather prioritizes thought and concept.[9] It is within this expanded field of fashion where Throup's fashion design practice can most comfortably be situated. Torres contends that like that of the evolution of sculpture, fashion designers in the twenty-first century are exploring the same space of idealism at the borders of the fashion discipline.[10] Here I discuss fashion in the expanded field in terms of the fashion garment being "one term on the periphery" of a wider pluralistic space of possibility. To guide Throup's creative practice within this expanded field, he has developed design principles that have formed a contextual manifesto that guide his practice.

Design Manifesto

Generally, a manifesto is a published declaration of the intentions, motives, and worldview of the producer, whether that is an individual or a group or ideological movement. Manifestos are prescriptive insofar as they present notions that they have every intention of carrying out. A manifesto is often artistic and has heralded in specific aesthetic, political, and cultural movements such as the 1909 nationalist-leaning Italian Futurist manifesto written by F. T. Marinetti in which a desire for speed and transformation of traditional culture was called for through artistic expression. Then there are the post–World War I Dada and Surrealist manifestos that heralded the arrival of avant-garde modernist movements, offering a different way of producing and consuming art.[11] These manifestos put forth a worldview to challenge the very nature of the sociocultural and political context in which they emerged during the tumultuous first half of the twentieth century. A manifesto focuses more directly on process over results and is in direct contact with time and place. The word "manifesto" as it comes into contact with "fashion" carries with it this particular historical and political resonance. The concept of the manifesto becomes part of the art or fashion movement or production itself. In 2008 Vivienne Westwood published *Manifesto*, in which the designer puts forward broad ideas about art and culture and the importance of their development for human societal progress.[12] However, Westwood's work has always been a form of resistance and social activism against the political structures. Since the late 1960s Westwood and then partner Malcolm McLaren gave a voice and a greater worldview to the "bohemians, misfits, miscreants and malcontents," which manifested in Punk style and the embodiment of an antiestablishment manifesto.[13] Before this, "fashion was largely defined and guided by wealth and class," and the dominant ideologies of culture that they espoused.[14] Vivienne Westwood contributed to the dismantling of the "trickle-down" flow of influence with regard to style and fashion as she championed subcultural styles of the masses.

Rei Kawakubo presented a manifesto for her spring/summer 2014 collection instead of a traditional press release. It displays a combination of "creative posturing and artistic vision" with the last paragraph of the manifesto reading:

> In order to make this SS14 collection, I wanted to change the usual route within my head. I tried to look at everything I look at in a different way.
> I thought a way to do this was to start out with the intention of not even trying to make clothes. I tried to think and feel and see as if I wasn't making clothes.[15]

Kawakubo outlines a process of ideation that focuses against the grain of typical fashion production and more on the conceptual space outside of the garment in this expanded field. Borderless fashion practice reflects designer's thinking processes confronting and translating their concepts and ideas through a diverse language.[16]

Like Abloh, Throup emphasizes a pragmatic focus on specific design principles that culminates in a manifesto and philosophy that the designer uses to frame his work, which facilitates Throup's expanded concept of fashion. New Object Research (NOR) is the name of the expanded research practice, philosophy, and manifesto of Throup's design studio, the first iteration of such was published in 2012 through his design studio A. T. Studio Ltd.[17] In the document, Throup prioritizes a focus on process through a "Justified Design Philosophy," stating that "all design features should be traceable back to the process, and therefore the narrative and concept."[18] The manifesto contends that for a design to have integrity "it does not need to rely on function," but through conceptual and narrative construct an expanded reason can be validated for the product's existence. Throup outlines a fundamental difference between art and design within the NOR methodology: "Artists create problems. Designers solve problems."[19] The manifesto employs a systematic methodology that incorporates both claiming that the transition from "concept to product—or from art to design—should be about distilling, not diffusing." To communicate this symbiotic relationship and distinction more, the manifesto negotiates the relationship between the designed object and art. It reads,

> Art: the narrative / conceptual framework, and the system of visual / physical metaphors and symbolism utilised.
> Product design: the unique design solutions generated and dictated by the concept.
> (Fashion): the way in which the work can be appropriated into people's lives. Much as utilitarian design classics have become appropriated into lifestyle products.[20]

This demonstrates the way in which art and design are in an oscillating dialogue in the practices of borderless fashion practice. The methodology of NOR is focused on design process with regard to Throup's studio, which functions more as a think tank or laboratory for experimentation and development. Evident in the manifesto is a resistance to the predetermined timelines of the seasonal fashion industry machine.

Throup's 2016 *The Rite of Spring/Summer/Autumn/Winter* project was a manifestation of NOR. For the installation performance he republished the manifesto in the form of a presentation press release.[21] Some of the key points conveyed in Throup's 2016 NOR manifesto developed from those points made in his 2012 manifesto, such as the designer's intentions not to let the brand become a "product brand," rather allowing the brand to be about the research of new objects and conceptual critical narratives. A desire to oscillate between art practice and the designed object that manifests in the fashion product and experience is still present. Throup's unconventional approach to commerce "creates an immersive platform, which allows an otherwise rare insight into the process and practices of the studio."[22] He opens up this process through behind-the-scenes imagery films on social media channels such as Instagram and YouTube by "presenting prototypes, patterns, sculptural tests, and general process artefacts."[23] This immersive platform that unveils process is also part of the expanded notion of Throup's practice and creative output. By unveiling this process of making, Throup opens the space for the audience to be active in its process, transparently oscillating their position between audience and participant.

In 2014 Throup produced a film titled *A Portrait of Noomi Rapace*, which opened with Throup's process of creating his specific three-dimensional mesh anatomical block patterns that are used across his many projects.[24] The film separates into seven acts mirroring the practice of Rapace's vocation: "The Identified Self," "The Loss of Identity," "The Casting Process," "The Growth of Identity," "The Directed Memory of Form," "The Directed Memory of Self," and "The Final Performance." In acts 1 and 2, Swedish actor Rapace walks into the frame and disrobes, taking off her own clothing and replacing them with a black full-body stocking, reducing her identity to anatomical form. In act 3, the scene shifts and Rapace is standing on a plinth as Throup and his design assistants, wearing contrasting white clothing, wrap and cast her body in gauze mesh fabric. The cameras record the designers as they mold each separate body part in the mesh with heat, as shown in figure 7.1. The face is the final body part to be cast before Rapace exits the scene. In acts 4 and 5, each piece is then sewn together by Throup, constructing the identity of the disembodied form limb by limb. In act 6, the human exoskeleton is then cast in black spray paint, "returning it, metaphorically, to its former self of Rapace clad in black," her original embodied form in act 1, evidenced in figure 7.2.[25] In act 7, the final performance takes place in which the constructed portrait is fitted to a suspended rotation device on the ceiling, thrown into relief by an encompassing white background (figure 7.3). Clothes are then molded onto the figure encasing its empty interior, installing the portrait in its final form, a "disembodied/re-embodied figure dangling alone and prone in space."[26] The film was not about the construction of garments; rather, as Geczy and

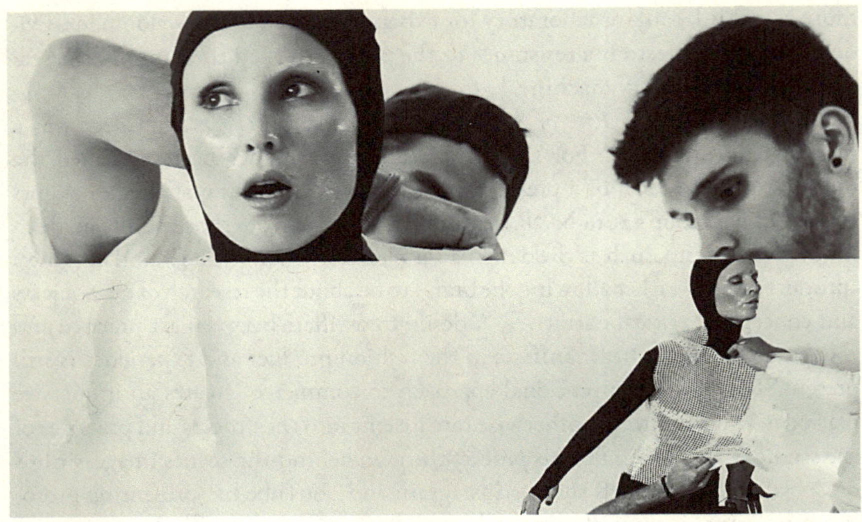

FIGURE 7.1 Screenshot of Aitor Throup Studio, *A Portrait of Noomi Rapace Act III*, 2014. Source: Nowness, https://www.nowness.com/story/noomi-rapace-by-aitor-throup.

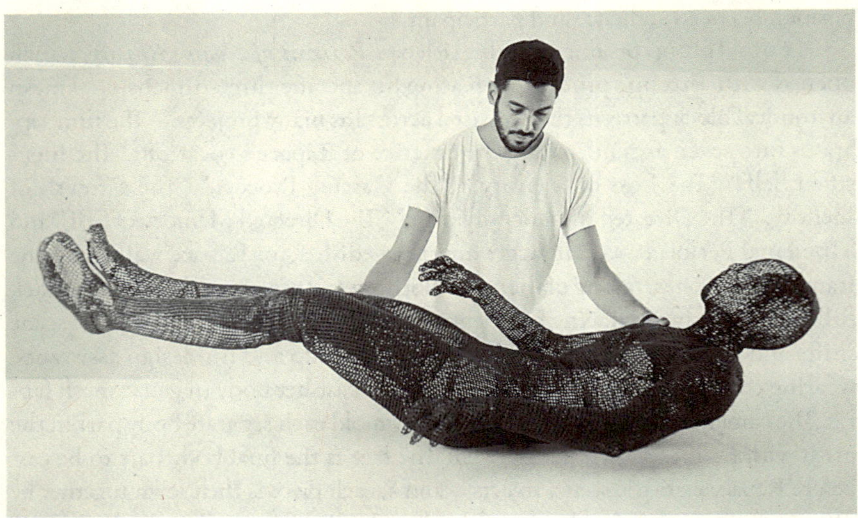

FIGURE 7.2 Screenshot of Aitor Throup Studio, *A Portrait of Noomi Rapace Act V*, 2014. Source: Nowness, https://www.nowness.com/story/noomi-rapace-by-aitor-throup.

Karaminas contend, it was about "making the carapace that leads to the garment," and "the living subject is made absent."[27] The shell becomes sculpture, an imprint of the mapped body blurring the binary between embodied and disembodied garment. This project presents the principles of Throup's manifesto in physical practice. There is a dialogue between artistic concept and designed product.

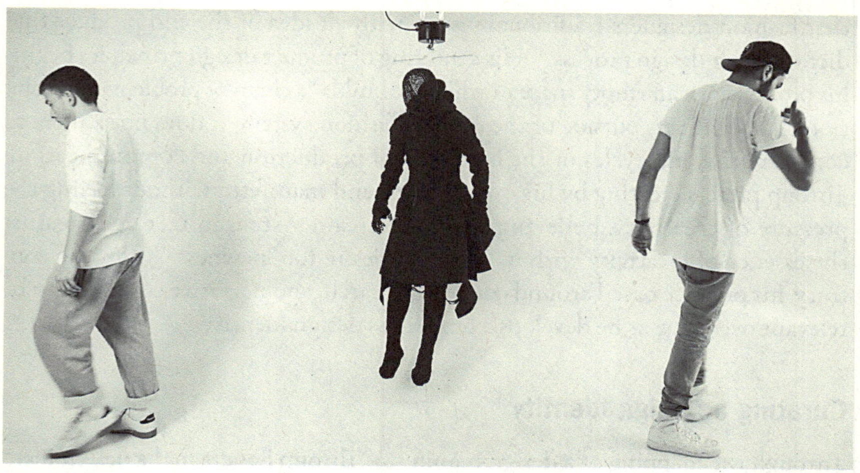

FIGURE 7.3 Screenshot of Aitor Throup Studio, *A Portrait of Noomi Rapace Act VII*, 2014. Source: Nowness, https://www.nowness.com/story/noomi-rapace-by-aitor-throup.

NOR is not a fashion line or even a brand; it is a working project whose very malleable nature is stated in the title. As the manifesto states, "'New Object Research' is a paradigm shift in the world of product brands. 'New Object Research' is a process brand."[28] "Research" is an open word that alludes to the seeking out of knowledge and the establishment of working theories. It is an ongoing process, like that of Throup's fashion practice.

The design process of fashion practitioners has always been somewhat of a rarefied mystery. Access is granted only to those who can afford designer products or those invited to witness their display. The twentieth-century assumption that this process is somehow esoteric has been shattered with the onset of digital media in the twenty-first century and the consequent democratization of fashion that has occurred. Fashion documentaries, designer high-street collaborations, and fashion's entrance into the museum and gallery space have all demystified the aura around the idea of fashion's great "creative director" that dominated fashion's narrative throughout the twentieth century and into the twenty-first. Throup makes the case for this by making his design process and design "codes" an open source for audiences and consumers. By way of making the process of creation transparent, Throup actions and solidifies his design principles allocated in his manifesto.

Throup uses the words "object" and "research" in describing his practice, which means that he is working to expand the fashion object, beyond just materiality. He has gained a reputation within the fashion industry as a conceptualist, championing the process of design with its problems and solutions over the actual end product, which is always meticulous. On his process Throup states that fashion designers traditionally start with an idea of the end product that dictates their design process.[29] His centering of product design principles begins his process with an empty space in which he builds "a chain of problems and solutions."[30] NOR acts outside of the cyclical fashion system; it does not adhere to commercial trend cycles or the hierarchy of production and communication. Throup prefers creating by his own systems and manifesto without feeling the pressure of creativity, believing the mainstream system in fact goes against the essence of creativity with its constant desire for "newness."[31] On the contrary, his practice based around concept, research, and narrative continues to be relevant over time as he develops a borderless design identity.

Curating a Design Identity

Through the mapping of a design manifesto, Throup has created a design identity that does not conform to the traditional branding of mainstream fashion practices like that of Abloh. Instead of branding through the development and placement of specific logos, Throup's work is identifiable through conceptual form. Throup has established a consistent design identity through slow design methods he has developed over the course of fifteen years. Attention to the human form's anatomy and movement identifies a conceptual focus on utility and streetwear signifiers. Throup's practice is fashion as a design process, a borderless fashion *practice*.

Practice derives from the Greek *praxis*, which to Aristotle meant an action that is valuable in and of itself, in contrast to those actions whose goal is making or creation.[32] To quote Marcus Boon and Gabriel Levine in their summation of "practice" within the realm of art, "The Greek *Praxis* had an ethical dimension, concerned with self-shaping or a decision as to how to live, as well as a political dimension concerned with the for in which one lived with other people."[33] The meaning of "praxis" evolved throughout time and different theoretical canons, throughout modernity philosophers such as Kant and Marx reframed ways of thinking from the individual to the collective and encouraged action as an articulation of human freedom through "the transformation of material conditions."[34] Speaking of the art world of the mid-twentieth century, they say, "Praxis, for artists drawn into the radical current of the times, meant the reformulation of life and art into a new fusion of critical thought, creative production and political action."[35] Borderless fashion emulates this current of "critical thought, creative production, and political action." They go on to state that "the ethical mandate that art has taken on via its confrontation with existing material conditions has resulted in a splintering of art into more and more diverse objects, events, and engagements—with the paradoxical result that basically anything that could be considered a practice might be considered art."[36]

It is within this definition of practice that borderless fashion manifests in multiple ways, being a garment, a performance, an installation, or a film. All of these can be defined as "fashion practice" due to the very definition of "practice" as multi-methodological and multidisciplinary. Throup's practice can be described as being situated in an "expanded field" because he liberates the garment from the body, placing emphasis on the external space, which holds the conceptual narrative. Design scholar Malene Leerberg proposes a rethinking of the definition of design in the contemporary disciplinary landscape in her research paper "Design in the Expanded Field" and asks, "How does design work?" rather than "What is design?"[37] Justifying this change in rhetoric she writes, "contemporary design increasingly transcends the idea of merely tangible, material objects to include more elusive creations such as interactions, strategies and systems."[38] As established in the opening chapters of this book, fashion design practice in the twenty-first century has become a hybrid practice of interdisciplinarity due to the changing fashionscape brought about by advances in technology, and a move toward more critical conceptual practices in fashion that started in the second half of the twentieth century. In relation to the question "How does design work?" Leerberg states that the idea of design is to communicate. She continues: "As a noun design refers to a product, be it an object, a scheme, a sketch, pattern or composition, the design is the output of a process. As a verb design is a process, which most commonly refers to design as an activity, the act of conceiving, creating or constructing a product."[39] Under this definition, the idea of "design" is both the process as well as the output. Borderless fashion practice benefits from this definition insofar as it can manifest in a multitude of ways via physical objects and via its communication, which includes real-life experiences (runway presentations, exhibitions, etc.) as well as videos and online images that show both process and product. Throup's "practice"-based fashion design focuses on critical thought and creative production with a focus on process and collaboration. Form and material are important and develop off the back of a narrative Throup has conceptualized, and he uses the garment as an art object to explore the human body as form and function. Reinventing design methods, such as the buttonhole or the shoulder seam, he creates complete sculptural looks that are both utilitarian and couture.

Throup as a creative practitioner is difficult to confine to a single creative label. His process is based around anatomical illustration, conceptual product design, fashion construction, and performative art practice. His process and communication expand beyond fashion as it relates to commerce, creating a practice that is situated between the material object and conceptual representation. Speaking on the products he creates, he says that "they are objects designed to interact with the human body, but when they're not interacting with the human body, they're inanimate objects, which have their own identity. They have a soul."[40] Throup goes on to say that "an object has achieved its own anatomy once it can ultimately be appreciated without the need for it to interact with the human body directly."[41]

Throup's aesthetic and conceptual design language emerges from a convergence of two things, football hooliganism and Italian avant-garde apparel brands. His fascination with the subculture of football hooliganism, unique to where he grew up in the north of England, began with looking at Italian apparel brands such as C. P. Company and Stone Island and the ways in which the subculture appropriated their aesthetic language. The dichotomy and oscillation between the two were something that instigated his interest in fashion, as he tells journalist Skidmore: "It's a whole contradiction of these two things; one's very avant-garde, the other's very narrow-minded [in reference to the hooligans]."[42]

Throup's Master of Arts graduate collection from 2007 deals with this dissonance and was even titled *When Football Hooligans Become Hindu Gods*, which is a critical comment on the violent and often racist disposition of those who exist within the subculture. Jo Turney comments that clothes can be "recognised, used and worn, as expressions of wider sociocultural and political concerns in contemporary everyday life."[43] Clothes are loaded with cultural meaning, but they are also performative insofar as they "perform the self (real or perceived)."[44] Throup's articulation of the human form always carries a conceptual narrative that drives their purpose or performs an identity. *When Football Hooligans Become Hindu Gods* references the act of identity metamorphosis through the transforming qualities of the designed product archetype. The concept narrative describes a story of redemption among a group of young football hooligans after the brutal murder of a young British Hindu boy. Throup states that the collection showcases the character's individual attempts at converting to Hinduism to eventually transform into Hindu gods.[45] He goes on to say that each design "represents a hooligan's metamorphosis into one of Hinduism's foremost deities."[46] Or it at least represents their attempt at absolution, which is contradicted by the appropriation of military design features into the garment construction. Such features include the M-65 American fishtail parka and British Navy overcoats that reinstate connotations of the character's violent pasts.[47] Caps featured throughout the collection morph into masks reminiscent of Garuda the Hindu bird god. This conceals the face to complete the oscillating metamorphosis of embodied identity.

Anatomy Design "Archetypes"

Throup's studio practice is based around the concept of creating new design archetypes such as those from *When Football Hooligans Become Hindu Gods*, much like that of Miyake's A-POC, which is the imperative focus of NOR.[48] In his manifesto Throup states that the term "archetype" in the specific context of his studio practice refers to the slow development of his conceptual style that then becomes elevated to the status of archetype through distillation over time. These archetypes are not "conceived or developed as a reaction to a specific style or trend, but rather as an organic and considered symptom of the original concept and process."[49] Anatomy to Throup works as a conceptual vehicle for the architecture of the garments he designs as well as the space in which they exist. The objective of his design process "is always to create anatomical objects which can create an instinctive—and hopefully emotional—connection with the viewer or wearer. Through an anatomical approach to design I aim to create symbols that remind us of our own systematically layered nature."[50]

Leonardo da Vinci, the original Renaissance man, was fascinated with the human body in all its parts. His anatomical sketches, more prolific than his painting practice, imposed the principles of geometry on the configuration of the human body, the proportions corresponding directly with the forms of a circle and square.[51] The 1490 anatomical drawing *Vitruvian Man* was an illustration of this theory, one that was in fact based on the proportional theories of the Roman architect Vitruvius. Da Vinci believed this chart of the human body represented an analogy for the symmetry of the universe. He went further in his analogy by comparing the aspects of the human embodied form to that of the natural world. The skeleton became rocks, which are the ballasts of the earth, and the delicate expansion of breathing lungs became the ebb and flow of the oceans.[52] This breakdown of the binary between man and nature was expressed through the study of many disciplinary fields and the acknowledgment of their interdependence. Da Vinci was a painter, an architect, a musician, a scientist, and an engineer who studied the mechanics of design and acknowledged their reflections of the workings of the natural world. Like Abloh and Throup, he created anatomical archetypes and design principles of graphic representation to determine an identity.

Throup's process begins with anatomical sketches that the designer has compiled into his "daily sketchbook series" of illustrations that present characters in mid-"metamorphosis."[53] He then translates these two-dimensional images into three-dimensional molded life-sized mannequin sculptures usually created using his own body proportions like the objects in *A Portrait of Noomi Rapace*, which he then builds his patterns from. Throup uses these sculptural figures as the basis to his work and act as design "archetypes" that have developed from the principles outlined in the NOR manifesto. Commenting on the archetype ideation process, Throup has stated that he is trying to capture a sort of "human essence, the human energy behind anatomy—whether it's a drawing, a painting, a sculpture or a garment."[54] He is trying to capture an authentic representation of human likeness through the construction of a garment actioned by the development of archetypes.

Lifeless clothing floating in space is uncanny; the direct absence of the live body welcomes the viewer to look at the details of the garment with more attention. The garment also leaves traces of the lived body behind, creating eeriness in the space around it. Elizabeth Wilson speaks about the "haunted" nature of clothing in the museum space in *Adorned in Dreams*: "We experience a sense of the uncanny when we gaze at garments that had an intimate relationship with human beings. . . . They hint at something only half understood, sinister, threatening; the atrophy of the body, and the evanescence of life."[55] This is speaking directly to the presence of costume in the museum setting, and the traces of human beings left on the clothes who are now "long since gone."[56] For Throup's work, not only does he conjure up the past through the uncanny "empty" nature of his figures; he also projects into the future, hypothesizing and reconstructing archetypal identities for a potential dystopia or utopia. Although the garment prototypes are never actually presented or communicated on a live human body, we can see the ways in which he takes every aspect of the lived body into consideration at their creation. This is due to the attention he gives to details such as a buttonhole or an individual seam and the movement with which they constrain or invite movement on individual parts of the body. Geczy and Karaminas use seventeenth-century philosopher Baruch Spinoza's theories of the body to examine Throup's research process in which he assembles a garment piece by piece onto his signature exoskeleton mannequins.[57] The same process is used to construct the shell mannequins as evidenced in *A Portrait of Noomi Rapace*. Spinoza theorized a systemic way of thinking regarding the body, nature, and God, which was in variance to the divine mind/body binary dualism espoused by his predecessor, René Descartes.[58] This intricate process predetermines the body as a site of multiple surfaces, and the garment is made up of a set of parts creating a whole that exists individually in space from the lived body. They are a confirmation of who the wearer is as a whole and act not as a set of hierarchies.

Anatomy is the undeniable basis of Throup's design philosophy, as writer Vanessa Hsieh comments: "Throup explores the ways in which the human anatomy functions to produce movement and shape, his designs act as both political intervention and cultural narrative."[59] The clothes themselves are based in concept and utilitarian function. Throup is not interested in the hierarchies and seductions of the fashion system, and this shows in his practice, particularly in how he represents his work. Installation is the primary means in which he does so, preferring an immersive experience, what Geczy and Karaminas theorize as an open or closed fashion installation, that the audience can wander through and engage with on multiple sensory levels rather than in a static runway show.[60] The value is then placed in the experience of the space beyond the garment rather than solely on a commoditized object for trade.

Hybrid Spaces

Lou Stoppard claims that "The work of designers whose creations take fashion beyond clothing into areas such as sculpture, performance and product design," is fashion installation.[61] Fashion "installation" is "where 'fashion' is primarily mobilised."[62] This manifests specifically in the commercial design of retail stores, more specifically in the shapes, sizes, and colors of bags and boxes that deliver the fashion product. In a broader sense, fashion installation is the multitude of spaces that communicates fashion's wider image or meaning. Therefore, on a noncommercial level, it is in these hybrid spaces of existence. This includes but is not limited to film, performance, virtual reality, exhibition, and social media feeds. Within this context, the space between the fashion product and the consumer dissolves "so that the consumer is made to feel like a participant in an active speculation as to where he or she fits within the particular fashion scenario."[63] Throup communicates his work solely through these acts of installation, as evidenced in *A Portrait of Noomi Rapace*.

Borderless fashion practice's primary means of communication is through installation. This is demonstrative in Throup's work, where he primarily communicates his concepts through a combination of performance and film. *The Funeral of New Orleans (Part One)* from 2007 is one of the designer's first collections after graduating from the Royal College of Art in London and was primarily communicated via the production of a fashion film. The collection witnesses traditional suiting that morphs into utilitarian clothing typical of Throup's practice. The conceptual framework of the collection is inspired by the designer's reaction to the 2005 natural disaster Hurricane Katrina that devastated the American city of New Orleans, in turn uncovering the systemic race divides of the cultural context. Throup references the importance of the funeral procession of musicians that makes up the soundscape of the city and represents the convergence of cultures specific to the city. The embodied garments morph in the film and peel off from the lifeless bodies onto the instruments, protecting them and breaking down the boundaries between body and object.[64] Initially presented in film format, the actual garments then went on to be displayed in a gallery setting. The fashion collection exists through film and static presentation.

As Stoppard states, Throup's installations present in two ways. One shows the process of the work manifesting in sketches, film, and sculptures; the other communicates his concepts in the form of performances, presentations, and exhibitions.[65] The former is exemplified by *The Funeral of New Orleans (Part One)*, where we see the process played out through the utilization of film. Commenting on the topic, Throup states that "with luxury products there is a growing public demand for proof of authenticity and integrity. Showing the process can prove that something is expensive for a valid reason, not just because it has a logo on it. It is about transparency."[66] These ideas of authenticity and transparency are common threads between the designers that I have described as *borderless*. The metamodern era requires these characteristics as fashion's democratization has made information travel faster and allowed exposure of brand and designer practices unlike ever before. This means hierarchies have been broken down within the system that places agency in the hands of the audience and the consumer. Throup champions this connection between the audience and his work by subverting the psychology of the way clothing is presented: "In a catwalk scenario the audience is passive and the work is active. That gives the work a hierarchy—it's the inherent pretentiousness in the fashion world."[67]

The spring 2017 men's collection for NOR, subversively named *The Rite of Spring/Summer/Autumn/Winter*, engages with this dynamic between audience and work. The project consisted of six individual looks, which were, as stated in the manifesto, "trans-seasonal prototypes."[68] It acted as a metamorphosis of Throup's illustrated two-dimensional archetypes into physical three-dimensional reality. These "prototypes" were dressed on life-sized marionette-like puppets, which were manipulated by four technicians down the runway at an almost excruciatingly slow pace. British fashion critic Tim Blanks noted the movements were "clearly physically taxing for them."[69] The performance took twenty minutes; white masks covered every face, giving the presentation an uncanny aura, the puppeteers acting as the negative white space beyond the garment prototype.

The mannequin's exoskeleton-like shell draped in Throup's intricately materialized and constructed garments struggled down what we would identify as a traditional runway in what Blanks described as "an arduous ritual—for the audience as well as the actors," to a soundscape of atmospheric pendulum music.[70] This ritualistic nature of the performance explores the boundaries between performer and viewer, and by doing so Throup creates self-awareness in the audience of their own discomfort within space and time. On this relationship, the designer commented, "I like that the objects are static and the audience is active. You're doing the work more justice and you're paying respect to the audience; they can view it for however long they want."[71] Throup's use of the word "prototype" reflects his insistence that he is a product designer first and foremost. Each pocket and panel are worked together on the archetypal form, building a relationship between each piece that adds to a collective whole. The outcomes are long, hooded anoraks and quilted coats and sportswear- and military-inspired layers including paneled motorcycle-style trousers. More than that, the garments encompass the figure as though it is dystopian armor, the face or head of the body often covered, at once erasing identity and constructing one around the narrative of the constructed clothes that are devoid of a lived body. Like Miyake and his A Piece of Cloth (A-POC) concept, Throup's process remains the same throughout his projects, always beginning with an archetype and then liberating from the imprint of the lived body. On this matter Throup states in his manifesto, "An object has achieved its own anatomy once it can ultimately be appreciated without the need for it to interact with the human body directly."[72]

For *The Rite of Spring/Summer/Autumn/Winter*, Throup presented the collection in the form of a traditional runway show that completely rejected the formal commercial structure. The performance subverted all of the traditional social constructs of a normative runway show. There were no live models except for the puppeteers, who were secondary to the main performance and only six painstakingly constructed "looks." The performance caused discomfort in the crowd and challenged their experience and understanding of what a fashion presentation is and what it can be beyond a commercial trade show. As Blanks recalls, "There was a walk-out or two, rolled eyes, raised brows. There was also unrestrained enthusiasm at the end, and an admiring throng clustered by the six puppets swaying in a row."[73] The audience had a chance to engage and move around the garments, seeing them in as much detail as they desired as they were promptly installed statically within a framed structure postperformance. The clothed figures are liberated from their moving human constraints. They are at peace, waiting to be activated once again as if by artificial intelligence. Afterward the mannequins were moved to Dover Street Market, the iconic London retail space and hub established by Rei Kawakubo, a supporter of new talent, in which designers could exhibit and sell their work; the mannequins were to be sold as complete looks, as though a sculpture or a piece of art rather than a garment to be worn by a human.[74] The trace of another is already left behind through the exoskeleton sculpture. These sculptural installations within a commercial retail environment further solidify the dismantling of hierarchies of a fashion show. The instant accessibility of the clothing both during the presentation and immediately after emphasizes the idea of feeding the contemporary audience's desire for authenticity and thoughtfulness in the way in which fashion is communicated and consumed. Throup's borderless fashion practice oscillates between the art experience and designed object connoting a tension between nihilism and optimism for the future projecting the essence of the tensions of the metamodern era. These projects potentially pose more questions than answers; at the same time, they dismantle preconceived notions of what fashion can be, whom it is for, and what it is able to say.

The Rite of Spring/Summer/Autumn/Winter was a total work of fashion encompassing the disciplines of design, fine art, architecture, and engineering to create unified synthesis. Soundscapes, spatial design, performance, and exhibition were all utilized within a production that lasted no more than half an hour. It was filmed, however, which adds a haunting element to the seemingly ephemeral nature of performance art, making it immortal. Technology and the ghostly image are spaces in themselves that designers are utilizing to represent and display their work, and as a consequence they are reaching a far wider audience than previously possible. The whole presentation transgresses the traditional runway from beginning to end. There were three main elements to the presentation as a whole. Held at the Holy Trinity Church at One Marylebone in London, as visitors arrived they were greeted with a static installation of four casts of Throup's own body wearing garments cast in white paint and laid on top of one another. Named *The Resting of the Past*, this initial static installation represented Throup's process of previous designs for the collection, acting as a nod to his practiced quest for product design "archetypes." The use of puppets to present the final clothes in a performative "catwalk" display acted like that of Alexander McQueen's 2001 show *Voss*, insofar as it asked self-reflection of the audience. Where McQueen's runway show literally reflected the viewer's image back at them through the use of mirrors, Throup enforced self-awareness over one's own body, his obsession with anatomy on full display as the viewer is made to look at every seam and pattern piece that bends and moves with the puppet's body. Fashion installation, with its democratic, collaborative, and interdisciplinary characters, is the primary means in which to describe the practice of contemporary borderless fashion designers working within an "expanded" definition of fashion.

Interdisciplinary Collaboration

Collaborations for Throup are not a matter of working for another brand to sell a certain product or story; they are a symbiotic partnership in which he works *with* rather than *for* others. This comes in the form of collaborations with other companies, brands, consultancy positions for larger corporate brands, and art patronage. Throup has practiced and collaborated within the realms of sportswear, music, film, dance, and art. It could be said that the more commercial collaborations, which connect with pop culture and streetwear brands, and his previous role at G Star Raw, offer the financial independence to be more experimental in his individual practice. This also highlights the progressive deconstruction of the hierarchies between high and pop culture as mentioned before. Rather than conforming to the fashion industry's cyclical system of newness, Throup has infiltrated a commercial brand in a mutually beneficial relationship in which the company gains cultural and artistic gravitas within the industry through hiring Throup as creative director, and Throup gains commercial credentials. The designer's initial interest in fashion was through sportswear and streetwear brands with their appropriation of the English football hooligan subculture, one that he was surrounded by after moving to Burnley from Buenos Aires when he was twelve years old.[75] His designs have been exhibited in both the Design Museum and the Victoria & Albert in London as well as concept retail space Dover Street Market, which furthers the discussion of fashion's dislocation from the runway to the museum and gallery sphere. Fashion exists across these disciplines within the expanded field and therefore is not hermetically sealed.

Some of Throup's earliest collaborations were with iconic Italian sportswear brands Stone Island and C. P. Company and the British apparel brand Umbro. In 2009 he designed performance wear in collaboration with Umbro for the English football team's kit, a design they still use to this day. Using his process of deconstructing the human form, he reconstructed the archetype section by section so that it fit the biodynamic of the human body better during a game.[76] His redesigns for the twentieth anniversary of C. P Company's goggle jacket were presented in an installation in 2009 as part of Milan's International Furniture Fair that Throup also curated. The collaboration was a celebration of the past and future for the Italian brand, the goggle jacket being a consistent product of theirs and one that was very present in the subculture that Throup lived in growing up in Burnley. Twenty archival jackets were displayed alongside his own original design. Through the presentation of the history of this piece, the continuous experimentation and transformation of one designed garment can be seen in its meticulous detail. Throup says of the jacket that even when the design is hanging in a shop or in a wardrobe, "it has a soul already," as though there is already someone inside it even when it's devoid of a lived body due to its engrained history.[77] For the installation, this sensation of the uncanny was exaggerated by suspending twenty archival goggle jackets in square framed boxes. The designer also created one original design to add to the C. P. Company archive. The jackets had impressions of a body hovering in space, the traces of character archetypes highlighted by spotlights against a black background. Throup states in response to the curation of the installation that sometimes the absence of the human body transforms garments from "fashion to product."[78] This way of displaying his product has become characteristic of Throup across all of his collaborations and projects, even in his work as creative director with G Star Raw. In his time for the Dutch denim company, Throup developed three research projects, Raw Research I, II, and III, to develop innovative ways of constructing denim into forms. Throup deconstructs the trope of utility through the archive and conceptualizes the new in reference to a garment's past through his meticulous product design. Mixing the traditional denim fabrics from G Star's legacy and the intricate prototyping of Throup's design archetypes, the pieces are not garments; they are product sculptures.

The borderless nature of Throup's practice manifests in his ability to work across creative disciplines. He has acted as creative director for the English rock band Kasabian since 2011, designing branding, album concept, and stage design much like that of Abloh's work with West. In 2014 for Kasabian's Glastonbury performance, Throup designed the stage set, and he designed the accompanying visual concept for their album *48:13*. For the performance, he designed and created a "white cube" for the band to perform in, projecting onto the canvas with flashes of images of the crowd and static text as the band moved through its set. Speaking about the project, Throup stated that "the ultimate way to showcase art in a powerful way is to put it in a beautiful white gallery, so you free it of context."[79] Although a completely different creative output, Throup's creative direction in the field of music includes directing conceptual music videos for Kasabian and Damon Albarn that take on the same design principles that drive his other disciplinary projects.

In 2017 Throup collaborated with British choreographer Wayne McGregor on his contemporary ballet performance titled *Autobiography*. Rather than creating theatrical costumes, McGregor asked of Throup to make *clothes* influenced by the designer's own archive of research and work. The performance explores the choreographer's own body as an archive and through research he collaborated with cognitive experts and scientists to sequence his individual genome.[80] These sequences were then fed into a computer algorithm that was used to organize twenty-three different sections that make up the whole production. Each night a different sequence determined in what combination the dancers performed the acts, resulting in no two performances being the same.[81] McGregor's focus on the body as a tool for design and transformation aligns with Throup's relationship with the body and his research and development of design archetypes. Throup created clothes for the dancers that allowed free interpretation and movement, saying of the process, "To reflect his (McGregor's) process of going into his past, we tried to replicate this idea of memory and fragments."[82] Throup and his team went into their studio archive and selected four pieces that made up an adaptable wardrobe for the dancers including a pair of shorts, a T-shirt, a tunic, and a jacket re-created out of light mesh in a monochrome color palette. Each product piece was designed to be refastened on different planes of the body, allowing a restructure and layering of forms that represent fragmented memories and traces. For example, the T-shirt could be fastened on the waistband of the shorts, creating a new silhouette for the dancers as their whole bodies changed their sequence of movement. The mirrored focus on the body for both Throup and McGregor relates back to Spinoza's theory that composition of the body "follows relationships not hierarchies."[83]

The process of creation for Throup's design archetypes starts from a point in which "neither body nor clothing exists."[84] They are assembled from nothing, the archetypes designed in pieces just like that of the garment itself. The hierarchy of a garment's assemblage has been destabilized and reconstructed. Dance is the perfect collaborative field for Throup's design process because of this. Dancers move their body through this relationship of compositions and a symbiotic process of cause and effect to stretch the body's natural ability.

Throup has built a career on subverting the status quo. He approaches designing a garment from the inside out, piece by piece, and to use his own words, by "unlearning the predetermined solutions that exist, the standardized solutions to a core problem. . . . To find new solutions to that problem has been what has driven my career."[85] This comes back to the idea of the mediation of the human form through the design of "archetypes." This constant process of research and development has enabled Throup to construct a design identity that diverges from the typical fashion designer archetype of the mainstream industry. As a designer, Throup is saying something through concept and narrative and transparent process that is not just about making clothes for the sake of making clothes. His ability to work outside of this fashion cycle by way of his multidisciplinary practice has created the opportunity to be successful and sustainable in both his own personal studio work and his work for larger brands. Throup's practice encapsulates key characteristics of the metamodern that underpin the proposition of borderless fashion practice. These include critical and conceptual frameworks, dialogue in the form of process, collaboration, and interdisciplinarity, which are fundamental to the making and communication of Throup's fashion practice.

The dissolving fashion runway brought about by the democratization and dislocation of fashion has allowed the emergence of "fashion installation," an umbrella term that describes the process and the communication contemporary fashion practitioners produce. Fashion as a result has evolved to a broadened definition and can manifest in the material and representational, and experiential immersive fashion comes in the form of "in real life" (IRL) presentations, exhibitions, and performances and "URL" (World Wide Web) fashion films and digital channel content. What is important about this cohort of designers is that they aren't making clothes for the sake of making clothes; they are utilizing the realm of fashion to say something. Rather than drawing on "themes" of architecture, filmmaking, graphic design, and science, the designers in this book *embody* these practices, making their identity important to the makeup of their overall fashion practice.

8

Iris van Herpen's New Couture

Technology could enable us to radicalize
the definition of what fashion means.
—Andrew Bolton, *Manus × Machina*

In 2016, the Metropolitan Museum of Art's Costume Institute's annual spring exhibition was titled *Manus × Machina*, meaning "hand" and "machine," respectively. The Apple Computer–sponsored exhibition explored the distinctions between the handmade and the machine-made in relation to fashion's history and technological development. The exhibition emphasized the dichotomy between the hand and machine in fashion practices, which has been perpetuated by the separate realms of the haute couture and prêt-à-porter systems. However, the exhibition also presented examples of how fashion designers have reconciled the two (the hand and the machine) across recent fashion history through representing the "spectrum or continuum of practice, whereby the hand and the machine are equal and mutual protagonists in solving design problems, enhancing design practices, and, ultimately, advancing the future of fashion."[1] One of the designers to most succinctly represent this symbiosis of *manus* and *machina* is Dutch fashion practitioner Iris van Herpen. The exhibition highlighted the importance of connecting with the process of how garments are made through technological technique, but it also brought to attention how Van Herpen's practice sits at the nexus of fashion technology and art, concept, and representation. However, her practice is so much more than an amalgam of the disciplines of technology, art, and fashion. Conceptual ideas and contextual narratives have just as much importance in her work and situate it within the framework of borderless fashion practice.

Taking characteristics from aesthetic and conceptual elements of metamodernism, explained in the theoretical framework chapter of this book, I analyze Van Herpen's practice through specific case study projects she has developed. Those metamodern characteristics include design identity, interdisciplinary collaborations, and hybrid spaces, which are consistent with the other case study chapters. I contextualize Van Herpen's fashion practice through a discussion of fashion, technology, and innovation. Van Herpen's oeuvre is the creation of fabrics through 3D technology, but she also experiments with nanorobotics and synthetic biology with the intention to push this practice from experimentation to customization.[2] "I use technology as a creative tool," Van Herpen says, "not as a functional end product. It's super exciting to use technology to push my skills and dreams forward; to create a shape, silhouette or structure that I cannot make by hand."[3] She does so to create fabrications that act and move in new ways in relation to the body and space, leaving ephemeral marks reminiscent of, as she has stated, a "fingerprint."[4] This begins a conversation surrounding the idea of *space in relationship to the body*, a concept that is increasingly more important to contemporary fashion designers in the communication of their work and reflects this idea that they are in fact working across design borders to push fashion practice forward. Van Herpen's studio is based in Amsterdam, but her practice is global in scope and is renowned for its "New Couture" creations that fuse technology with traditional haute couture handcraft techniques.[5] Following her first collection of womenswear in 2007, she went on in 2011 to be invited to present her work at haute couture fashion shows in Paris as a guest member of the Chambre Syndicale de la Haute Couture, an unprecedented move due to her young age, the newness of her studio, and her relatively small group of technical staff. It is a position she still holds today, and one that tethers her to the traditional fashion system of seasonal runways and commercial clients. However, Van Herpen has managed to create a successful fashion business that is not necessarily reliant on fashion's commercial market. She moves between disciplines, bringing in collaborators from other fields to work on projects with experimental concepts and techniques. It is within these collaborations that she gains commerciality and capital to produce her designs where sustainability and innovation are at the center of every concept.

The process and research behind each of Van Herpen's collections are as important as the finished product. The designer claims that the research that goes into the creation of each "collection" takes longer than the actual production and making of the garments.[6] Aesthetically she is known for neo-futuristic silhouettes that are unlike anything ever imagined before. Frequent collaborator photographer Nick Knight describes her practice as both allegorical and scientific, going on to state that "Her approach to her work is rooted back in a time, centuries ago, where the teaching of science and the teaching of art were considered as equal and nobody could regard themselves as educated unless they understood and practiced both approaches. This makes her, in my opinion, one of the most exciting designers working today."[7] The designer herself stated that for her, "art and science are the most powerful media of transformation."[8] This is what enables Van Herpen's practice to transcend fixed descriptions of creative disciplines. Her practice is hard to pin down and define in simple terms or even with any categorical certainty. It "filters the many currents that inform our everyday," utilizing fashion not only as a statement but also as a challenge to envisage potential futures.[9] Like Abloh and Throup, Van Herpen is expanding the scope and concept of what it means to be a fashion designer in the twenty-first century and changes the way fashion is read, consumed, and articulated. I will articulate the ways in which she has curated a recognizable practice through the development of a design identity based around aesthetic design principles, a focus on process, and elaborate conceptual frameworks. The inclusion of Van Herpen in this book is due to the nature of her hybridic design identity, her collaborative approach to fashion practice, and her transcendence of normative business structures within the fashion system. She champions *process*-driven making, where emphasis is placed on the development of new techniques or conceptual ideas rather than solely on the effect or affect of the final product/garment and experience. Futurism, new materialism, surrealism, and transformation are all expressions one can use to describe the work of the designer.

After graduating, Van Herpen trained with Alexander McQueen and then worked for artist and textile designer Claudy Jongstra, where she developed working on conceptual frameworks with a focus on process.[10] Since 2007, her design studio has produced some of the most mind-bending material designs and installations the fashion industry has seen, often manifesting in runway performances, which I discuss in relation to the hybrid spaces in which borderless fashion practices exist. Although she does work within a seasonal framework for her couture presentations, Van Herpen's garments, rather than being referential of the season with which she is presenting, reference the technology and concept that she used and conceived of for the collection. Instead of presenting her work on a traditional runway, she creates elaborate installations that speak to her commitment to immaterial concept and statement and utilization of projected collective fantasy and atmosphere on her audience, much like that of designers such as Alexander McQueen did throughout the nineties and early millennium. Rather than going into mass production, the collections are often purchased by museums or sold to a handful of couture clients, effectively making her exist on the outskirts of fashion's retail environment, but through these commissions and collaborations her business is commercially viable. Van Herpen's practice is immersive when consumed in real life and online, and her experiments at the in-between of materiality and immateriality linger at and transcend the borders of space and time. Interdisciplinary collaboration with other designers, scientists, and architects are at the center of her work, and that enables Van Herpen to occupy liminal and interdisciplinary spaces within the primary practice of fashion, which I believe is fashion's future beyond its end and what I define here as borderless fashion practice.

Celebrities and creatives such as Solange Knowles, Naomi Campbell, Gwendoline Christie, and Cara Delevigne have all stepped out to events dressed in Van Herpen's designs, in turn, giving commercial validity to her work while at the same time giving the wearers cultural cachet. High-profile collaborators to work with Van Herpen include Icelandic musician Björk, Nick Knight's platform Showstudio, and Swiss crystal conglomerate Swarovski as well as long-standing collaborator architect Philip Beesely. The recognizability of her garments, with their melded forms and phosphorescent fabrication, has created a uniform aesthetic that denotes a utopic sensibility unlike other designers who change their general "look" season to season.

Technology, Innovation, and Sustainability

Sci-fi aesthetics and the advancement of "technology" have been referenced in relation to fashion throughout the twentieth century with designers such as the retrofuturists of the 1960s: Paco Rabanne, André Courrèges, and Pierre Cardin, as well as Thierry Mugler in the 1980s and Alexander McQueen in the 1990s and early 2000s. Aesthetic references such as chained metal dresses, space boots, and metallic shift dresses saw a projection of the future in the middle of the twentieth century. Thierry Mugler in the eighties and nineties imagined otherworldly futuristic femmes fatales, reappropriating the corset and transforming it into robotic armor integrated into the wearer's flesh, presented most memorably at Mugler's infamous twentieth-anniversary fashion show spectacle in 1995. The armor was made in collaboration with artist Jean-Jacques Urcun, a designer specializing in aircraft bodies.[11] At the onset of the millennium in 1999, as Y2K panic was setting in, Alexander McQueen created a collection for Givenchy that projected a future beyond the world's end. Sharp metallic tailoring and elongated silhouettes echoed dystopian genre pop culture artifacts like the film *Blade Runner* (dir. Ridley Scott, 1982). Artificial intelligence was referenced in the final look, a Tron-inspired plastic bodice fitted with a circuit board and LED lights built in collaboration with Studio van der Graaf.

In terms of the communication of fashion through runway presentations, McQueen was the most experimental when it came to utilizing technology as a means to do so. In 2006 for the designer's autumn/winter collection, Kate Moss appeared as a hologram trapped in a glass pyramid moving in circles enveloped by the billowing fabric of her dress until the three-dimensional image slowly dematerialized into thin air. It was created by video artist Baillie Walsh and was what Sarah Mower described as an "astonishing feat of techno-magic."[12] The visual movement and wonder at witnessing a new technological means of communicating in the "fashion" space feels reminiscent of *The Serpentine Dance*, the Lumiere Brothers' film of Loïe Fuller performing the dance in 1896, which is an example of early motion picture recordings. The dancer wears layers of gauzy cloth and as she moves her arms up and around; she holds onto the folds of the fabric, creating the mesmeric movement. The Serpentine Dance was an excellent subject for film, as it highlighted the medium's ability to represent light and movement. These examples exemplify an ingrained interest in the practice of fashion designers that conveys a forward-thinking nod to the future but also presents how they engage with contemporary digital technologies. Hussein Chalayan is another designer who combines these two factors and evolves the scope of fashion through technological transformation. Along with his autumn/winter 2000 presentation that saw garments transform out of furniture, other collections focus on themes of transformation and metamorphoses. For the spring/summer 2016 season, Chalayan presented two garments that dissolved off the body when touched by water. The two models walked out onto the runway wearing couturier, or even scientist-like, white coats then stood on two plinths in the middle of the catwalk that formed a bridge over a constructed pool of water. From above, two streams of water showered over the models as the coats slowly dissolved and disintegrated into thin air, revealing dresses veined with thick black stitching and appliqued petals adorned with Swarovski crystals.

Chalayan is a designer who has set the playing field for Van Herpen's practice through his conceptual work that utilizes technology not only in how he constructs a garment but in the performative nature of how he communicates his work. As academic Sandy Black contends, "Fashion is harnessing emerging science and technology to enhance both the functional and emotional experience of clothing, creating new scenarios that were previously only imagined."[13] Propositions of an expanded field of fashion offered by designers such as Chalayan have helped develop this intersection of the "functional and emotional experience of clothing." This happens as more avant-garde concepts, represented on the runway and increasingly in design collaborations, inspire other practitioners, leading to a "normalization" of such practices.[14] Black goes on to say that due to fashion's fixation on technology in the twenty-first century, potential has been created for the "unprecedented convergence of disciplines to create intelligent and responsive textiles and fashion."[15]

Van Herpen transcends the kitsch tropes of sci-fi and futurism and integrates new material technological fabrications, what Anneke Smelik uses as an example of "new materialism," and communicates them through narrative concepts and immersive installations.[16] What makes her practice different from that of her predecessors such as Chalayan is that it moves beyond the spectacle. Technology intersects with Van Herpen's practice at every step of the process. For her collection *Crystallization*, she created a 3D dress for the first time collaborating with London-based architect Daniel Widrig, the first successful attempt at creating a wearable item from a digital file. Technology by its broadest definitions, that being the sum of knowledge, skills, systems, and processes to advance human existence, has been intrinsically linked to fashion for as long as humans have been clothing their bodies in the evolving ways it is produced and constructed as well as how it is communicated. The idea of "technology" can span from the development of looms to nanotechnology and even digital media. The relationship between fashion and technology can be separated into two categories, one in which we see the direct impact of technology on how garments are constructed and then another in which technology is utilized in the communication of the work, such as in the runway show, or installation. Van Herpen's practice, I argue, is a manifestation of the two. The fabrications she uses are predominantly synthetic: latex, molded and laser cut, then hand sewn, or the finest laced metal. Then of course there is 3D printing, a technology Van Herpen has not only championed but also pioneered in terms of fashion making. Through her practice it has evolved immensely from a tool that created simply solid sculptural garments to one that the designer has combined with the knowledge of fabric making, evolving the practice of 3D printing directly onto tulle fabric to manifest the flexibility of a woven fabric.[17] Van Herpen's "skeleton" dress, from her fall/winter 2011 collection *Capriole*, is an example of the former. Now owned by the Metropolitan Museum of Art, it is one of her first examples of 3D printing experimentation in relation to fashion, made from white polyamide. The latter dress I describe was from the couture project *Ludi Naturae* from spring/summer 2018, which was inspired by the macroscopic aerial photography by artists such as Thierry Bornier. The dress was engineered using thermosetting polymers expelled by a 3D printer then set using ultraviolet light and tulle fabric that was inserted into the printer during the 3D printing phase.[18] Unable to be printed in one single print, the dress was created in patches that were then sewn together to create the whole, which is evident in the scale-like texture of its fabrication. These pieces blur the boundaries between the biological and the synthetic and over the past ten years have built up an identifiable aesthetic for Van Herpen's material practice. Connections to the scientific realm go beyond that of aesthetics. In 2013 Van Herpen collaborated with Massachusetts Institute of Technology (MIT) professor Neri Oxman on another 3D-printed dress. Oxman runs the Mediated Matter research group at MIT, a lab that focuses on "nature-inspired design and design-inspired nature" conducting "research at the intersection of computational design, digital fabrication, materials science, and synthetic biology."[19] They then apply this knowledge to many different design methods and scales, blurring the design methodologies between macro (architecture) and micro (ecology) processes. Sustainability of design instigates this oscillation between the natural world and the manmade, seeking to connect the fields of art and science that since the Western Age of Enlightenment have become increasingly dichotomous. Rather than massproducing product for the capitalist consumer market, Van Herpen experiments with new technologies for a projected utopian future, occupying a space of sustainable experimentation. Van Herpen, too, seeks to mediate between humans, objects, and their environment like the MIT lab, integrating a convergence of hardware and software technologies to create garments that contribute to a wider visual and experiential story that oscillate between body, space, and time.[20] The collaboration with Oxman manifested in a 3D-printed garment generated by Stratasys, a leading manufacturer of 3D printers that can produce prints made out of various material properties.[21] The garment worked as a "second skin" for the body in motion. Through 3D printing technology, designers can create fabrications that speak to not only the garment's form but also its motion.

Curating a Design Identity

The dominant underpinning to this book is the idea that fashion practitioners are becoming more collaborative and interdisciplinary in terms of how they approach their projects. This in turn curates a unique design identity that moves away from the cyclical trend-driven brand identities of the mainstream. Instead, we see a uniformity of design sensibilities, as evidenced in the case studies of Abloh and Throup. At the center of this book is the crumbling of disciplinary borders in art and design. The two, I argue, go hand in hand: the evolving terrain of cultural creativity and design, and the identity of those practitioners driving it. Disciplines are becoming less fixed, and the realm of fashion is a place in which this can be palpably witnessed. Van Herpen herself rejects the fixed nature of disciplines in relation to her own design identity and hopes that this fixation on homogenized definitions will evolve: "If we think about a fashion designer today, we have a very specific idea of what that is, and that's a person who is designing with fabric, making garments. I think, and hope, that disciplines will become much less fixed in terms of what we understand them to be, and interact much more."[22] Van Herpen sees fashion as unbound, which is how she defines herself apart from the traditional confines of fashion, that is, something primarily utilitarian, trend based, and intrinsically tied to the body and socioeconomic conditions.[23] This desire to not limit herself in terms of boundaries of what defines "fashion" enables her to create metamorphic artifacts that act more as stand-alone objects than garments to be worn. In some ways it is this very "unboundness" that leads to some defining her as an "artist" rather than a fashion designer. I would argue, in line with the broader hypothesis of this book, that Van Herpen's identity as a practitioner is borderless and "meta" in terms of her process and creative output but that it still firmly sits within the realm of design and fashion. As Marco Pecorari has noted, the discourse that has occurred since the 1990s to compare fashion to art paralyzes the "understanding of the dialogues between these two distinct disciplines" and in turn transforms analysis "into a void comparison of practices where fashion is represented as a sort of emulation or mimesis of art."[24] Rather than claiming her as an artist and relegating her to the realm of fine art due to the inability to pin her down in terms of mainstream definitions of fashion, a redefinition of the term "fashion" within the contemporary industry is more pertinent, and that is what I propose here. As Annamari Vanska notes in her analysis on posthumanism and fashion, "a new definition of fashion beyond the commodity" is needed in critical fashion scholarship that expands beyond that of just criticism of the unsustainable manufacturing landscape.[25]

Van Herpen acts as a creative director, researcher, curator, and practitioner for her brand. Her borderless fashion practice integrates brand image, technical innovation, and visual storytelling.[26] These three elements intersect to curate a design identity. Rather than investing in a lifestyle, consumers and audiences of Van Herpen's work invest in an identity and character that are communicated in her aesthetic and conceptual narratives. Her pieces act as an extension of the wearer's skin, to use an analogy from Canadian media theorist Marshall McLuhan.[27] This concept returns to the idea that Van Herpen's garments embody the form but also the motion of the wearer as it comes into contact with the exterior space. Fashion critic Nicole Phelps noted in her review of Van Herpen's 2019 couture collection *Omniverse* that "writing about Iris van Herpen, one can find oneself mired in the technicalities of her creations."[28] It is true that Van Herpen uses new technologies to produce her work, such as 3D printing, laser cutting, and mylar bonding; however, her pieces are equally made by hand. This is the way in which she has constructed a design identity, through a practice that oscillates between the *hand* (*manus*) made and the *machine* (*machine*) made. Through this symbiosis, Van Herpen has curated a design identity that disrupts the binaries not only between creative fields but those that have created a dualism between mind and body, body and space, and nature and humanity.

New Materialism

New materialism, as defined in the context of fashion by Anneke Smelik, is a way of understanding "materiality in an age of technological innovation."[29] Smelik goes on to write that "Materiality refers not only to materials like fabrics or the garment, but also to the wearer's body, and, at large, to the world of production and consumption."[30] Adding the "new" as a prefix presents the notion that fashion, art, objects, and even the human body are made of matter, meaning they are a combination of mineral, vegetable, and synthetic materials.[31] Smelik highlights this concept as placing agency in the "nonhuman" factors in the field of fashion that have come about through developments in technology such as raw and smart materials, and I would argue that this could also include the importance of the space beyond and in between the body where Van Herpen creates fashion installation. For Van Herpen's practice the symbiotic relationship between the material object and immaterial experience is of equal importance. New materialism as a lens or perspective in which to look at fashion then "decentres the human subject, expanding fashion beyond the frame of the human body and human identity to the non-human world of technology and ecology."[32]

Van Herpen is a practitioner who is known for her performative conceptual designs, as well as her engagement with emerging technologies and her focus on natural phenomena. The combination of technology and nature extends to the use and development of metamaterials. "Metamaterials" comes from the Greek *meta* (beyond) and *materia* (matter) and refers to any material that is engineered to not have naturally occurring material properties. An assemblage of multiple elements is constructed from materials such as metals and plastics fashioned into repeated patterns much like that of naturally occurring biological phenomena. In other words, *metamaterials* translates to *beyond matter*. These materials then become biomimetic; for example, in 2018 Van Herpen created silicone-pleated material garments for her *Syntopia* project that emulated the motion of a bird's wing. Another example from 2019 uses metamaterials to mirror the central nervous systems of deep-sea organisms. Van Herpen constructs these materials into wearable garments that are inspired by the logic and symmetry of unseen natural phenomena. In other words, her practice brings scientific data and natural phenomena to life in material aesthetic form. This sentiment is much like that of the British conceptual art duo Semiconductor, who create large-scale image and video works that translate scientific data from the natural world, creating immersive visual installations that render the invisible visible. Van Herpen utilizes scientific technology such as 3D printing and the construction of metamaterials to make these ephemeral phenomena not only visual but tactile, too, which is testament to fashion's ability to connect and communicate unlike any other creative medium. Unlike Throup, whose practice starts off with anatomical illustrations, Van Herpen free drapes and constructs after material development. Her designs often look beyond this world insofar as there is no recognizability in the fabrications and designs. She visualizes data unknown to the human eye, creating chimera-like creations in which she "resurfaces the contours of the human body."[33]

In 1985, Donna Haraway published "A Cyborg Manifesto" in the journal *Socialist Review* (later to be published in *Simians, Cyborgs and Women: The Reinvention of Nature* in 1991) in which she uses the concept of the *hybrid cyborg* to propose a rejection of the rigid boundaries between human and machine, human and animal, and the physical and nonphysical. Haraway was writing within the context of feminist posthumanist theory and claimed that high-tech culture challenges canonical binaries put in place by the dominant Western patriarchal system and discourse. Problematic dualisms such as male/female, culture/nature, self/other, and truth/illusion, Haraway argues, have subjugated women, people of color, workers, animals, and nature.[34] She goes on to say, "In our time, a mythic time, we are all chimeras, theorized and fabricated hybrids of machine and organism."[35] This once again alludes to the breakdown of the binary between *manus* and *machina*; rather than creating trope-like cyborgs where the garments act as armor, like that of Mugler, Van Herpen's garments act in unison with the body expanding beyond it and into the space that surrounds it.

"A Cyborg Manifesto" is seen as a classic postmodern text. However, I would argue that Haraway's focus is on a world not dominated by binaries dictating culture by the Western patriarchal agenda but aligns with that of metamodernism. Haraway writes about borders and boundaries when she states that the idea of the cyborg is our ontology; it is the image of "imagination and material reality," which she argues is at the center of any possibility of historical transformation.[36] The romantic utopian notions of boundary breakdowns are relevant to apply to the work of Van Herpen as she transcends not only disciplinary borders but also the borders of this "imagined" and "material" reality as defined by Haraway. Van Herpen's work alludes to Haraway's human cyborg, "a creature of social reality, as well as a creature of fiction."[37] *Shift Souls* was a collection inspired by representations of mythological and astrological chimeras, particularly by Harmonia Macrocosmica, a collection of celestial atlases created by German cartographer Andreas Cellarius and published in 1600.[38] The designer focused on the "evolution of the human shape" and the different idealized shapes this has taken throughout time through the hybridization of the human form.[39] In the referenced celestial charts, chimera figures from mythology ornament the frame; winged human torsos morph into reptilian bodies, hybridizing the relationship between humankind and the natural world. While referencing ancient imagined mythological creatures, Van Herpen brings the idea into the twenty-first century, noting that genetic and DNA engineering technologies have developed material outcomes in the form of "cybrids"—human/animal hybrids.[40] This is a manifestation of Haraway's "imagined and material realities," in which humankind's mythological dreams have become scientific reality. The ethical ramifications of such engineering are still unknown; however, *Shift Souls* makes clear that it is a technological reality. The collection consisted of voluminous layering, and otherworldly fabric gradients in the form of the "Symbiotic" garments, which are made from dyed silks multilayered into sculptural shapes using a fine 3D laser-cut frame of polyethylene terephthalate glycol, a lightweight thermoplastic polymer. Through this materialization, hybrid bird shapes in gradient colors move in symbiosis with the human body manifesting in a fashion chimera. Other similarly made wearable sculptures hide anamorphic faces in the layers of synthetic and organic fabrics creating spectral apparitions. 3D-printed face adornments, named "Cellchemy" by the designer, were custom made by the Delft University of Technology through individual generative designed 3D face-scanning technology, mapping the lines of the face. The wiry topographical markings do not just act as adornment but mutate the contours of the human face, creating an organic cyborg. Through references to mythology and the natural world, Van Herpen harks back to a moment in scholarship in which the study of science was symbiotic with that of art. As a designer, she utilizes new technological processes like no other, effectively creating feats of wearable-engineered architecture that breaks down boundaries not only between disciplines but also between the human body and the world in which we live. This manifests not only a hybridized design identity but a hybridized way in which fashion can be perceived, that is, not something to solely be consumed but a unique medium in which to explore the human condition and our relationship with technology and nature.

For her spring/summer 2016 collection *Quaquaversal*, Van Herpen expressed the powerful merging of nature and architecture. Van Herpen was inspired by the "living tree bridges" found in India's northeast region, which are as they sound, bridges made by local villagers out of woven tree roots that grow and strengthen over time, manipulated by the human hand for the utilitarian use of getting over a river safely. The name of the collection refers to the geological term for a formation that is directed outward in all directions from a common center. The clothing in this collection "executes a new approach to garment construction, mixing the techniques of cutting, weaving, folding, and growing into a process that transcends the boundaries of traditional clothes-making."[41] The runway performance was centered around actress Gwendoline Christie lying down on a circular plinth clothed in a fishnet-like fabric that over the course of the runway show appeared to grow, fanning out all around her in a circular halo or in a "quaquaversal" motion. Three robotic arms that combined 3D printing, laser cutting, and weaving to effectively "grow" Christie's gown in real time using magnetic technology orchestrated the performance. The concept comes from a previous collaboration Van Herpen had with product designer Jólan van der Wiel in 2013 in which the collection was based around this magnetic weaving technique to manipulate and sculpt the fabric. The sculptural magnetic material being made out of iron filings mixed with resin while the material is still in molten form, it is then subjected to magnetic forces that morph the surface, creating miniature spiked formations that look organic by nature, furthering the themes of the morphing of the human body and nature that weave throughout Van Herpen's practice. It also provides an example of the use of technology in both how the work is produced and how it is communicated. This manifests a practice that combines aesthetic design uniformity, visual and conceptual storytelling, and technical innovation.

Hybrid Spaces

Van Herpen reimagines space into experiential installations in which her fashion is "mobilized" and the space between the fashion and the audience "dissolves." This tactic of using fashion installation to communicate a conceptual project is consistent with both Abloh and Throup's projects that work to create this "total" practice in the "expanded field of fashion" as outlined in each chapter. For the presentation of *Shift Souls*, which presented eighteen works or looks, Van Herpen collaborated with artist Nick Verstand, producing an ephemeral laser light installation by creating a dreamscape of oscillating cloud formations on the ceiling, plunging the audience into darkness and highlighting the models as they criss-crossed around the space beneath the synthetic clouds. The way in which Van Herpen communicates her couture work imagines atmospheric presentations that arrest and affect, creating collective fantasy that projects the viewer into hypothetical future environments. Although Van Herpen's practice looks and feels otherworldly, in reality it is filled with projections of an imagined humanoid future, based on human's relationship with the elements. It is utopian in the sense that with each presentation she endeavors to provide a somewhat dystopian projection with a utopian resolution, through the mobilization of fashion via installation. This metamodern characteristic manifests in her couture collection from July 2017 called *Aeriform*. For this project Van Herpen collaborated with Danish underwater artists Between Music, who "challenge the relationship between the body and its elemental surround, in a subaquatic environment where air is absent."[42] Presented in the basement of the infamous Cirque d'Hiver in Paris, to emulate the echoing abyss of the ocean, the performance appeared to make the impossible possible through a hijacking of nature. Between Music set the soundscape performing affecting auratic accompaniment to a collection of wearable objects and clothes that were biomorphically molded to the form of the human body and were a comment on the relationship between our bodies and the natural earthly elements of air and water, the manifestation of the intangible. Between Music has worked with deep-sea divers, physicists, and neuroscientists to create the biophonic "sound sculpture."[43] The musicians were submerged in larger-than-life tanks with their custom-built instruments, the sound escaping both the instruments and musicians in anguished yet harmonic symphony that enclosed the viewers in what Geczy and Karaminas label as a "closed" or "sealed" installation, which refers to the audience being in a darkened setting, their bodies submerged in the performance.[44] This is also the experiential affect created in *Shift Souls*, which combined the sensorial experiences of sight and sound to design the expanded space beyond the garment.

The press release for *Aeriform* reads, "Air and water are the structural and visual components of the eighteen elaborate silhouettes of the collection and have influenced the development of both the textiles and garment construction, which is reflected in their volumes, rippling patterning and translucent layering."[45] For *Aeriform*, Van Herpen designed work in tandem with motion and form, establishing the garment as a "second skin" through the biomimetic function of the metamaterials. The press release further establishes this notion: "Biomorphic structures include a feathery-light metal lace of geodesic floral patterns in collaboration with Philip Beesley, which floats around the body like a silver cloud.

Echo waves of mylar bonded cotton ripple across the skin mapping the surface of the body and painting its contours."[46] The details of the fabrication, such as the metal lace and mylar bonded ripples, are the physical manifestation of, and Van Herpen's interpretation of, waves, both sonic and water based. The conceptual narrative that Van Herpen established through this collection and the consequent presentation of it is that of harmony between the human body and the earth's elements, a poignant if not fantastical response to the earth's impending climate changes. The auratic atmosphere constructed by the combination of the musician's underwater music and Van Herpen's biomorphic designs created an all-encompassing sense of our vulnerability against the earth's elements but also evoked the precarious harmony with which we symbiotically exist with these elements. The two lead vocals of the underwater band remained in a constant state of strain to maintain the underwater sound. The ephemeral performance was earnest and emotional: one reviewer stated that the overall effect was transfixing to the extent "that it might have been hard to concentrate on the models walking around the tanks, had van Herpen's designs not been equally defiant of convention."[47] Speaking of the uncanny vibrations of sound that the musicians were projecting, Van Herpen commented that what she found most profound is the fact that the instrument itself did not create the sound but rather the interaction between the water, glass, and instrument.[48]

Looking at Van Herpen's body of work and aesthetic, what Elizabeth Wilson calls "utopic impulses" are communicated through the garments, conceptual narrative, and installation that all make up the total practice.[49] Modernity's cultural idealism created entire fictional utopias in literature and art representations that ultimately failed to materialize. Postmodernity, as Elizabeth Wilson states, became an "aestheticisation of dystopia," or the anti-utopia, that acknowledged the macabre ambivalence to the horror of "the destructive excess of Western consumerist society," and then turned that into a commoditized aesthetic.[50] Van Herpen's practice, I argue, is a projection of a future that oscillates between imaginings of utopia and dystopia, what Alice Payne refers to as "fashion futuring."[51]

The Anthropocene is the current informal geological epoch used to define humanity's impact upon the earth having started with the Trinity nuclear bomb test in the United States in 1945. The acceleration of this human impact upon the earth has direct ties with the industrial production of fashion and the environmental degradation that has happened as a result to mass production and consumption starting from the Western Industrial Revolution of the nineteenth century. Payne describes the Anthropocene by stating that it "reflects the ways in which human activity has become a world shaping force, and highlights the urgent need for planetary stewardship to ensure a sustainable future for human society and the nonhuman world."[52] In her discussion on sustainable fashion in the Anthropocene, Payne references ethicist Clive Hamilton's nomenclatures of "Prometheans" and "Soterians" as a means to "identify two narratives of sustainable fashion and trace the way the actions proposed by each narrative may entwine."[53] Hamilton's work examines the ethical and philosophical implications of climate change, including geoengineering, using these two analogies to illustrate the tensions that exist in envisioning and planning for the future. Within these two narratives, Payne argues the Prometheans remain within the paradigm of the present fashion industry in which a "techno-enabled cornucopian future" is embraced by the fashion industry that includes "wearable technology, speed, and efficiency."[54] The Soterians apply a more cautious approach proposing fashion "return to a new localism and valuing of the hand-made in a time of shrinking resources."[55] I argue that Van Herpen's practice is situated between these two analogies. Van Herpen's innovative practice transforms fabrication and production techniques, and although at the laboratory research stage, they act as somewhat of a utopic resolve, antidote, or even uniform to the effects of the Anthropocene.

Van Herpen's garments often move as though they are sentient and autonomous from the lived body, giving them life beyond the catwalk and the human wearer. Wilson has stated that "clothes act as an extension of self and body; in a very immediate way they represent culture" or at least the dominant values of a given culture.[56] She looks to the future with a sense of fantastical utopic idealism looking at what fashion can be beyond its rhetorical "end." These utopic impulses also loop back on the potential of dystopia, or the post-human world in which the environment reclaims what was lost. An erasure of life as we know it. She attempts to propose resolutions to predicaments that are arising in fashion due to the Anthropocene, creating what I call here "meta-utopias" that serve as both a critical comment and potential resolution to the current unsustainable fashion ecosystem. The meta-utopias exist through this installation of fashion and its "dislocation" from traditional systemic formats and spaces that comes in the form of immersive performances/presentations, curated exhibitions, or static presentations. In these hybrid installation spaces the expanded notion of fashion is explored. Aileen Ribeiro, channeling the "anti-utopia" narratives of British author Aldous Huxley, concedes that perhaps "to create a perfect utopia, there are no rules about dress."[57] She goes on further to state, "Perhaps the moral is that Utopia can only be achieved in the mind; the word itself, after all, taken from the Greek, means nowhere." She contends, however, that when writing or proposing a fantasy of utopia the author/maker "reveals as much about the sartorial tastes and aspirations of their own time as they do about their visions of the future."[58]

Meta-Utopias

In 2015, Van Herpen was included in an exhibition entitled *Utopia Bodies: Fashion Looks Forward* at Stockholm's Liljevalchs Konsthall art gallery curated by Serge Martynov and Sofia Hedman. Her magnetic dresses designed with van der Wiel were shown alongside other avant-garde fashion designers such as her predecessors Chalayan and Dutch Fashion designers Viktor & Rolf, as well as contemporaries such as Craig Green and Pauline van Dongen. The central aim of the exhibition was to present the power of fashion as a vessel for visions of the future through ideas such gender, memory, and society. As I have outlined in this chapter, her fashion practice oscillates between creative disciplines, fields of research, materiality, and physical space, which amalgamates into what I define as a borderless fashion design. Rather than representing utopian impulses through the design of an aesthetic uniform, Van Herpen does so through the experimentation of new materials and their interaction with body and space. Her practice utilizes already existing and invented avant-garde technologies to create a utopian proposition for the future. This future that Van Herpen proposes is one that integrates art, technology, and science, as well as one that links the earth's natural phenomena with that of the human experience. This borderless convergence can provoke empathy and feeling into our relationship with the earth. Although Van Herpen does not overtly critique the state of global environmental politics, it is hard to read her work separately from conversations of the Anthropocene. She creates meta-utopias through her process-driven installation of fashion.

The concept of Utopia was integral in the idealism and emotion found in international modernist aesthetics particularly in the interwar period, art creating beauty out of misery, architecture breaking from the formal past to project ideal unbreakable designs of the future. Utopia is a place imagined, however, and not necessarily realized, as Richard Noble states in his essay on the topic of this "utopian impulse" in contemporary art.[59] He writes that

> The utopian impulse or tendency is present in many of our foundational works of art, literature, and philosophy. It has been central to most of the dominant political ideologies of modernity . . . is present in virtually every future-oriented activity humans engage in, from the aura of hope surrounding the purchase of new clothes or planning a holiday, to the commitment to a better world implicit in medical research, constitution writing and making art.[60]

These optimistic ideals were rejected at the onset of postmodernism in the mid to late twentieth century or had no position in the cynical and ironic era of simulacra, in which everything became a copy of a copy.[61] The cynicism that arose in fashion through designers such as Rei Kawakubo, Maison Margiela, and Alexander McQueen during this time manifested in the deconstructed fracturing of the body via the garment. Physical garment attributes included rips and tears on fabric and exaggerated proportions distorting the body, which mirrored the cynicism toward the close of the millennium with a fixation on what Caroline Evans stated in *Fashion at the Edge* (2003), death, decay, alienation, and trauma.[62] This was also emulated in the spectacular fashion shows that these designers put on as the integral tool of communication for each collections concept. The fashion of today combines these ideas of cynicism and deconstruction, however, with critique and resolution that manifest both in the literal garment construction and in the way in which they are communicated, which is becoming more multifaceted as designers move beyond the runway spectacle and into the gallery space with ephemeral installations that are simultaneously physical and digital.

The metamodern, an oscillation between modern and postmodern sensibilities, then has utopic tendencies in its earnest approach to the future as well as a resigned self-awareness of its current sociocultural context. Thomas More's sociopolitical satire *Utopia* (1516) was set in a socialist society and fashion was represented through the description of identical uniforms. The idea of the social collective continued into the nineteenth- and twentieth-century canon of thought, but in the twenty-first century the utopian in relation to fashion is more multifaceted. It is less literal and more metaphysical in the sense of inclusivity, diversity, and environmental awareness being driving concepts and prerequisites in the production and communication of fashion brands. Those designers and brands that are most successful have a sense of community and collaboration in the way they create and communicate their work.

Interdisciplinary Collaboration

Van Herpen's most consistent and interwoven collaborative relationship is with Canadian interdisciplinary designer Phillip Beesley, who specializes in architectural design, public art, and experimental installations. The duo not only collaborate on projects; they actively create *together* offering both their technical skill and adept creativity on an equal playing field inventing new material technologies and structures transforming fashion into a borderless practice of fashion design architecture. What initially drew Van Herpen's eye to the practice of Beesley was his work with the concept of sentient architecture, essentially buildings with feelings, named Hylozoic Ground. *Hylozoism* is the concept or idea that all matter around us is alive, life manifesting or emerging from matter. Beesley's conceptual installations suggest that a future city could operate as a living being through a combination of materials, electricity, and chemistry; he creates immersive environments that breathe and shift as people walk through and interact on a sensory level with them.[63] The difference in scale of how both practitioners work, public buildings and space versus wearable sculptures on the human body, is vast; however, the shared ethos of wanting to improve human experience through new materialism is what drives their collaboration forward. Van Herpen created her collection *Hybrid Holism* in 2012, paying tribute to Beesley's practice, and it was actually Beesley who made contact with Van Herpen after seeing this collection. Beesley and Van Herpen's collaborative relationship is not transactional or purely based on practicality. They share personal research and ideas with one another to collectively make something new.[64]

Van Herpen finds the space between materiality and immateriality is most interesting in her fashion practice experimentations.[65] Her work often occupies these spaces between "commonly accepted dichotomies" such as the organic and synthetic or the natural and technological.[66] The "meta" nature of her practice indicates that it is the synthesis of these dichotomies or rather an oscillation of presumably opposite elements. This oscillation or synthesis is apparent not only in the way she makes her garments and the materials that she uses to do so but also in her interdisciplinary collaborations undertaken to complete projects. Her work is driven through interdisciplinary collaborations. Every project and collection are a collaboration with scientists, engineers, and architects in the construction of the garments. Van Herpen then collaborates with visual and sound artists in the construction of the performative installations that she creates to communicate and present the physical work. This collaboration is intrinsic to the reading of her practice insofar as it opens up her work to audiences wider than that of the mainstream fashion industry, much like that of Abloh and Throup. Van Herpen notes the difference between collaborations in which she designs *for* another project such as a ballet performance and when she works *with* a particular architect, scientist, or artist on a design much like that of Throup's collaborative practice. She states:

> In those situations where the creative processes are touching each other, they're not interwoven. There is still a natural distance, and it's two artists that still have their own islands. But when I work on the actual dresses with an architect or a scientist, then we have to understand each other on a different level. It's like a friendship that goes deeper, because you want to have both of your creative visions expressed in one thing.[67]

Van Herpen's fashion experiments are successful only by way of collaboration and exist not just in their finished form but also in the transient, immaterial concept of their process and presentation. Often the "how" is more important than the "what" in relation to Van Herpen's practice, which is what makes her work so interesting and what relates her work to that of the other designers I have chosen to interrogate in this research project. It exists not only between the borders of disciplines but at the borders of commerciality, artistic pursuit, and technological design innovation: fashion, art, and commerce in unifying harmony. Van Herpen's studio acts more like a think tank than an atelier, in which she brings multiple collaborators who utilize their own expertise to help build a project. While she produced ready-to-wear collections between 2013 and 2016, her practice fundamentally is situated within the space of experimental concept and innovation to drive the industry forward in a design and process-driven way. She elaborates on this idea further in an interview with *Vogue* magazine:

> I see couture as the laboratory of the bigger picture of fashion (the ready-to-wear), and my aim is to show that couture is not about yesterday. [That] it can be the place of innovation and collaboration to help push production,

materiality, and sustainability forward. [I hope to] make haute couture the engine of progress in our rapidly changing digital age.[68]

Nick Knight's Showstudio Platform

One of Van Herpen's consistent champions and collaborators is fashion photographer Nick Knight. At the turn of the millennium Knight launched the online multidisciplinary fashion platform Showstudio as a vanguard means to communicate fashion at a time when the digital was progressing so rapidly. Experimental fashion film and the moving image were pioneered by Knight and his team of editors, photographers, and collaborators encouraging fashion to engage in what was at that time a new medium in the digital age.[69] Self-describing the platform as "the home of fashion film," Knight and his collaborators have built up a community that although based in London, is international by scope, emulating the democratic nature of the internet in the twenty-first century. Fashion film continues the lineage of fashion communication that was forged by fashion illustration and fashion photography, the difference being the ability of the viewer to experience fashion in motion. Knight established a platform to showcase fashion film like American *Vogue* did for photography in the 1930s when it started publishing color photographs rather than illustrations. Another reason for Knight's launch of the platform was about access to the systems and creative processes of the fashion industry. Throughout the twentieth century, a complex web of hierarchies was constructed within the fashion system that came from the social class system established in the nineteenth century. The void between the artist and the designer, as well as between the audience and the consumer, was in part because the masses did not necessarily have access to communication technologies (such as fashion plates or magazines) and "fashion" was generally only created and communicated for high society. Access to the internet enables the consumer to access Showstudio live, or stream to a fashion show, or even view a film Nick Knight has made in collaboration with a designer.

Showstudio's aim is to change the way we as an audience perceive fashion through an interactive network of online media, which involves the fashion consumer through collaborative projects, blogs, and use of interactive digital technology.[70] Through the multichannel site, which broadcasts live panel discussions, interviews, works in progress, and behind the scenes of photo/film shoots, the general public gains access to see the process of making and creating fashion. This democratization of fashion is one of the most important side effects of the digital technetronic age and one that Showstudio has spearheaded and innovated. Showstudio represents the crumbling of disciplinary borders that began to occur at the onset of the new millennium and informs this idea of "borderless" fashion practice. More than just showcasing fashion from some of the most innovative vanguard fashion designers of this generation, Showstudio also acts as an access point to the spectacle of fashion week, offering livestream panels of academics, editors, and writers as well as artists and designers, who critically discuss the periodic state of the fashion industry, acting as an "alternative" coverage of international fashion weeks.

Van Herpen utilizes technology to help the handwork of haute couture–style fashion making, not to make the production of garments easier or faster as in ready-to-wear but in the creation of imagined garments that have never been made before. This is case in point for her conceptual "waterdress," which Van Herpen created in response to an architectural work of Benthem Crouwel Architects in 2010 (a museum Van Herpen likened to the shape of a top of a bath), which was her first cross-disciplinary collaboration.[71] She wanted to capture in freeze frame the motion of water wrapping itself around the human form, visualizing water as a garment. Becoming frustrated with the growing impossibility of how to create this quotidian moment, Van Herpen turned to a new technology she saw her collaborators using, 3D printing. Although in this instance she had to hand make the waterdress out of Perspex and a blowtorch (3D technology in 2010 could not print transparently), this triggered her practice-defining experimentation with new technologies. This technique was further put to experiment in 2013 in collaboration with Knight and Showstudio. Knight captured creative avant-garde, and patron of Van Herpen's work, Daphne Guinness, using a high-speed camera, as she stood statuesque on a plinth, being splashed with black and clear water as seen in figure 8.1. Those photographs, the water seemingly draping her body like a piece of fabric, were then analyzed frame by frame by Van Herpen, who then chose one that she could turn into a one-of-a-kind dress.[72] The whole process was captured by Showstudio and posted online through a live weeklong broadcast and consequently turned into an editorial with Guinness modeling the final dress. The project also manifested in a film and soundscape by artist Geoffrey Lillemon and sound artist Salvador Breed, and a static exhibition in SHOWstudio's *SHOWcabinet* space. The curator of the project, Niamh White, stated that the project in all of its manifestations came from "a desire to push a concept to its furthest forms, mining an idea for everything it could offer. . . . The object [the *Splash!* dress] is activated by all those installations around it."[73] The final version of the garment was not envisioned at the start, but was predominantly a project dedicated to the intricate and collaborative nature of process. Speaking about the multifaceted and multidisciplinary project, Lou Stoppard commented that it "suggests that the future of installation in fashion lies with work that moves seamlessly between the 2D and 3D worlds, embracing and contrasting different media—from film to sculpture to wearable dress—to create one unified concept."[74] The work relies on the borderless nature of the process, from conceptual ideation, to the physical making, then to the communication and interpretation. No one part is more important than the other. The transparency of this practice creates an authenticity of making. We see behind the curtain, a privilege only fashion editors and buyers were

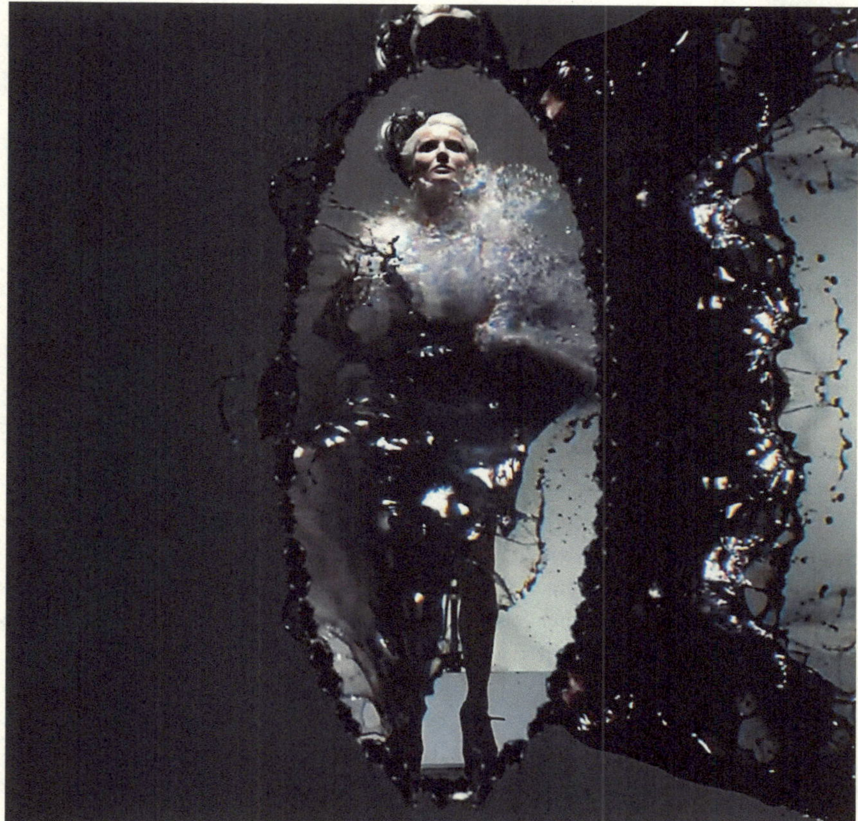

FIGURE 8.1 Screenshot of Iris van Herpen, Nick Knight, and Daphne Guinness Showstudio collaboration *Splash!*, 2013. Source: Nick Knight, https://www.showstudio.com/projects /splash.

allocated until the rise of digital media. This relates to the idea of delocalization, and the concept that what constitutes and defines "fashion" is no longer solely contingent on the lived experience of the body and the final product. It is in the process of making and collaborating and in how that work is communicated and experienced.

Dance and Movement

Movement in relation to fabrication and the body as well as immaterial phenomena such as sound are important in the all-encompassing sensory experience of Van Herpen's practice. In July 2019 the collection *Hypnosis* was presented, focusing on just that—the phenomena of hypnotic kinetic movement. In this collaboration of Van Herpen with artist Anthony Howe, the centerpiece of the presentation was a sculptural work that floated in oscillation as the models glided through underneath the structure.

Like many fashion designers before her, Van Herpen has designed costuming for dance companies. What piqued Van Herpen's interest in the medium of fashion was her personal experience in growing up with dance and her consequent fascination with the connection it creates between the body and space.[75] The transformative power of dance through bodily movement is something she found she could produce through the creation of sculptural garments.[76] The thought of movement is inherent to Van Herpen's design process. Once a fabrication is chosen, or discovered, then she starts draping and imagining what the fabrication could be on a moving form. Designing costuming for dance is not something out of the ordinary for fashion designers, particularly those whose practices are inherently theatrical or avant-garde. Christian Lacroix has designed for the Paris Opera Ballet, Coco Chanel designed for the Ballets Russes in 1924, and even Chalayan created costumes for *Gravity Fatigue* at Sadler's Wells Theater in 2015, also helping with the choreography in terms of how the costumes integrated with the dancers' bodies and movement. Van Herpen collaborated with German choreographer Sasha Waltz in 2018 on the contemporary dance production *Kreatur*, performed at the Gilman Opera House in New York.

Utopic thought in relation to technology and sustainability that we see occurring in Van Herpen's practice is reactionary to the era of global capitalism, which has seen a regression to nationalistic conservatism and a rise of neoliberalism that has unveiled the trajectory toward ecological disaster and further economic inequality across borders.[77] Van Herpen proposes ideas and solutions to these issues rather than mass-producing clothes for consumption. The reemergence of the trope of Utopia in contemporary aesthetics can be connected to these conversations. In turn, these contemporary discourses are inadvertently tethered to the rhetoric around the end of fashion, which picked up traction at the onset of the new millennium. The end-of-fashion discourse itself is related to ongoing conversations surrounding the end of art brought to attention by theorists such as Arthur Danto who claimed that the art of the late twentieth century broke from the master narrative becoming pluralistic in both practice and concept. Although Danto's philosophical thought sits outside of paradigm rhetoric, this language of the "end" is relevant in shaping the contemporary fashionscape looking toward the future. Fashion designers today can be artists, curators, or architects who just so happen to work in the realm of fashion. The fashion they create is contingent on the performative material and immaterial spaces within which it exists. Van den Akker and Vermeulen go on to say on this recurring theme that "Utopia—as a trope, individual desire or collective fantasy—is once more, and increasingly, visible and noticeable across artistic practices that must be situated in, and related, to, the passage from postmodernism and metamodernism."[78]

9

Eckhaus Latta's Community-Led Brand

Fashion is obsessed with gender: [it] defines and redefines the gender boundary.
—Elizabeth Wilson, *Adorned in Dreams*

For spring 2013, Eckhaus Latta created a dress with a photograph of American fashion designer Michael Kors printed on the front. It was an ironic meme connoting the brand's ethos, which is based around holistic self-awareness and community. Kors is one of the most monetarily successful fashion brands in North America, while Eckhaus Latta is a community-led young brand. Eckhaus Latta, although successful too, acts somewhat as an antithesis of Kors's monolithic commerciality with their very grassroots authentic community-driven brand. However, Eckhaus Latta is beyond the irony and mimesis of many millennial brands. It is both commercial and noncommercial, occupying a space in which its commercial output within the traditional fashion industry is bolstered but also grounded by its collaborative project-based practice. As writer Alec Leach states, "50% clothing brand, 50% an eclectic explosion of interdisciplinary ideas."[1]

Eckhaus Latta is a multidisciplinary North American bicoastal brand started by Mike Eckhaus and Zoe Latta in 2011. They met at the Rhode Island School of Design, where they both graduated in 2010. Eckhaus studied sculpture, while Latta studied textile design, a foundation that has attributed them the descriptor of "art school brand," which is a title that has a longer history connected to other New York City–based brands from the turn of the millennium such as ASFOUR, now threeASFOUR, that were practicing in the in-between experimental spaces of creative fashion practice. The multidisciplinary educational grounding they both have enables them to work in a more pluralistic and borderless way due to their ability to envision their practice outside the confines of the commercial fashion system. Their design identity, collective collaboration, and interdisciplinarity defy the classic market-led brand strategies of the commercial fashion system. They have a *practice* that happens to be centered on the fashion garment. This practice is project-based with the end product not being a collection as such but, as Josie Thaddeus-Johns states, is "more like an inspirational starting point that is developed and honed throughout different media over the six months the collection is out."[2] Eckhaus Latta does not intentionally create commoditized fashion moments through big-budget commercial art and fashion collaborations or runway spectacles. It offers more authentic propositions, whether that is through using "nonmodels" in its fashion shows or contributing to projects by the designers' artist friends. Eckhaus Latta maintains a sense of agency in its practice that then places value on the products it produces.

In this chapter I propose Eckhaus Latta's success in the cultural fashion sphere reflects upon the changing fashion landscape and the crumbling of disciplinary borders in the practice of contemporary fashion designers. It speaks to wider discussions of transparency and authenticity that have bubbled to the surface in the contemporary fashion industry that has given agency to the audience and consumer. I propose that Eckhaus Latta inhabits a space in the fashion industry that sees the brand become a conceptual artwork. Eckhaus Latta's work, like that of the other designers in this research project, is not only consumed in terms of the physical garment but also in the representational collective world that the designers offer. This is achieved because Eckhaus Latta's practice exists in an expanded field of fashion beyond that of just the runway. It exists on the internet, in social spaces, in museum and art galleries, and on film. The way in which the brand communicates its work, the marketing strategy in which it undertakes, conveys a holistic image of the brand that is based more around the experience of being a part of the community rather than a consumer.

The "borderless" nature of the brand is not solely limited to the crumbling of disciplinary boundaries that emerges in the process of their total practice; it is also evident in the idea of making a brand and a collection of garments and the accompanying imagery borderless in terms of gender. The fashion system of the twentieth century relied on the separate markets of "women's" and "men's" collections, and although more mainstream fashion brands still separate the two, it does not reflect the contemporary world in which we live—one in which the rhetoric around gender and sexuality is acknowledging fluidity and the fact that the two are not mutually exclusive. As Judith Butler stated, fashion adornment performs gender identity. As much as it creates the binary, it can just as effectively dismantle it.[3] Eckhaus Latta creates uniforms free of gendered stereotypes for the millennial generation and reflects diversity through the casting of "non-conventional" models. This casting is not tokenistic, however; often the models consist of creative practitioners from the designers' own community. The "experimental, gender neutral, textural designs" of Eckhaus Latta transcend the parameters of the traditional fashion system that has relied on a separation of gendered collections and the stereotypical trappings of commerce, such as classical runway shows, editorials, retail spaces, and advertising campaigns.[4] Eckhaus Latta has emerged alongside other brands that practice in similar ways. Some of these include Vetements and Telfar, which present their androgynous or genderless designs on creative collaborators rather than just models.

In this chapter I will use the lens of the metamodern to argue that like Abloh, Throup, and Van Herpen, Eckhaus Latta has created a new design identity that breaks down previously engrained boundaries between not only creative disciplines but also gendered boundaries of the body and its representations. I will analyze specific projects that Eckhaus Latta has created through the metamodern principles of design identity, collaboration, and interdisciplinarity that have created a new economy of value for contemporary audiences and consumers through what I define as borderless fashion practice. Discussing the developments around understandings of gender and "postgender" fashion emphasizes the need to create a critical discourse.

Fashion Communities and Collectives

Andy Warhol's Pop Art practice of the twentieth century paved the way for a lot of interdisciplinary and experimental practices, but even before Warhol, the radical utopian gestures of the Dadaists, Duchamp, and the Bauhaus challenged the notions on what defines art and design. That legacy is the deliberate blurring of boundaries between high and low culture, and art and commerce, crumbling the boundaries between disciplines and media to make consumers and audiences question the status quo around them. Heralding in Pop Art, Warhol surrounded himself with a collective of artists, actors, and models at his physical centerpoint: The Factory. As Four did the same with its home/studio space, colloquially called the Silver Cage, both of which were based in the lower Manhattan suburbs of Midtown and Chinatown, respectively.[5] What makes this idea of a collective creative community different for Eckhaus Latta from that of its predecessors is the brand's delocalization. Eckhaus Latta's community manifests through the multiplatform multidisciplinary approach to its brand, existing on the internet through content creation and social media as well as through its two physical retail sites and intermittent live performances, installations, runway performances, and exhibitions. The brand has created its own style tribe based on the community of collaborators that surround it. Eckhaus Latta is "anti-fashion" insofar as the designers do not adhere to the trend-based fashion system. Polhemus articulates that "anti-fashion style tribes" have emerged in recent years, differing from the subcultures of the previous century, that utilize adornment in an attempt at "subcultural stability and as a bulwark against a world where change is forever gathering pace."[6] Community fashion brands reflect the taste and cohesion of the people who surround them. In this case, musicians, artists, and writers all wear the Eckhaus Latta "look," but more than that, they live it. As subcultural styles "bubbled up" in the closing decades of the twentieth century, fashion communities today "trickle across" the fashionscape, acting more like utopian uniforms than antiestablishment armor.

Eckhaus Latta fits into a historical narrative of fashion practice that relates to the likes of New York City fashion collective As Four (Mike Eckhaus interned for Threeasfour in 2007). The collective, which still practices today under the new title Threeasfour, was made up of four creatives, Ange, Adi, Kai, and Gabi, who came of age at a point in time just before and after the new millennium. As Four did not fit within the commercial fashion system. Rather, it sat at the nexus of fashion and art creating work collaboratively using its studio as a base for community, operating in the space that can be described as "avant-garde," due to its conceptual approach to the design process. The collective lived and created in the same communal studio space, colloquially naming itself the "United Nations of Fashion," referring to each member's immigrant status. Each member was from Tajikistan, Israel, Palestine, and Germany, respectively. The decade in the lead up to the new millennium was a pre–social media utopia, relatively undocumented in comparison to today's oversaturated, image-saturated mediascape. As Four remains in the historical fashion lexicon through cultural consciousness and oral histories rather than being one that is thoroughly documented.[7] This exudes an authentic community sensibility that parallels that of Eckhaus Latta. The difference today is that this representation of authentic community building and unveiling of creative process is documented through social media. As Four's first live "runway" show, and first public communication of their practice, was set during New York Fashion Week in 2000. Fashion journalist Kim Hastreiter curated a tent at Bryant Park to showcase young vanguard designers, including American designer Rick Owens alongside the As Four collective. The "collection" was called "Puppen Couture" and composed of between 100 and 150 cheap plastic wind-up hula dolls, bought from Canal Street in Downtown Manhattan. With their doll heads removed, they were dressed in miniature versions of the collective's signature curvilinear looks.[8] The performance took place in a separate room, and as members of the audience entered, they were invited in by dramatic classical Wagner music playing in the background.[9] The dolls were placed on large platforms covered in fabric and raised to chest level so that the audience could view them at eye level. As the audience moved around the room, the miniature dolls danced and spun around to the music.[10] They were uncanny, breaking the barriers "between the animate and the inanimate, bridging the worlds of the living and the dead."[11] This tactic of using miniature mannequins to present designs to clients has been utilized by dressmakers and couturiers since the Renaissance. The utilization of miniature mannequins, in fact, saved the couture fashion industry in post–World War II Europe when morale and resources were in deficit.[12] In 1945, Parisian couturiers were commissioned by the French government to create collections of miniature fashion dolls so that the country's capital could remain the center of creative culture, to uphold the textile industry, and to keep the employment of couture laborers.[13] The group played with installation to experiment with the parameters of the fashioned garment as it interacted with an audience rather than the wearer.

Another New York City fashion collective that preluded the new millennium and transgressed from the commercial mainstream was the Bernadette Corporation, a collective of interdisciplinary conceptual creative practitioners who dominated the New York City "downtown" scene of the late 1990s and early 2000s including as principal members Bernadette Van-Huy, John Kelsey, and Antek Walczak. They incorporated film, literature, events, performances, exhibitions, and product into their practice to protest the homogenized corporate landscape of the time. Bernadette Corporation was a purely postmodern concept collective whose name itself uses irony and detournement to hint at the very anticorporate sentiment of the 1990s. Formed in 1994 in a Manhattan nightclub, the collective instigated social gatherings and events much like that of the happenings of 1950s and the Situationist International interventions of 1960s art scenes. During the mid-1990s the collective worked under the guise of an underground fashion label, but its members were also writers, creating the fashion and French theory magazine *Made in USA*, and eventually collectively authoring a book titled *Reena Spaulings* about post-9/11 New York City, which became an example in multiauthorship and creative collectivity with fifty unnamed authors. The Bernadette Corporation worked across many formats of the culture industry, such as magazine, film, photography, literature, and object-making.[14] It was postmodern by nature, appropriating the very aesthetic signifiers of consumerism that it was critiquing. As writer Malte Fabien Rauch notes, its practice was "camouflaged with a visual language that appropriates the knife's edge of the commodity fetish."[15] The Bernadette Corporation's practice has produced a zone of indeterminacy between the critique of total commodification and the total commodification of critique.

The Bernadette Corporation is situated more in line with the Situationist Internationals, a postmodern Marxist social revolutionary organization made up of avant-garde artists, writers, and theorists in the mid-twentieth century who critiqued advanced capitalism through the concept of the "spectacle." In 1967 Debord theorized that mass media had become a spectacle that alienates individual lived experience, and he stated that "when culture becomes nothing more than a commodity, it must also become the star commodity of the spectacular society."[16] The experimentation of Bernadette Corporation's interdisciplinary practice left it at the borders and in the liminal spaces of creativity outside the fashion system to critique the absurdity of capitalism. Although Eckhaus and Latta are not militant anticorporate conceptualists, they borrow the satirizing mimetic energy of collectives like Bernadette Corporation to simultaneously work within the capitalist system and live off it while also maintaining a sense of the authenticity through a critical practice that transcends disciplines. The point is, fashion collectives such as Bernadette Corporation and As Four experimented at the borders of art and fashion and contribute to the factors that led up to the development of borderless design.

Eckhaus Latta blurs the boundaries between art collective and fashion brand. The very foundations on which the designers established their practice was based around the formation of fashion and clothing as a communicative tool that reflects the social context. I argue the work produced reflects the contemporary democratization of fashion that offers the fashion experience to more people as well as reflects a sense of authenticity that is built on an oscillation between individuality and conformity. Eckhaus Latta's garments are tactile, textured, and entirely unconventional.[17] Naturally died denim, shrunken and oversized T-shirts, handmade knitwear, and tactile outerwear are common patterns in the designers' practice. However, rather than designed to fit a certain gender and demographic of people, these clothes are crafted to fit all types and shapes of people, hence the brand's low-key success. The design of clothing in the contemporary context is no longer singularly about trends; it's about building a recognizable uniform to fit an eclectic array of collaborators. Cult items such as the denim and the multipieced lapped T-shirts with tiny "Eckhaus Latta" branding hint at the duo's subconscious knowledge of the hype economy of streetwear and cult items that Abloh favors in contrast to the highly conceptual pieces of Throup and Van Herpen's practices. At the brand's retail store in New York City's Chinatown, which opened in late 2018, there is a separate "denim bar" that caters to all shapes and sizes and acts as a space for customers to spend time with the garments and get the right fit before purchasing.[18] The space itself acts as a serene environment high above the commercial streets of Manhattan on the second floor of "Chinatown Mall." This separation from the foot traffic that usual fast fashion retailers bank on separates the brand from the usual trappings of commerce and creates an experience and space for the community rather than a service. This community also expands globally beyond the physical space into the democratizing space of the digital, creating a globalized style tribe of individuals not only wearing the Eckhaus Latta brand but also engaging in its key values and design principles.

Curating a Design Identity beyond Hierarchies and Binaries

Discussion around the dismantling of boundaries and binaries in relation to fashion practice eventually leads to the discussion of gender and the gendered body, as fashion is for the most part an embodied practice, as Joanne Entwistle has noted.[19] Geczy and Karaminas discuss this intrinsic link by saying that "discourses of gender control the body in similar ways to how fashion governs and dictates the body's appearance."[20] Gender has been fixed into a restrictive binary through the colonizing Western, and Christian, perspective discourse that perpetuated aesthetic signifiers of what was deemed "masculine" or "feminine" adornment. Judith Butler challenged this discourse in the 1980s with her book *Gender Trouble*, claiming that gendered characteristics are social constructs and therefore performed.[21] She generally claims that if the appearance of "being" gender is culturally constructed, then a solid universal gender does not exist and is open to interpretation and "resignification."[22] Rather than use the word "performance" in relation to theatrics, she spoke of it in relation to performed social constructs within a heterosexual matrix that perpetuate binary notions of gender in terms of and through "masculine" and "feminine" signifiers. It is important to note critics of Butler theorize that this idea of gender performativity when used as a lens can imply that transgender identity is not real, authentic, or material. This can enforce a misreading of gender that sees it as a choice, something that can be picked up or put down like a mask. As Butler comments:

> Gender performativity is not a matter of choosing which gender one will be today. Performativity is a matter of reiterating or repeating the norms by which one is constituted: it is not a radical fabrication of a gendered self. It is a compulsory repetition of prior and subjectivating norms, ones which cannot be thrown off at will, but which work, animate, and constrain the gendered subject, and which are also the resources from which resistance, subversion, displacement are to be forged.[23]

Entwistle contends that "Sex, gender, and sexuality are often conflated so that there would appear to be a 'natural' and inevitable link between them."[24] In the twenty-first century, as communities converge and collaborate through the channels of the internet, an intersectional discourse has reemerged that completely dissolves these entrenched binaries and ideas of "natural" identity signifiers. "Intersectionality" was a term coined by American philosopher and lawyer Kimberlé Crenshaw in 1989 to address the systemic oppression of Black women in society due to their sex and race.[25] It was a reaction to the privileging of white femme bodies and social hierarchies that were prevalent in the second-wave feminist movement. In the twenty-first century it can be understood in an expanded notion in relation to intersections of social identity, encompassing race, gender, sexuality, sex, class, and ability, among other factors, that comment on systems of representation and power in society.

Eckhaus Latta has established a community that is based on principles of intersectionality. It creates imagery and garments that are inclusive of all social identities and do not conform to the previous cycle of representation in the fashion industry that centered white, thin, and cis-gendered bodies.[26] Authenticity is at the center of this, within the current metamodern zeitgeist, and particularly within the fashion system, authenticity has become not only an aspiration but also a necessity and a bankable commodity. This is due to the changing value system of the audience and consumer, which has been instigated by the access and agency offered by the internet, and in particular social media. Consumers are buying into the formation of a collective identity or a "style tribe" that reflects this desire for authenticity in who is represented. Entwistle has noted that from the nineteenth century, "clothing began to connect more closely to the body and individuality of the wearer" and was read for its "authenticity"; however, it still conformed to exterior signifiers bound by social class.[27] Postmodernism, as a product of the sociocultural context of the twentieth century, dismantled these hierarchies of class, which offered a new perspective on self-referential authenticity. Borderless fashion practice oscillates between these notions. Rather than buying into trends, consumers are buying into an identity that is often communicated in the expanded spaces of fashion practice and the communities that congregate within them.

In Virginia Woolf's often-cited literary masterpiece *Orlando* (1928), the protagonist wakes at the beginning of the novel as a young nobleman in Tudor England, while it ends with her as a noblewoman and writer in 1928. The centuries in between see Orlando change gender from male to female and back again, moving with ease through androgyny as situations see fit. The novel was dedicated to Woolf's lover Vita Sackville-West, a fictional biography of her life that includes portraits of Sackville-West, a novel shaped as a nineteenth-century biography. Not only does *Orlando* blur gender boundaries; it also demarcates those of genre, too. *Orlando*, both the novel and the 1992 film directed by Sally Potter, have informed intertextual references and inspired fashion in recent years.[28] Beyond inspiring specific garments and how they are styled on the traditional runway, the gender-fluid identity taken on by the story's protagonist has become a point of early reference in the modern Western zeitgeist. Referring to "zeitgeist" in regard to fashion, argues that fashion responds to social and political changes.[29] In November 2019 at the Business of Fashion's annual VOICES conference, gender nonconforming performance artist and poet Alok Vaid-Menon spoke of a need to completely "de-gender" the fashion industry.[30] Vaid-Menon stated that the fashion and beauty industries want the "aesthetic of diversity, but they don't actually want us. I am not an idea. I am not a symbol. I am not a prop. I am a person."[31] Vaid-Menon urges the industry, the makers and communicators, not to tokenize but to represent in an authentic way. Representing the spectrum of gender in an agentic manner, that is, centering a diverse array of perspectives both through who is behind the scenes and who we see in the accompanying imagery. Vaid-Menon goes on to say that "gender-neutrality is not the death of fashion, it is the Renaissance of fashion."[32] Eckhaus Latta understands this notion, breaking gender identity from its binary, much like that of Woolf's *Orlando*.

The mainstream fashion industry has become increasingly more open to blurring the gender binary in terms of the models it casts in runway shows, editorials, and campaigns. Transgender models such as Andreja Pejić, Teddy Quinlivan, and Hari Nef are regulars on fashion runways and in editorials and campaigns. Models and practitioners who identify as gender nonconforming or nonbinary are also being centered and represented in visual storytelling narratives. In an editorial for *SSENSE* in 2018, model Meetka Otto, photographer Richie Shazam, and stylist Thistle Brown all stand contrapposto, mimicking the power poses of 1990s supermodels or the harmonious stance of a classical Greek sculpture. Their photograph was published on the niche fashion website SSENSE and was taken by Eckhaus Latta friend and collaborator Michael Bailey Gates. Rather than offering an idealized version of a man or woman, however, the trio all identify as gender nonconforming, nonbinary, or gender-neutral, subverting preconceived notions and subsequently subverting any notion of an "ideal" body in fashion. Gender is not projected or inherent. It is performed, and there is an unlimited spectrum of gender representation that can be performed and communicated. As writer Jake Hall has stated, "The ways in which designers choose to work with the silhouette creates the meaning behind fashion; some choose to deform, cloak, or reconfigure it entirely, creating new possibilities as to what a 'human,' 'male,' 'female,' or 'non-binary' shape could be. Decisions like these are crucial given the ongoing politicisation and policing of bodies."[33] Representation of real life and real people in their total eclectic form dominates Eckhaus Latta's imagery, in the form of editorials and advertising campaigns as well as noncommercial projects, and offers a glimpse into the collective world Eckhaus Latta has created. Rather than leveraging the concept of gender-neutral or nonbinary clothing as a tokenistic tactic to sell its product, Eckhaus Latta's garments are inherently neutral and represent people with agency over their own representation and narrative in the accompanying editorial campaigns, films, and exhibitions. Entwistle notes that clothing imbues the "body with significance, adding layers of cultural meanings, which, because they are so close to the body, are mistaken as natural."[34] This means that rather than revealing the body, clothing and fashion embellish it.[35] Eckhaus Latta uses "nonmodels" in their presentations and campaigns, continuing the legacy of other postmodern fashion designers who experimented with similar "street-casting," such as Jean Paul Gaultier and Margiela. Contemporary artists, stylists, actors, and general creative practitioners such as artist Susan Cianciolo, multidisciplinary creative Bobbi Salvor Munez, photographer and model Richie Shazam, actor Hari Nef, stylist Thistle Brown, filmmaker Alexa Karolinski, model Paloma Elcessor, and photographer Michael Bailey Gates are frequent collaborators and are often present in runway shows and campaigns. Martin Margiela and contemporary brand Vetements have utilized this tradition too, but what makes Eckhaus Latta's use of "nonmodels" more authentic is the fact that they represent a more diverse mix of people in terms of size, race, gender, and age. Through their familial

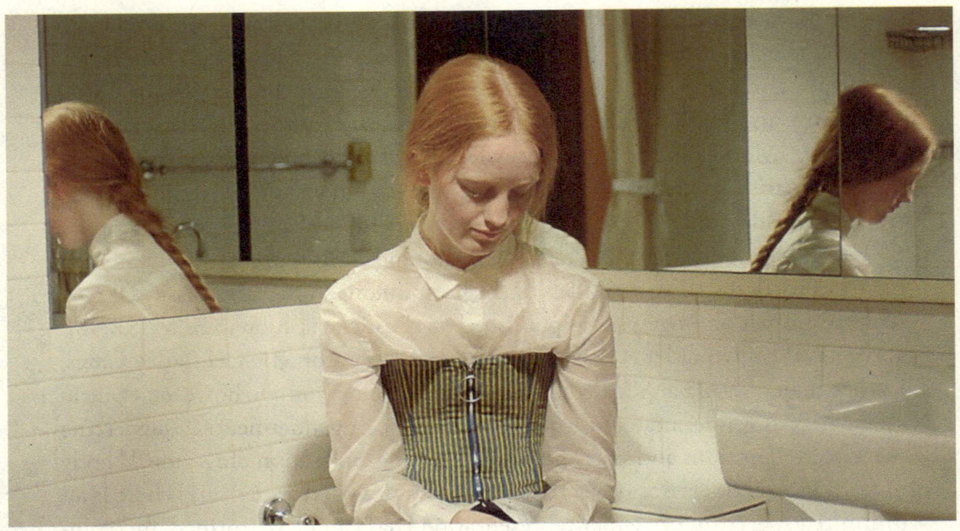

FIGURE 9.1 Screenshot of Eckhaus Latta and Alexa Karolinski, *Coco*, 2017. Source: https://world.eckhauslatta.com/world/.

collective of friends and collaborators, not only do Eckhaus and Latta overthrow gender norms; they also redefine the Western heteronormative notion of a nuclear family that has been perpetuated through mainstream fashion imagery that is particularly evident in their film collaborations with Alexa Karolinski, which I will go on to discuss further in this chapter. I also acknowledge that this practice is part of a wider historical move away from binary notions of Western society represented through fashion practice and that this analysis is in direct response to fashion in the twenty-first century being a borderless metamodern practice.

In 2017, Eckhaus Latta created a film with Karolinski that acted more of a confessional therapy session for their community rather than an advertising campaign for clothes. Titled *Coco*, the forty-minute film was shot in a nondescript bathroom, the subject/model alone but with a camera and a selection of discussion prompts that ranged from true love, identity, and family history. The designers described the project as "actual reality TV," their diverse community of friends confessing secrets and personal anecdotes dressed in Eckhaus Latta garments.[36] The film was installed at New York's Museum of Arts and Design as a part of its *Fashion after Fashion* exhibition that aimed to promote fashion's expanded scope and ability to exist in many different representational forms beyond the runway.[37] As presented in figure 9.1, the film is a compositional triptych. The subject's profiled reflections frame the candid face-to-camera confessionals. The designers are selling authenticity not only by casting "nonmodels" but by having them talk about their subjective experience of the world. It breaks the fourth wall of fashion imagery that usually creates a fantastical and aspirational barrier between subject and viewer. This break is a familiar tactic in still photography, however, when established in the context of a moving film, as the eye contact is more disarming for the viewer. Here the gaze is set for everyone, welcoming the viewer into the Eckhaus Latta community.

This tactic of agentic representation continues across more traditional communication material such as the photographic advertising campaign. For its spring/summer 2017 advertising campaign, Eckhaus Latta captured a diverse cast of couples of all genders and sexual orientations having real-life sex adorned in the duo's designs. Heji Shin, who had previously photographed a sex education book for German teenagers in 2011, shot the campaign. They cast real-life couples, some friends of the designers and others hired through Craigslist (a community website in the United States), and styled them in the latest collection from the brand. Eckhaus Latta confronts the classic "sex sells" tropes of traditional fashion campaigns, producing an unconventional but real collection of photographs that reconstruct notions of authentic sexuality not based around gender and sexuality binaries. To quote the designers, "We live in a time where there is still tension between individualised freedom of expression (especially online) and puritanical approaches to sex that are deeply encoded in culture."[38] The highly sexualized campaign imagery of the early 2000s from fashion houses, such as Gucci (Tom Ford was creative director at the time), ostracized and shocked audiences rather than invited them in with its brand of sex appeal. Tom Ford's campaigns were a nod to the 1970s imagery of fashion photographers such as Guy Bourdin and Helmut Newton, who embedded codes of erotic suggestions in their fashion work. However, Ford's campaigns "celebrated female sexuality in ways that problematize simplistic understandings of production and reception."[39] In one famous image from 2004, a model stands against a wall naked from the waist down with a Gucci "G" shaved into her pubic hair while a male model kneels before her. As in this image and so many others from this era of Gucci, the models are "headless and limbless." Constructed into objects through the erasure of their identity, they become "sets of fleshy folds and orifices, passively awaiting penetration."[40] Eckhaus Latta's sex campaign, however, normalizes diverse sexual expression, breaking down hierarchies of gender and sexuality that images such as Ford's for Gucci perpetuate. By confronting the idea of commercially stylized sexuality with real censored images of real couples having sex, Eckhaus Latta calls out a consuming audience by subverting or even hijacking the hegemonic gaze.

Interdisciplinary Collaborations

Eckhaus Latta is known for establishing and uplifting a collective community of friends and collaborators. As Eckhaus Latta has found success, so have those that it has worked on projects with. As Latta has stated, "I think, unintentionally, the reason we work with clothing has to do with the way that it engages other people."[41] In August 2018, Eckhaus Latta staged an installation at the Whitney Museum of American Art in New York City, the first fashion-centered show at the gallery since an Andy Warhol exhibition called "The Warhol Look/Glamour Style Fashion," which was staged in 1997.[42] The legacy of Warhol and The Factory, and the way they converged high and low culture, makes it possible for fashion practitioners such as Eckhaus Latta to have exhibitions in revered spaces such as this. The postmodern breakdown between what was perceived as "high" and "low" culture opened the scope for definitions of "art" to be expanded. Warhol's practice did just that, incorporating screen-printing, fashion, and mass production into his creative output.

The title of Eckhaus Latta's Whitney exhibition was *Possessed* and was a collaboration between curators Christopher Y. Lew and Lauri Freedman (the gallery's director of product development) and Eckhaus and Latta.[43] The title alludes to the convergence of commerce, art, and fashion manifested in the exhibition. The press release for the show states, "Through collaborations with artists, musicians, and others, and an approach that plays with and against industry conventions, Eckhaus Latta addresses the crosscurrents of desire, social relations, and consumption."[44] In this age of metamodern fashion, clothes have become somewhat superfluous or secondary to the creation of content across media platforms and physical spaces. Fashion exists in this expanded field that critically engages with social issues such as politics, race, gender, sexuality, and class. *Possessed* presented a convergence of retail, exhibition, and performance that connects to wider practices that integrate retail signifiers with installation and curated exhibition. The practice of scholar and curator Matthew Linde works in this space. Linde is the founder of Centre for Style, which was an experimental performance retail space in Melbourne Australia between 2013 and 2016, which put on presentation events consisting of runway, retail, and performance. Similar projects include *Prada Marfa*, the installation in Texas erected in 2005, the projects of the Bernadette Corporation, and of course Abloh's museum retrospective.[45]

Possessed consisted of three separate rooms, and installed within were three phases of the shopping experience. The first installation was an ode to traditional advertising with multiple light boxes illuminating photographs in the style of classic fashion campaigns by the likes of Irving Penn or Steven Meisel of models dressed in the duo's clothes.[46] Famous millennial supermodel Gemma Ward was a recognizable addition in one of the shots and was also the image used to advertise the museum exhibition. Latta commented on the reasoning of Ward's inclusion in the exhibition by saying, "You don't need to know her name, but you know that she's sold you something before," in reference to the recognizability of the model's look. The second room was the "retail" space in which visitors could touch, try on, and ultimately purchase products. The furnishings of the space were made in collaboration with artist friends such as Susan Cianciolo. Subverting the traditional rules of a "white-cube" exhibition space that traditionally centers around the inability to touch the fine art that usually dominates the space democratizes the experience and creates a unique and rarefied environment in which to shop. Emulating Eckhaus Latta's fashion practice as a whole, the exhibition was a self-conscious look at what it means to be sold product in the current socioeconomic climate bridging the gap between art and commerce.

Discussion of the rise of installation and performance in the art world that occurred in the mid-twentieth century now takes place with regard to the expanded concept of borderless fashion practice. Installation and performative practices are the result of artists' aims to produce a living art long sought after in painting and sculpture: "They also present a new aesthetic response to changed historical conditions, social practices and political divisions of space as well as to changing environments and new technology of representation and reproduction; they can also be seen as a result of the increasing urgency for responsible social action and interaction."[47] This is a sentiment reflected in the current Western fashion industry, the backdrop of which is a crumbling capitalist system that only touches lightly upon the damage it is doing environmentally, socially, and culturally. In one room of the exhibition, a dark room of surveillance camera footage is presented on a grid of television monitors. This is the last room that visitors entered, and they were confronted with voyeuristic footage of the previous gallery spaces as well as camera footage from other international retail locations that stock Eckhaus Latta.

Connecting to the wider discussions of fashion's democratization that I have emphasized throughout this book, *Possessed* was a "shoppable" exhibition that allowed visitors to touch, try on, and purchase the clothing displayed in the main exhibition space. Prices ranged from USD$24 to USD$7,200.00, and the products ranged from tote bags and socks to handmade beaded garments in upcycled materials. Through this tactic, the designers usurp the function of the rarefied white cube gallery space in which rules and regulations are institutionally ingrained. These historically have placed a barrier between the visitor and object on display, restricting interaction. Eckhaus Latta has not necessarily turned a gallery space into a retail space, but through highlighting the importance of commerce in an artistic institution it has redefined the value of a fashion object, or at least it is asking this question of the visitor/audience, as well as calling into question the art world's uncomfortable relationship with commerce. Fashion has always been up-front about its entanglement with commerce, whereas other creative disciplines such as fine art and architecture have always placed themselves at a distance even though their very existence relies just as much on the labyrinth of capitalism. *Vogue* magazine stated in a review of the show that "with *Possessed*, the duo is deconstructing the ways the fashion industry sells us things."[48]

Eckhaus Latta takes on a marketing strategy that is based upon a holistic take on the experience economy. Their brand exists across multiple media channels as well as across disciplines in an agentic way rather than utilizing tokenistic collaborative gimmicks as a marketing tool like larger fashion houses might. As previously mentioned, the experience economy argues that the memory of an experience in relation to a brand becomes the product. Through interdisciplinary collaborations, borderless fashion practitioners create multidimensional design and communication projects that rupture the fields between art, fashion, film, and design and the expanded spaces in which they occupy.

Like Abloh, Throup, and Van Herpen, Eckhaus Latta has dedicated commercial collaborations that give it a boost in commercial attention while offering an aura of cultural cachet to the large corporate companies. It also acts as way to put into practice some of the more conceptual ideas the designers have percolating. The brand brings cultural cachet and an element of "cool" to otherwise everyday utilitarian companies. Through collaborating with highly commercial companies like Camper and Ugg, Eckhaus Latta subverts the boundary between high and low culture again by handing over the artistic conceptual aura of its brand. These collaborations work much like that of the limited-edition "drop" model mentioned previously in relation to Abloh's practice. The limited-edition nature of the collaboration as well as the juxtaposition of a cult brand against an accessible everyday corporate brand creates a convergence that attracts the attention of a consumer and audience that want to "buy in" on a brand's experiential aura.

Eckhaus Latta's first large commercial collaboration was with Spanish shoe company Camper for their *Camper Together* series of seasonal collaborations. Camper has been savvy with what designers it has aligned itself with in the last decade. Previously the company has created capsule collections with more conceptual critically minded designers such as Bernhard Wilhelm, Dai Fujiwara, and Kiko Kostadinov. Like other fashion collaborations such as Rick Owens × Birkenstocks and Balenciaga × Crocs, Camper sees the importance in what *Highsnobiety* called "buzz × bland" collaborations that have dominated the fashion industry over the past five to ten years.[49] That is the mixing of high-street commercial brands that proliferate across mainstream culture with high-fashion design practitioners.

For their 2016 collaboration, Eckhaus Latta and Camper designed a knitted shoe consisting of an athletic sock merged with a block heel. Eckhaus stated that the shoe's concept stemmed from a long design process of wanting to mix Eckhaus Latta's off-kilter knitwear with footwear.[50] To communicate the collaboration, a film was made directed by Karolinski that saw actor and model Hari Nef and performance artist Martine Gutierrez roaming around the Spanish island of Mallorca. The low-fi nature of the filming is juxtaposed with audio of the two models discussing everything from ghosts to what their preferred juice flavor is, a tactic to create a mundane and relatable soundtrack to the film and similar to the "confessional" nature of *Coco* (2017). They sit in a square drinking wine and run through an orange grove crushing oranges under their Camper-clad feet, as seen in figure 9.2. It is this "everydayness" evoked through Eckhaus Latta's visual language that creates the authenticity that Eckhaus Latta

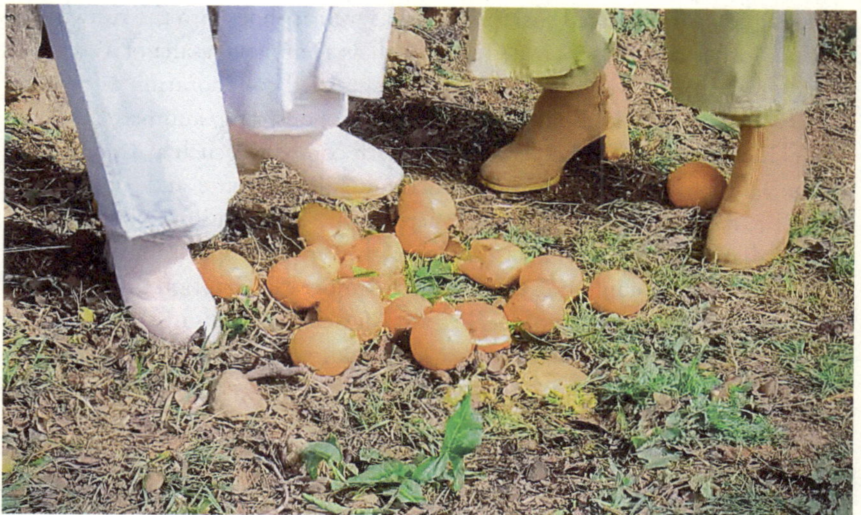

FIGURE 9.2 Screenshot of Eckhaus Latta × Camper collaboration, 2016. Directed by Alexa Karolinski. Source: https://world.eckhauslatta.com/world/.

is known for. Eckhaus Latta and Camper invite the audience not only to buy their product but to become a part of their community. Authenticity is also achieved through Camper's wholesome reputation. Since 1975, Camper has been a family business in Spain producing ethically minded shoes that avoid trends. Rather, Camper makes staple classics such as the rubber-soled Pelotas and the classic Twins, in which a pair of shoes has two different designs on each foot. Then there is the Kobarah sandal, an abstracted all-rubber modular heeled shoe in bright pink, orange, and blue that became an instant hit, selling out around the world due to the products' jolie laide (attractive but not conventionally so) essence, not despite of it. Camper has the underlying values of "comfort, sustainability, and casualness by design" underscored with notions of irony, humor, and honest original design that align with the values of Eckhaus Latta's borderless fashion practice.[51] A sense of beauty is connoted in the ugliness of the everyday imagery and everyday stories that Eckhaus Latta represents and tells.

After the brand's Whitney Museum exhibition success, Australian American company Ugg approached the designers to collaborate on a capsule collection for its fall/winter 2019 seasonal offering. Ugg is synonymous with the surf culture of Australia in the 1970s and then California. In the early years of the new millennium, pseudo-celebrities such as Paris Hilton and Nicole Richie made Ugg enter the mainstream vernacular. After a decline in popularity, the past five years has seen resurgence due to the introduction of limited-edition fashion collaborations. Streetwear-focused designers such as Heron Preston and Y/Project have collaborated previously, adding a value of cool cultural cachet and hype to the traditionally kitsch brand. This collaboration with Ugg was more symbiotic, as the designers incorporated shearling coats as well as shoes into the runway collection. Other contemporary designers such as Demna Gvasalia of Vetements collaborate in this way that sees a more ingrained collaboration of product intertwined with the high-fashion runway items. For spring/summer 2017, Vetements included seventeen collaborations with companies such as Levi Strauss, Brioni, Church's, Champion, Manolo Blahnik, Juicy Couture, and Alpha Industries. The collection utilized the signifiers of all these brands, mixing and converging diamond-encrusted Blahnik heels with oversized Alpha Industry bomber jackets and Champion hoodies, creating a democratized notion of luxury and once again destroying any borders between definition of "high" and "low" culture, much like that of Abloh's work with branding.

Hybrid Spaces

Film has been one of the more important platforms in which Eckhaus Latta has communicated its design language. Eckhaus Latta has done so through its ongoing collaboration with aforementioned filmmaker Alexa Karolinski, who is German born and New York City based and whom the designers met after they produced their first collection.[52] Commenting on the inception of the collaborative relationship, Karolinski has stated, "It was a special time because when we started our conversation it wasn't just about what shall we do for the next video, but what should video be and how do we develop a video language together."[53] These films represent the immaterial cultural production of the brand. However, unlike big fashion houses that utilize the medium of big-budget cinematic short films that show the latest collections, the collaboration between Karolinski and Eckhaus Latta is an ongoing artistic project that seeks to communicate the authentic world they have created around the clothes. These films also present an uncanniness of the everyday, as touched upon previously. The tropes used in each film, whether it is the location, the movements, or human gestures, morph the everyday social interactions into something that is both humorous and often uncomfortable due to the uncanny nature of actions that take place. I will look at the early films *Uniform*, *Dinner*, and *Smile* to extrapolate on the ways in which Eckhaus Latta the brand entices its audience through affective means. As stated previously in this book, consumers are no longer just that; they are audiences who value cultural appeal and connection, the immaterial, as the luxury "product" of a brand.

Film and fashion have evolved in symbiosis since the development of the moving image in the late nineteenth century. The ability to capture the body in movement is inextricable from the body's relationship to fashion. Nick Rees-Roberts states in his book on the topic that fashion film today is "primarily understood by those within the fashion industry to refer to the production of digital video content and branded entertainment commissioned by designer labels and fashion houses as a promotional tool."[54]

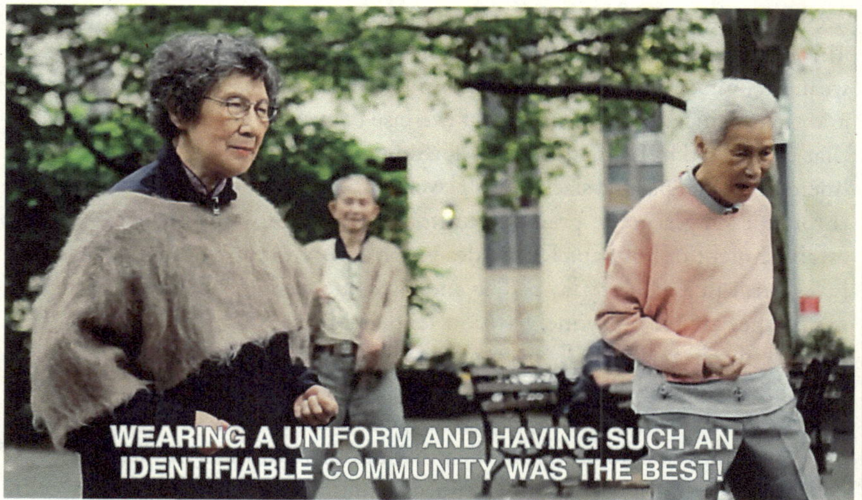

FIGURE 9.3 Screenshot of Eckhaus Latta, *Uniform*, 2012. Directed by Alexa Karolinski. Source: https://world.eckhauslatta.com/world/.

He argues that since the new millennium, the consumption of online video has steadily risen as fashion houses morph into multimedia producers that create both material objects and digital content.[55] Rees-Roberts goes on further to state, "As a product of multimedia convergence-cultural, economic, and technological-fashion film exists as a hybrid genre, a mixed form of online filmmaking mostly produced in short-form to display fashion in motion."[56] This blurring of boundaries or convergence of media acts as an advertising tool not only to sell product but to convey the aura of the brand, and its aesthetic as well as cultural principles. With the emergence of online platforms such as Nowness and Showstudio in the twentieth century, a space opened up for the production of collaborative art house fashion films. This is the context in which Eckhaus Latta's film collaborations operate.

In the film *Uniform* (2012), hosted by online digital interface platform Nowness in collaboration with Eckhaus Latta, Karolinski captured a community group of New York City residents and their daily morning routine that takes place in Chinatown's Columbus Park.[57] For thirty years the group has gathered daily to practice *luk tung kuen*, a specialist Chinese form of exercise with roots in Hong Kong. The group of predominantly women were given a selection of Eckhaus Latta's pieces to choose from to wear as they moved through the movements and poses while Karolinski filmed them. A voice-over of interviews with some of the participants is played over shots of the collective moving in Zen synchronicity. As the film unfolds, the voices of the group transcend the fourth wall. It becomes apparent that clothing and fashion have been utilized in a casual way by the group as a means to unify, as one states: "Wearing a uniform and having such an identifiable community was the best!" (figure 9.3). They used to all dress in yellow; however, as they grew older, they became less and less "uniform." Through this video, Eckhaus Latta offers an eclectic uniform for the women to wear, a reunification through sartorial unity. The searing earnestness of the group and their dedication to the ritual of exercise convey an authentic everydayness that is reflected in Eckhaus Latta's clothing: mohair felted knits, sheer blouses, linen shirts, and pleated slacks are all layered upon each member as they all move through each gesture in practiced uniformity. This film was made early in the establishment of Eckhaus Latta's design philosophy, but what it conveys is an investment in real, everyday people and an acknowledgment that Eckhaus Latta's clothes are for everyone. Fashion scholar Marketa Uhlirova explains that fashion film has principally been motivated by the "kinetic and metamorphic possibilities" of dress and adornment since the dawn of cinema in the late nineteenth century.[58] In *Uniform*, the fashion garments emulate their wearers' synchronized movements, unifying them in a utopian, or meta-utopian, world of collective familial practice. Once again, a communal identity and experience are on offer rather than a particular commodity.

Dinner (2013) occupies more carnal elements of the everyday. Featuring a cast dressed in Eckhaus Latta's spring/summer 2013 collection, the film opens with guests preparing for an eminent dinner party, preparing food and occasionally cutting away to shots of them doing one another's hair and painting each other's nails. Grooming is happening while simultaneously vegetables are peeled and pureed into bright green and pink cocktails, two acts of the everyday that when instigated in unison invite an abject reaction. *Dinner* descends into the grotesque from there as the guests cover the clothing with clear plastic ponchos that act as full-body napkin bibs before sitting at a pristine white banquet table lit with a cold fluorescent light. The guests laugh while serving each other handfuls of rice, hummus, and cauliflower, all monochrome foods, before drizzling the green and pink purees over the top. They devour the food, emulating a bacchanal tableau as the pristine white tablecloth and plates become covered in the detritus of their feast. The convergence of the actions makes apparent the somewhat arbitrary processes set around feeding and beauty rituals.[59] Adding to the uncanny nature of these everyday actions, the film is set to the backdrop of a soundtrack of the guests' own conversations and movements in reverse, adding to the uncanny and self-referential aura of the film. The actions of the guests as they merrily and collaboratively construct their meals and delight in each other's company offers a parallel vision to the creation of an Eckhaus Latta collection. Although grotesque, the juxtaposition is mesmerizing and enticing, as demonstrated in figure 9.4. The film is not about the clothes; it is about the sharing of rituals, creation, and practice. Eckhaus Latta is inviting the viewer to experience the brand's aura and buy into the brand through the action of watching and engaging. In its formal language, metamodernism encompasses a "structure of feeling," the aesthetics of which reflect a new sincerity, new materialism, and new romanticism.[60] These aspects can be found in Eckhaus Latta films such as *Dinner* that have a

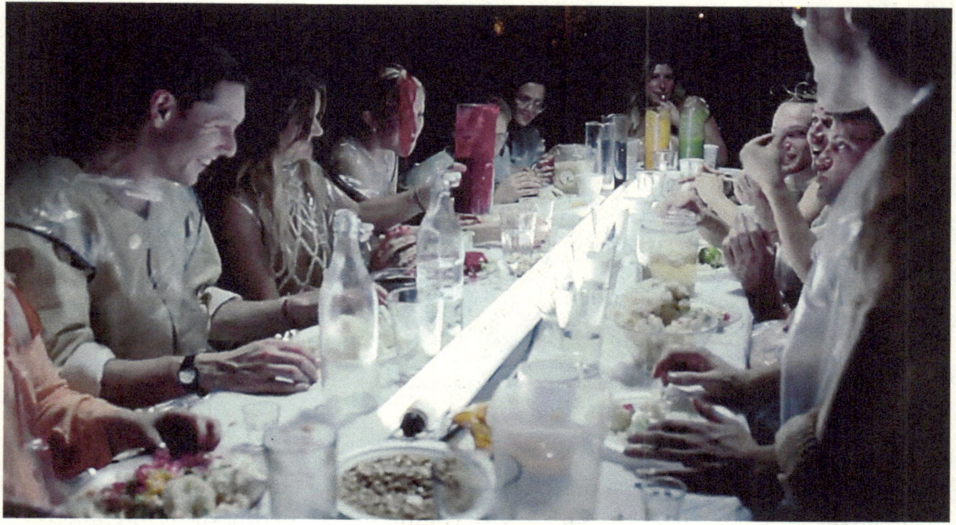

FIGURE 9.4 Screenshot of Eckhaus Latta, *Dinner*, 2013. Directed by Alexa Karolinski. Source: https://world.eckhauslatta.com/world/.

focus on communing together in some form to create a multifaceted ritualistic performance.

In 2015, the trio collaborated again to communicate the spring/summer 2016 collection. Named *Smile*, the film was set in the sun-drenched Los Angeles mid-century modernist–style Kappe Residence with mezzanine floors, wood paneling, and floor-to-ceiling glass windows.[61] The film was made not only as an accompaniment to the brand's 2016 collection offering but also as a commission for the Hammer Museum's biennial exhibition, *Made in L.A. 2016: a, the, though, only*. Another everyday setting is used as the backdrop to *Smile*, enticing the viewer into a sense of familial comfort. In the first shot, an eclectic mix of people wearing the brand's clothes walk into the frame and sit around a woman (architect Miggi Hood) who is looking directly into the camera. They all smile widely and sit close together surrounding the woman, touching and looking into each other's eyes before breaking the fourth wall. The film was originally intended to be a photo shoot, but Eckhaus and Latta decided to explore the artifice of a photo shoot instead and create a film that captures the in-between moments, the chatter, the moving in and out of frame, and the spectrum of emotional expressions, seen in figure 9.5. Karolinski framed these moments as though taking a family portrait, lingering the camera on the model characters as their moods shift between smiles and anguish in what Latta referred to as capturing a "manic energy that is a bit more honest than 'incredibly stoic' or 'fierce,'" which are general attributes and tropes used in traditional fashion advertising campaigns.[62] The eclectic nature of the group resembles that of a utopian (or dystopian) family cult that throughout the film engages in acts of dancing, kissing, crying, and

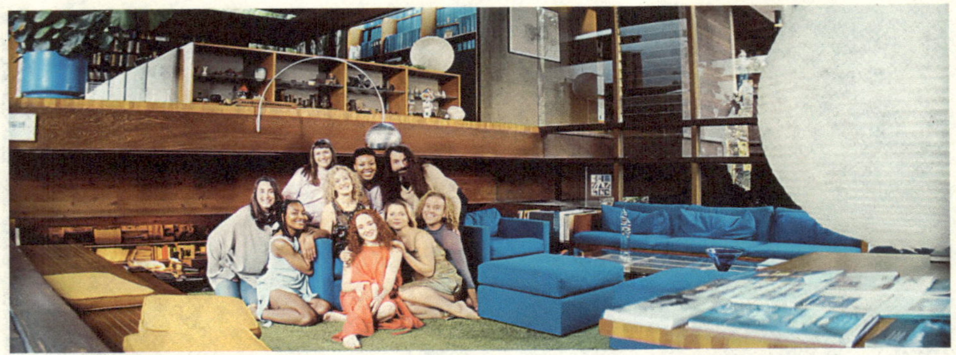

FIGURE 9.5 Screenshot of Eckhaus Latta, *Smile*, 2016. Directed by Alexa Karolinski. Source: https://world.eckhauslatta.com/world/.

laughing. Karolinski's own practice focuses on ideas of family and community. Having grown up in a close-knit Jewish community in Berlin, she is interested in the ways in which people interact and relate to one another in contemporary modernity.[63] This notion is a reaction to the sociocultural climate of the twenty-first century in which political divisions and debates have moved ever more insidiously into the home. To quote the artist, "I really believe that, in this weird political situation, communities are going to become more important than ever, we have to turn to the communities of loved ones and people we can identify with, because in the near future we're probably not going to be able to count on governments or systems."[64]

Eckhaus Latta's film collaborations with Karolinski rebrand the concept of "family" without the cult-like connotations. Utilizing modernist tropes of a utopian societal community, they juxtapose this with the deconstruction of traditional branding exercises to reconstruct the metamodern definition of a fashion "brand." The metamodern principle of collaboration and community acts as a central element to the building of their brand that evokes a sense of authenticity. Through breaking down the tropes of a traditional fashion brand, those that relate to individual success and beauty and that are perpetuated through campaign imagery, the duo turn a fashion brand into an art practice that has the grounding principles of collective and collaborative creativity.

Through this dedicated ongoing collaboration with Karolinski, Eckhaus Latta reflects a commitment to interdisciplinary creativity that rejects the siloing of creative practices and promotes collaboration. These films present a holistic image of the Eckhaus Latta brand. They do not use traditional waifish supermodels, nor do they focus on selling an individual product. They promote and experience, an attitude, and a lifestyle. As Elizabeth Moor establishes in her writing on branded spaces, contemporary marketing attempts to approach consumers in an "expanded range of everyday spaces."[65]

This metaphysical world building appears across a multitude of projects and mediums that Eckhaus Latta has developed. In late 2017 the brand edited and curated the annual concept publication *A Magazine Curated By*, which sees a different fashion designer/group/house take full control over the publication for one issue, communicating their creative universe and behind-the-scenes access to the process of this creativity. They bring on their own collaborators to convey their creative world to express not only their aesthetic but also their values. To quote the publication, "Each issue celebrates this designer's ethos: their people, the passion, their stories, emotions, fascinations, spontaneity, and authenticity."[66] Formerly designers such as Martin Margiela, Iris van Herpen, and Gucci's Alessandro Michele have been chosen to curate their own issue. The publication in itself acts as a limited-edition object: as they sell out, they appreciate in value until they are all sold. This tactic creates an aura around both the magazine object and the brand. The consumer can gain access to the practitioners' design philosophy that they have not had access to previously. This creates a sense of the authentic through experiential marketing. If the fashion brand is the "aura" of our age, as Alice Hines states, and the evolution of the fashion show into the concept of fashion installation is the vehicle of the brand's aura, then forms of communication such as "niche" publications like *A Magazine Curated By* contribute to this immersive communication.[67] "Niche" fashion magazines, as defined by Ane Lynge-Jorlén in 2017, are independent publications that speak to a "highly fashion literate readership and mix the codes of style magazines, glossy women's magazines and art catalogues."[68] This style of fashion publication is a site in which we see the further blurring of borders of creative disciplines as writers, art directors, curators, fashion designers, graphic designers, photographers, and even architects collaborate to communicate their borderless creative practices. As Lynge-Jorlén states, "They are often produced and read by people engaged in the business of creating fashion taste."[69] Publications such as *Vestoj Journal*, *Business of Fashion*, *System* magazine, and *A Magazine Curated By* fall under this umbrella, offering critical long-form essays and profiles on practitioners and the culture of fashion. They offer a convergence of critical academic perspectives with journalistic topics and tone. The democratization that has occurred through the contemporary fashionscape has enabled the audience and consumer to have agency over what they consume. Value is placed within this type of cultural production of fashion and designers and practitioners who partake in this obtain cultural cachet. Niche fashion magazines have become more prolific as readers' desire for authenticity becomes more dominant.[70] Eckhaus Latta's curation of *A Magazine* offers a glimpse into the designers' creative process, their creative relationships, and their own personalities and taste. Buying a copy of *A Magazine Curated By: Eckhaus Latta* is an accessible, but still luxurious due to the publication's limited nature, way to buy into the brand.

Eckhaus Latta's issue played on classic tropes of the traditional "glossy" fashion magazine, in particular satirizing or parodying the tradition of the "September issue" made famous by Conde Nast's *Vogue* magazine, the most important and largest issue of the year. To quote the publishers, "Eckhaus Latta's avant-garde approach to fashion is brought to light through its adoption and subsequent subversion of existing structures."[71] They use familiar categories such as "Beauty" and "Interiors" and open the publication up to collaborations with friends and family. Susan Cianciolo edited the "home" feature, while Tim Blanks wrote the Letter to the Editor, and Juliana Huxtable wrote an advice column. In one spread they present an "Out and About" section called "They Are Just Like Us," photographed by Rob Kulisek with paparazzi-style photographs of friends, models, and collaborators seemingly going about their daily routine. The shots are emulating the classic "Out and About" sections from the second half of glossy magazines where the upper echelons of high society can be seen rubbing shoulders at event parties, or they parallel the shots of celebrities going about mundane daily life that fill tabloid-esque publications. Eckhaus Latta senior designer Bobby Andres is captured grabbing a coffee on a rain-soaked street, while model Camilla Deterre is captured by a surveillance-like camera riding her bike through the streets of New York. Another feature mirroring a classic beauty section of a fashion magazine is titled "Uncanny Silicon Valley: Beauty for the Forward Thinker," a collaboration with interdisciplinary artist Bailey Scieszka and photographer Sharif Hamza. Models are adorned in psychedelic face paint and handcrafted jewelry made from found objects such as toys and costume jewels. The results are reminiscent of Leigh Bowery's famous beauty looks, which transcended boundaries of gender and the body, taking them to their most performative uncanny limits. The cover of the edition featured a model wearing the aforementioned Michael Kors dress from the designer's spring/summer 2013 collection. The model is throwing her head back and laughing, looking at the camera through scrunched-up eyes, which is an antithetical image to ones we are used to seeing on the front covers of more traditional mainstream publications. The fact that the model is a person of color is also in contrast to the status quo of magazine publishing, which although it has attempted to be more inclusive in the past five years still is dominated by white, thin, and cis-gendered identities. As a fashion brand and as fine art practitioner, Eckhaus Latta blurs the boundaries between "scrutiny and celebration" of the fashion industry. Through this very "meta" balance of celebratory subversion, Eckhaus Latta has found success due to the self-conscious nature of its practice.

As Eckhaus Latta's brand evolves and adapts through the current democratized fashionscape, the collective of artists, writers, actors, models, and multihyphenate creative practitioners that the designers surround themselves with grows and progresses, in turn crumbling the boundaries not only between creative disciplines but also between preconceived notions of what defines value and luxury. The design duo can be defined as critical borderless fashion practitioners insofar as they engage in and add to social discourse around issues such as gender representation, inclusivity, and sustainability through bridging divides between high and low culture and art and commerce. With a focus on collectivity, collaboration, and interdisciplinarity, Eckhaus Latta articulates the everyday through a soft satirization of the commercial fashion industry. This in turn, breeds an authenticity that is reflected in the aura the designers create around the brand, which is evidenced in the multiple collaborations and project-based practices that they engage with.

Conclusion

Metamodernism does not necessarily prescribe a utopian ideal of the now or the future. In this book, I have used it rather as a lens to critically articulate developments in the field of fashion practice, which I believe has moved well beyond the fractured notions of the postmodern era. What has emerged is the development of *borderless fashion practice*, a conceptual framework that maps and describes how fashion practitioners are working in the current sociocultural context. The first half of this book was a contextual narrative that analyzed key factors I identified as intrinsic to contemporary borderless developments in fashion practice. These factors included fashion's shift into the academy, fashion's democratization, the oscillating relationship between fashion and art, and the development of conceptual fashion. In order to support this discussion around borderless fashion and its developmental factors, I concentrated on the analyses of case studies that articulate the total practices of four contemporary practitioners working in the field of fashion.

This book and its development of a conceptual framework proposes the expansion of fashion, or rather, fashion in the expanded field, considering it beyond the physical garment and in terms of the spaces that it occupies and represents. Multiple spheres of creativity have converged on fashion as it manifests in the fashion show spectacle model of the twentieth century that was dominated by fashion designers such as Thierry Mugler, John Galliano, and Alexander McQueen. However, as fashion transcends the commercial runway system, it bleeds across other fields, making advancements in scientific materialism, conceptual product development, creative methodologies and technologies, and understandings of identity and social connection.

Borderless fashion breaks down barriers set within Western capitalist society that have hierarchized different aspects of culture and created binaries such as those between man and woman, human and machine, high culture and low culture, and art and science. Designers have become creative directors, driving their practice with a focus on process, concept, communication, and representation. Chapters 1–5 set up a contextual framework to help map the reasons *why* contemporary fashion designers in the second decade of the twenty-first century are working conceptually and collaboratively across disciplines.

This research has conceptualized a framework through which to analyze the practices of contemporary fashion designers, which I have named *borderless fashion practice*. This book adds to an already existing body of knowledge about the nature of the contemporary fashion practitioner. I hope it also adds to the mapping of knowledge regarding the development of wider creative fields and the ways in which they have evolved and changed based on their sociocultural, political, economic, and historical context. More specifically, *borderless fashion* speaks to the body of knowledge that explores the practice of fashion in the expanded field, that is, fashion's cultural value beyond that of just the physical garment. Audiences and consumers turn to fashion for existential reflection as well as its ability to directly reflect the zeitgeist and its *structure of feeling*. A shift in focus is evident and has moved from the dominance of the physical garment to that of the expanded field of fashion—consumers no longer desire just a well-made physical garment, but instead seek an authenticity of process and message that is communicated through digital communication technologies.

It is important to reiterate that the practitioners introduced here are representative of a wider generation of fashion practitioners who are engaging with the field of fashion in collaborative and multidisciplinary ways. The selection of these specific designers was based on their eclecticism in terms of identity and output. Hypothesizing the threads of significance between the practitioners, this study revealed that the designers have all constructed an identity that is *authentic* to themselves and an output that is accessible—not in terms of economic accessibility but in terms of cultural accessibility and the fostering of community. They establish this through the "open source" nature of their process—recording and disseminating videos, photographs, and illustrations in the form of behind-the-scenes content—which offers an opening up of creativity that democratizes the very field of fashion, a field that in the twentieth century was established as one that was rarefied and closed off to the masses. I chose these specific practitioners as case studies because they are broadly representative rather than exclusive. Borderless fashion practice going forward will act as a framework in which to articulate the industry's shift away from the fixation on the commodified garment and into the realm of representational and experimental space in which fashion most predominantly and most democratically exists. The intentions of this book were to theorize a new conceptual framework in which to analyze the practice of contemporary fashion designers in the digital age who are challenging this "old guard" hierarchy.

Through the mapping of twenty-first-century rhetoric around the proclamation of "the end of fashion," I traced the development of borderless fashion practice. The designers included in the case studies all maintain practices that are informed by other creative disciplines such as sculpture and fine art, architecture, civil engineering, and product design. The work these fashion designers produce also oscillates between the disciplinary realms of music, art, architecture, technology, and science, manifesting in a contemporary fashion practice that breaks with the stark boundaries produced by a claustrophobic modern commercial fashion system. Virgil Abloh emerged from civil engineering and architecture training to become a highly influential and innovative multihyphenate fashion practitioner and image-maker. Aitor Throup was trained in fashion design; however, he approaches his design practice from a conceptual framework that is very much rooted in articulating what a physical garment can say regarding its context. Throup has established a fashion practice that focuses on iterative process and research rather than on a commercially viable product. Iris van Herpen's design identity is filtered through a synthesis of science and technology; once again, rather than focusing on a commercially viable product, she centralizes research and process. Eckhaus Latta's two designers come from an art school background, and their approach to design emerges from a desire for community and a rupturing of hierarchies and binaries. Other threads of significance that were mapped across all of the designers' practices and outputs were these oscillations between fields, constructions of authentic design identities, and collaborative methodologies. These, I argue, relate directly back to the principles outlined in the theoretical framework of metamodernism articulated in chapter 1. Bourdieu theorized that a "field" is a structured social space with its own rules, whether that be arts, education, law, or politics.[1] Borderless fashion expands this field, renegotiating these rules to produce sustainable models of creativity and consumption.

Beyond disciplines, borderless fashion tentatively hints at geographical borders and the globalizing effect of digital media technologies and the democratizing access of knowledge and information that these technological developments have instigated. This has changed fashion's cultural production and consequently the ways in which the consumer and audience interact with a fashion garment and fashion media. The designers I mapped as having a borderless practice have three main characteristics that remain apparent across all four case studies. The first of these was the curation of a design identity, which is based around the design practitioners' value systems regarding cultural context, design process, and conceptual framework. The second characteristic was a focus on sustained interdisciplinary collaborations on a corporate commercial level and an artistic level, which relates to the mutually beneficial economic capital as well as cultural capital all parties gain in such collaborations. The final characteristic was the "delocalization" of fashion in terms of the spaces that fashion occupies beyond that of the garment, which encompasses the definition of fashion installation outlined by Geczy and Karaminas and which I have called here "hybrid spaces."[2] Analyzing the context, training, and background of each designer gained prominence in this book due to an emphasis on the design codes developed by each practitioner. Although all practices are aesthetically and conceptually different from one another, the mapping of similarities in terms of these factors connected to process and communication is what binds them together.

This book focused on developing the metamodern as a speculative paradigm in which to situate borderless fashion practice. I articulated metamodernism through the accumulation of multiple discussions to gain a comprehensive understanding of how and why it mirrors the current sociocultural moment in time.[3] The concept of oscillation introduced by Vermeulen and van den Akker reflected the "in-between" nature of the fashion practices that I was engaging with. That is, practitioners who work across disciplines, their work appearing in the form of films, exhibitions, performances, and research. This concept of oscillation also reflects the incorporation of both modern and postmodern principles, predominantly collaboration and interdisciplinarity. The oscillation between utopian and dystopian projections manifested in the spaces that fashion is now represented, which is mainly in the format of fashion installation, are dislocated from the hermetic space of the runway.

The examined factors that have led up to borderless fashion's development were discussed to map the historical and sociocultural context in which borderless fashion has emerged, the first of which in chapter 2 discussed the entrance of fashion into the academy. Fashion's shift into academia in the form of the development of fashion studies as a discrete disciplinary field in the 1990s saw the breakdown of the hierarchy of the academy that had previously ostracized fashion from academic spaces due to its "frivolous" connotations.[4] Critical reflections of fashion practice opened up the field to more experimental work that acknowledged fashion's ability to change our embodied experience of the world. The design processes and modes of communication discussed in this book are directly linked to the background of interdisciplinary design methodologies that were fostered by fashion's entrance into the academy through the establishment of fashion studies as well as studio practice at design schools. By this I refer to the action of approaching the practice of fashion design through the lens of other creative disciplines. This occurs when a practitioner has been academically trained in another creative field or in an institution that encourages cross-disciplinary collaboration, as demonstrated in Edelkoort's hybrid design studies course and Parson's transdisciplinary master's degree program. This approach to design in the context of fashion also refers to the utilization of techniques that sit outside of traditional dressmaking design methodologies—this I have labeled in the case studies as "curating a design identity." This emphasizes the importance of context and the oscillation of focus between the physical objects and the metaphysical or representational meaning beyond them, which is central to the conceptualization of borderless fashion.

The second factor I have discussed in this book is fashion's most recent democratization brought on by the technological developments of social networking platforms that have systematically changed the ways in which we communicate. As value systems change and audiences are able to engage with the culture of fashion in much more accessible ways, hierarchies within the field based around wealth, class, and access have been disrupted. Digital access through social media technologies have democratized the fashion show since the onset of the new millennium through platforms such as Showstudio. Not only have they done this, they have also expanded the definitive borders of what fashion is, how it is communicated, and consequently how it is consumed. Authenticity has become the primary value system of the consumer, which is reflected in the emergence of the experience economy. Individuals oscillate between creating and consuming content and product, which sees an increased interaction among audiences. A holistic system of exchange occurs in this economy that focuses on community and the breakdown of societal class barriers that have defined luxury fashion. Audiences and consumers of fashion can now *experience* it—not through the primary means of buying a garment, but through experiential digital engagement.

Borderless fashion has its earliest manifestations with its experimentations and collaborations with art through designer and artist projects. This relationship has developed on the basis of fashion offering access to commercial capital, while art has provided a level of cultural cachet. This discussion was important to include in this book, as art and fashion have occupied symbiotic space through time. They both represent the specific actions and thoughts of a certain time and place. Borderless fashion is a product of this symbiotic relationship that has allowed fashion to bleed across multiple creative disciplines and into spaces previously unoccupied by fashion, such as the art gallery. Abloh's retrospective exhibition *Figures of Speech* at the Museum of Contemporary Art in Chicago in 2019 is a direct example of this. Fashion has escaped the confines of the fixed commercial runway system through leveraging critical experimentation and reflection via conceptual installation both on and off the runway.

The fourth factor identified as intrinsic to the development of borderless fashion considered fashion as concept and the primacy of the idea within creative methodologies. Conceptual fashion has enabled fashion to become a mediator of cultural criticism in these installed spaces. The primacy of the "idea" or "concept" has empowered fashion to question the parameters of its own field, which relates to issues of sustainability that have entered contemporary discussions around the impact of fashion on the earth. Self-reflexive practices challenge what fashion's purpose is and what in fact fashion actually is and how it can be defined within the metamodern age. Borderless fashion as a conceptual framework challenges preconceived notions of these boundaries that confine fashion as a star commodity of the capitalist system.

Borderless fashion as a conceptual framework has come into further relief with the onset of the COVID-19 pandemic. The 2020 commercial fashion weeks shifted to online communication technology platforms through digital installations. Virtual reality and artificial intelligence in some specific instances replaced physical fashion shows. One of the largest European luxury fashion houses, Valentino, communicated its haute couture fall/winter 2020 collection through a filmic presentation that was debuted as a "conversation" between Valentino's head designer/creative director Pierpaolo Piccioli and Showstudio's Nick Knight. Van Herpen produced a film directed by Ryan McDaniels and starring actor Carice van Houten. Abloh created an animated film that captured the concept of his new collection for Louis Vuitton. Throup has entered the realm of nonfungible token creation, further blurring the boundaries between the digital and the physical. The convergence of fashion with the conceptual framework and method of creating a work of art manifests in these instances through an activated installation. This transforms fashion from the ties of the physical garment to the metaphysical cultural product oscillating once again between designed object and art piece.

As the reality of our daily lives shifts in and out of the digital realm, an acknowledgment of the changing ways in which we consume fashion has occurred. *Borderless Fashion Practice* contributes insights into the growing rhetoric around the crumbling of creative disciplinary borders, centering fashion as a space that incorporates multiple design methods and multiple physical and metaphysical manifestations. Thus, the conducted research builds new knowledge about global contemporary fashion practitioners, who signify a shift toward a more interdisciplinary fashion practice that moves beyond that of the commercially produced garment.

Fashion is a field that has the power to mirror society. Maria Luisa Frisa endorses this sentiment by saying, "Fashion is the most incredible platform to understand the arts of our century; fashion is the place where everything collapses."[5] Fashion is the common platform of the arts of the twenty-first century, and one of the aims of this research was to express this sentiment. Fashion is a system that generates ideas, content, values, and communication across a global terrain. *Borderless Fashion Practice* proposes a freedom of creative identity rather than an illusory spectacular dream. It encapsulates and illuminates the critical earnestness that the contemporary zeitgeist asks us to use as a lens of reflection, which is in oscillating opposition to the cynical notions of the postmodern era. Also, it maps the power fashion holds as a vessel of cultural significance and influence. Curator Andrew Bolton, in conversation with Caroline Roux, has commented on this idea, stating that "People like fashion for its immediacy, democracy and idealism. That's what gives it its power."[6] Through this, fashion can then "collapse the boundaries between high art and popular culture . . . to challenge the old-fashioned hierarchy."[7] Conceptualizing the framework of borderless fashion practice seeks to map the development of fashion practice within the context of this new social world. It emphasizes fashion's ability to be situated in the blurry, "meta" spaces between fiction and reality, the digital and physical, transcending and challenging long-held binaries symptomatic of the Western cultural context. Metamodernism's oscillating nature collapses rigid boundaries within our sociocultural contexts: history is not linear, creative fields are not siloed or fixed, and conventions can change. The sincerity we find in contemporary fashion practices invites us to critically reflect, question, explore, and experiment.

Acknowledgments

The guidance, encouragement, friendship, knowledge, and trust I have been offered over the course of this research has directly supported and made possible the fruition of this book. I am so very lucky to have acquired many mentors during this time, mainly my two doctoral supervisors, Professor Vicki Karaminas and Distinguished Professor Sally Morgan. Their intellect, candidness, and generosity have been invaluable and so very, very appreciated.

Dr. Sarah Gilligan has been an endless stream of support since our first meeting at the End of Fashion conference held at Massey University in Wellington, New Zealand, in December 2016. Dr. Gilligan established the international Fashion, Costume, and Visual Culture network in the summer of 2017, which has instigated many scholarly friendships and conference experiences that I will be eternally grateful for.

I would also like to acknowledge and give thanks to Massey University. Without the support of the doctoral scholarship I received from the university, I would not have been able to embark on this journey. I am also deeply thankful to the College of Creative Arts School of Design for its acceptance of my earnest applications for travel bursaries and research support that in turn have enabled me to attend overseas conferences and research trips.

I also want to take a moment here to acknowledge the importance of critical thinking and research in the field of arts and humanities. Internationally we are seeing a decline in the centering of such fields of research and education, which have been the conscious cornerstones of culture for millennia. The value in cultural criticism and reflection as practice has never been more pertinent.

The late Virgil Abloh said, "The end goal is to demonstrate that collaboration is a modern language." An artist/DJ/entrepreneur/designer/curator, Abloh was and is the ultimate metamodern borderless fashion practitioner, and I'm honored to include a chapter about his work in this book. I earnestly thank the

Abloh family and estate for the permission to reproduce images of his work in these pages.

Finally, I would like to thank my amazing family and friends, who are one and the same, never offering anything but unconditional love and support.

A version of chapter 6 was published in a peer-reviewed article in the Intellect journal *Critical Studies in Men's Fashion*. See Vanessa Gerrie, "On Metamodernism: Virgil Abloh's Borderless Fashion Practice," *Critical Studies in Men's Fashion* 7, no. 1 (2020), 1–18, https://doi.org/10.1386/csmf_00018_1.

A version of chapter 7 was presented as a conference paper at Popular Culture Association of Australia and New Zealand (POPCAANZ) in Wellington, New Zealand, June 2017.

A version of chapter 8 was presented as a conference paper at POPCAANZ Auckland, New Zealand, July 2018.

Notes

Introduction

1 Irina Aleksander, "Sweatpants Forever," *New York Times*, 6 August 2020, https://www.nytimes.com/interactive/2020/08/06/magazine/fashion-sweatpants.html.

2 A term defined by Vicki Karaminas as the way in which fashion visual imagery flows and impacts across the globe as fashion becomes a digital media artifact. The term borrows from the work of Arjun Appadurai, who in 1996 discussed the new "global cultural economy" that reflected the globalization of the late twentieth century. This he ordered as being made up of "technoscapes," "mediascapes," "ethnoscapes," "financescapes," and "ideoscapes." See Arjun Appadurai, *Modernity at Large: Cultural Dimensions of Globalization* (Minneapolis: University of Minnesota Press, 1996).

3 See, for example, Julianne Pederson, "Meta-Modernism in Fashion and Style Practice: Authorship and the Consumer," in *From Production to Consumption: The Cultural Industry of Fashion*, ed. Marco Pedroni (Oxford: Inter-Disciplinary Press, 2013), 59–75; Marcia A. Morgado, "Fashion Phenomena and the Post-postmodern Condition," *Fashion, Style & Popular Culture* 1, no. 3 (2014): 313–339.

4 Lidewij Edelkoort, *Anti_Fashion: A Manifesto for the Next Decade* (New York: Trent Union, 2015).

5 Edelkoort, *Anti_Fashion*, n.p.

6 Edelkoort, *Anti_Fashion*, n.p.

7 Edelkoort, *Anti_Fashion*, n.p.

8 Vicki Karaminas, "Image: Fashionscapes—Notes towards an Understanding of Media Technologies and Their Impact on Contemporary Fashion Imagery," in *Fashion and Art*, ed. Adam Geczy and Vicki Karaminas (London: Bloomsbury, 2012), 177. See also Appadurai, *Modernity at Large*.

9 Karaminas, "Image," 177–178.

10 Karaminas, "Image," 178.

11 Patrizia Calefato, "Fashionscapes," in *The End of Fashion: Clothing and Dress in the Age of Globalization*, ed. Adam Geczy and Vicki Karaminas (London: Bloomsbury, 2019), 3.

12 Calefato, "Fashionscapes," 3.

13 Calefato, "Fashionscapes," 4.

14 Marshall McLuhan, *The Gutenberg Galaxy: The Making of Typographic Man* (Toronto: University of Toronto Press, 1962).

15 See Adam Geczy and Vicki Karaminas, "Lady Gaga: *American Horror Story*, Fashion, Monstrosity and the Grotesque," *Fashion Theory* 21, no. 6 (2017): 714.

16 Adam Geczy and Vicki Karaminas, *Fashion Installation: Body, Space and Performance* (London: Bloomsbury, 2019), 7.

17 See Adam Geczy and Vicki Karaminas, *Critical Fashion Practice: From Westwood to Beirendonck* (London: Bloomsbury, 2017).

18 See the introduction to Geczy and Karaminas, *The End of Fashion*.

19 Elizabeth Wilson, *The Contradictions of Culture: Cities, Culture, Women* (London: Sage, 2001), 50.

20 Florence Müller, *Art and Fashion* (London: Thames and Hudson, 2000); Alice Mackrell, *Art and Fashion: The Impact of Art on Fashion and Fashion on Art* (London: Batsford, 2005).

21 Peter Wollen, *Addressing the Century: 100 Years of Art and Fashion* (London: Hayward Gallery, 1999).

22 Nancy Troy, *Couture Culture: A Study in Modern Art and Fashion* (Cambridge, MA: MIT Press, 2004).

23 See Mas'ud Zavarzadeh, "The Apocalyptic Fact and the Eclipse of Fiction in Recent American Prose Narratives," *Journal of American Studies* 9, no. 1 (April 1975): 69–83; see also Timotheus Vermeulen and Robin van den Akker, *Metamodern: Historicity, Affect, and Depth after Postmodernism* (London: Rowman and Littlefield, 2017).

24 Vermeulen and van den Akker, *Metamodern*.

25 Robert K. Yin, *Case Study Research: Design and Methods* (Los Angeles: Sage, 2014), 37.

26 Geczy and Karaminas, *Critical Fashion Practice*, 132.

27 Jennifer Morey Hawkins, "Textual Analysis," in *The Sage Encyclopedia of Communication Research Methods* (Los Angeles: Sage Reference, 2017), 1755.

28 Hawkins, "Textual Analysis," 1755.

29 Claire Hewson, Carl Vogel, and Dianna Laurent, *Internet Research Methods* (Los Angeles: Sage Publications, 2016), 1.

30 Hewson, Vogel, and Laurent, *Internet Research Methods*, 1.

31 Hewson, Vogel, and Laurent, *Internet Research Methods*, 1.

Chapter 1 On Metamodernism

1 Timotheus Vermeulen and Robin van den Akker, "Notes on Metamodernism," *Journal of Aesthetics & Culture* 2, no. 1 (2010): 57.

2 Gilles Deleuze and Félix Guattari, *A Thousand Plateaus: Capitalism and Schizophrenia*, trans. Brian Massumi (London: Continuum, 2004).

3 See Adam Geczy and Vicki Karaminas, *Critical Fashion Practice: From Westwood to Beirendonck* (London: Bloomsbury, 2017).

4 Stephen Knudsen, "Beyond Postmodernism: Putting a Face on Metamodernism without the Easy Clichés," *Artpulse Magazine*, http://artpulsemagazine.com/beyond -postmodernism-putting-a-face-on-metamodernism-without-the-easy-cliches (accessed 13 August 2019).

5 Knudsen, "Beyond Postmodernism."

6 Marcia A. Morgado, "Fashion Phenomena and the Post-postmodern Condition," *Fashion, Style & Popular Culture* 1, no. 3 (2014): 314.

7 See David Rudrum and Nicholas Stavris, *Supplanting the Postmodern: An Anthology of Writings on the Arts and Culture of the Early 21st Century* (London: Bloomsbury, 2015); Nicolas Bourriaud, *The Radicant* (New York: Lukas & Sternberg, 2009); Alan Kirby, *Digimodernism: How New Technologies Dismantle the Postmodern and Reconfigure Our Culture* (New York: Continuum, 2009); Gilles Lipovetsky, *Hypermodern Times* (New York: Wiley, 2005); Timotheus Vermeulen and Robin van den Akker, *Metamodern: Historicity, Affect, and Depth after Postmodernism* (London: Rowman and Littlefield, 2017).

8 Morgado, "Fashion Phenomena," 332.

9 Julianne Pederson, "Meta-Modernism in Fashion and Style Practice: Authorship and the Consumer," in *From Production to Consumption: The Cultural Industry of Fashion*, ed. Marco Pedroni (Oxford: Inter-Disciplinary Press, 2013), 63.

10 Pederson, "Meta-Modernism in Fashion," 61.

11 Pederson, "Meta-Modernism in Fashion," 64.

12 Pederson, "Meta-Modernism in Fashion," 60.

13 Pederson, "Meta-Modernism in Fashion," 61.

14 Pederson, "Meta-Modernism in Fashion," 66.

15 Daniel P. Görtz, "Metamodern Values Explained," *Ted Talks × Berlin*, 5 September 2019, https://www.youtube.com/watch?v=5USomyB3mZQ.

16 Vermeulen and van den Akker, "Notes on Metamodernism," 2.

17 Plato, *Symposium*, c. 385–370 B.C.

18 Warren Linds, "METAXIS Metaxis: Dancing (in) the In-Between," in *Dialogues of Theatre and Cultural Politics*, ed. Jan Cohen-Cruz and Mady Schutzman (London: Routledge, 2006), 38.

19 Vermeulen and van den Akker, "Notes on Metamodernism," 12.

20 Yves Millet, "Atopia and Aesthetics: A Modal Perspective," *Contemporary Aesthetics* 11 (2013): 1.

21 Millet, "Atopia and Aesthetics."

22 Morgado, "Fashion Phenomena and the Post-postmodern Condition."

23 Vermeulen and van den Akker, "Notes on Metamodernism," 6.

24 Seth Abramson, "Ten Basic Principles of Metamodernism," *Huffington Post*, 27 April 2015, https://www.huffingtonpost.com/seth-abramson/ten-key-principles-in-met_b_7143202.html.

25 Abramson, "Ten Basic Principles."

26 Rudrum and Stavris, *Supplanting the Postmodern*, 306.

27 Rudrum and Stavris, *Supplanting the Postmodern*, 306.

28 Abramson, "Ten Basic Principles."

29 Abramson, "Ten Basic Principles."

30 See Mas'ud Zavarzadeh, "The Apocalyptic Fact and the Eclipse of Fiction in Recent American Prose Narratives," *Journal of American Studies* 9, no. 1 (April 1975): 69–83.

31 Robin van den Akker and Timotheus Vermeulen, "Periodising the 2000s, or, the Emergence of Metamodernism," in *Metamodernism: Historicity, Affect, and Depth after Postmodernism*, ed. Robin van den Akker, Alison Gibbons, and Timotheus Vermeulen (London: Rowman and Littlefield, 2017), 5.

32 Michael Arlen, "The Living Room War," *New Yorker*, 15 October 1966.

33 Zavarzadeh, "Apocalyptic Fact," 70.

34 "Post-truth" was named word of the year in 2016 by Oxford Dictionaries. See Alison Flood, "'Post-Truth' Named Word of the Year by Oxford Dictionaries," *The Guardian*, 15 November 2016, https://www.theguardian.com/books/2016/nov/15/post-truth-named-word-of-the-year-by-oxford-dictionaries.

35 Abramson, "Ten Basic Principles."
36 Alexandra E. Dumitrescu, "What Is Metamodernism and Why Bother? Meditations on Metamodernism as a Period Term and as a Mode," *Electronic Book Review*, 4 December 2016, https://electronicbookreview.com/essay/what-is-metamodernism-and-why -bother-meditations-on-metamodernism-as-a-period-term-and-as-a-mode/.
37 Alexandra E. Dumitrescu, "Towards a Metamodern Literature" (doctoral thesis, University of Otago, 2014).

Chapter 2   Fashion in the Academy

1 Christopher Breward, *The Culture of Fashion: A New History of Fashionable Dress* (Manchester: Manchester University Press, 1995), 2.
2 Arthur Coleman Danto, *After the End of Art: Contemporary Art and the Pale of History* (Princeton, NJ: Princeton University Press, 1997).
3 Rosalind Krauss, "Notes on the Index: Seventies Art in America," *October* 3 (Spring 1977): 68.
4 Krauss, "Notes on the Index."
5 Christopher Breward, "Cultures, Identities, Histories: Fashioning a Cultural Approach to Dress," *Fashion Theory* 2, no. 4 (1998): 302.
6 Breward, "Cultures, Identities, Histories," 302.
7 Breward, "Cultures, Identities, Histories," 311.
8 Edelkoort quoted in Marcus Fairs, "Li Edelkoort Introduces Hybrid Design to Parsons 'to Loosen Things Up,'" *Dezeen*, 6 July 2015, https://www.dezeen.com/2015 /07/06/li-edelkoort-new-hybrid-design-studies-department-parsons-school-design -new-york/.
9 Marcus Fairs, "Products and Buildings Are the Same Says Heatherwick, as Designers Turn to Architecture," *Dezeen*, 1 July 2015, https://www.dezeen.com/2015/07/01 /products-and-buildings-the-same-thomas-heatherwick-designers-turn-to-architec ture/.
10 Efrat Tseëlon, "Outlining a Fashion Studies Project," in *Critical Studies in Fashion and Beauty Volume One*, ed. Efrat Tseëlon, Ana Marta Gonzalez, and Susan Kaiser (Bristol, UK: Intellect, 2012), 8.
11 Tseëlon, "Outlining a Fashion Studies Project," 8.
12 Tseëlon, "Outlining a Fashion Studies Project," 12.
13 Tseëlon, "Outlining a Fashion Studies Project," 12.
14 Tseëlon, "Outlining a Fashion Studies Project," 13.
15 Tseëlon, "Outlining a Fashion Studies Project," 13.
16 Alice Newall-Hanson, "The Graduates," *T Magazine*, 13 April 2020, https://www .nytimes.com/interactive/2020/04/13/t-magazine/royal-academy-antwerp.html.
17 Newall-Hanson, "The Graduates."
18 Newall-Hanson, "The Graduates."
19 Henry Jenkins, *Convergence Culture: Where Old and New Media Collide* (New York: New York University Press, 2006).
20 Parsons New School of Design, MFA Transdisciplinary Design course description, https://www.newschool.edu/parsons/mfa-transdisciplinary-design/?show=program -profiles (accessed 27 November 2019).
21 James Hunt, "Letter from the Editor," *Journal of Design Strategies* 5, no. 1 (2012): 6.
22 Hunt, "Letter from the Editor," 6.
23 Hunt, "Letter from the Editor," 8.
24 Hunt, "Letter from the Editor," 8.

25 Alex Coles, *Design and Art: Documents of Contemporary Art* (Cambridge, MA: MIT Press, 2007), 10.

26 Coles, *Design and Art*, 10.

27 Adam Geczy and Vicki Karaminas, *Critical Fashion Practice: From Westwood to Beirendonck* (London: Bloomsbury, 2017), 102.

28 Adam Geczy and Vicki Karaminas, "What Is Critical Fashion" (unpublished, 2019), 2.

29 Geczy and Karaminas, "What Is Critical Fashion," 2.

30 Geczy and Karaminas, "What Is Critical Fashion," 1.

31 Geczy and Karaminas, "What Is Critical Fashion," 5.

32 Geczy and Karaminsa, "What Is Critical Fashion," 1.

33 Geczy and Karaminsa, "What Is Critical Fashion," 3.

34 Geczy and Karaminas, "What Is Critical Fashion," 3.

35 Taylor Prince-Fraser, "A-COLD-WALL*: Brand or Art Project? Live Panel Discussion—Autumn/Winter 2020," Showstudio, 14 January 2020, https://www .youtube.com/watch?v=vLwvkl5IFTk.

36 Geczy and Karaminas, "What Is Critical Fashion," 1.

37 Geczy and Karaminas, "What Is Critical Fashion," 1.

38 Geczy and Karaminas, "What Is Critical Fashion," 10.

39 See Slavoj Žižek, *Living in the End Times* (London: Verso, 2010).

40 Žižek, *Living in the End Times*.

41 Yuniya Kawamura, *Doing Research in Fashion and Dress: An Introduction to Qualitative Methods* (Oxford: Berg, 2011), 121.

42 Kawamura, *Doing Research in Fashion*, 122.

43 Kawamura, *Doing Research in Fashion*, 122.

44 Marcia A. Morgado, "Coming to Terms with *Postmodern*: Theories and Concepts of Contemporary Culture and Their Implications for Apparel Scholars," *Clothing and Textiles Research Journal* 14, no. 1 (1996): 44.

45 Marcia Morgado citing Jean Baudrillard in "Coming to Terms," 44.

46 Morgado citing Douglas Kellner in "Coming to Terms," 44. Kellner's quote is originally from 1989.

47 Yuniya Kawamura, *Fashion-ology: An Introduction to Fashion Studies* (London: Bloomsbury, 2018), 114.

48 According to Baudrillard.

49 Fredric Jameson, *The Cultural Turn: Selected Writings on the Postmodern, 1983–1998* (London: Verso, 1998), 75.

50 Jameson, *The Cultural Turn*, 75.

51 Fredric Jameson, *Postmodernism, or, the Cultural Logic of Late Capitalism* (London: Verso, 1991), x.

52 Jameson, *Postmodernism*, x.

53 Jameson, *Postmodernism*, x.

54 Adam Geczy and Vicki Karaminas, "Time, Cruelty and Destruction in Deconstructivist Fashion: Kawakubo, Margiela and Vetements," *Zone Moda Journal* 10, no. 1 (2020): 67.

55 Osman Ahmed, "Lumps and Bumps at Commes des Garçon S/S97," *Another Magazine*, 5 January 2016, http://www.anothermag.com/fashion-beauty/8174/lumps-and-bumps -at-comme-des-garcons-s-s97.

56 Ahmed, "Lumps and Bumps."

57 Ahmed, "Lumps and Bumps."

58 Ahmed, "Lumps and Bumps."

59 See Arthur Danto, "The End of Art: A Philosophical Defence," *History and Theory* 37, no. 4 (1998): 127–143; Fredric Jameson, *The Cultural Turn: Selected Writings on the Postmodern, 1983–1998* (London: Verso, 1998).

60 See Teri Agins, *The End of Fashion: The Mass Marketing of the Clothing Business* (New York: William Morrow, 1999); Lidewij Edelkoort, *Anti_Fashion: A Manifesto for the Next Decade* (New York: Trend Union, 2015); Adam Geczy and Vicki Karaminas, *The End of Fashion: Clothing and Dress in the Age of Globalization* (London: Bloomsbury, 2019).

61 See Francis Fukuyama, "The End of History?," *The National Interest* 16 (Summer 1989): 3–18.

62 Tim Adams, "Francis Fukuyama: 'Trump Instinctively Picks Racial Themes to Drive People on the Left Crazy,'" *Guardian Online*, 16 September 2018, https://www .theguardian.com/books/2018/sep/16/francis-fukuyama-interview-trump-picks -racial-themes-to-drive-people-on-the-left-crazy.

63 Imran Amed, Achim Berg, Leonie Brantberg, and Saskia Hedrich, "The State of Fashion 2017," McKinsey, December 2016, https://www.mckinsey.com/industries /retail/our-insights/the-state-of-fashion.

64 Edelkoort, *Anti_Fashion*.

65 Edelkoort, *Anti_Fashion*.

66 Agins, *The End of Fashion*.

67 Caroline Evans, *Fashion at the Edge: Spectacle, Modernity and Deathliness* (New Haven, CT: Yale University Press, 2003).

68 Evans, *Fashion at the Edge*, 10.

69 Evans, *Fashion at the Edge*, 10.

70 Evans, *Fashion at the Edge*, 10.

71 Morgado, "Coming to Terms," 45.

72 Alison Gill, "Jacques Derrida: Fashion under Erasure," in *Thinking through Fashion: An Introduction*, ed. Agnes Rocamora and Anneke Smelik (London: I. B. Tauris, 2016), 251.

Chapter 3   Fashion's Democratization

1 Adam Geczy and Vicki Karaminas, *Fashion's Double: Representations of Fashion in Painting, Photography and Film* (London: Bloomsbury Academic, 2016), 120.

2 See Georg Simmel, "Fashion," *International Quarterly* 10, no. 1 (October 1904): 130–155; Thorstein Veblen, *The Theory of the Leisure Class: An Economic Study of Institutions* (London: Taylor and Francis, 2017).

3 Peter McNeil, "Georg Simmel: The Philosophical Monet," in *Thinking through Fashion*, ed. Agnes Rocamora and Anneke Smelik (London: I. B Tauris, 2016), 75.

4 See Ted Polhemus, *Street Style: From Sidewalk to Catwalk* (London: Thames and Hudson, 1994).

5 Polhemus, *Street Style*, 12.

6 Geczy and Karaminas, *Fashion's Double*, 120.

7 Geczy and Karminas, *Fashion's Double*, 121.

8 Yuniya Kawamura, *Fashion-ology: An Introduction to Fashion Studies* (London: Bloomsbury, 2018), 114.

9 Kawamura, *Fashion-ology*, 115.

10 Kawamura, *Fashion-ology*, 115.

11 See Pierre Bourdieu, *The Field of Cultural Production* (New York: Columbia University Press, 1993).

12 Agnès Rocamora, "Pierre Bourdieu: The Field of Fashion," in *Thinking through Fashion: A Guide to Key Theorists*, ed. Agnès Rocamora and Anneke Smelik (London: I. B. Tauris, 2016), 241.

13 Bourdieu, *The Field of Cultural Production*.

14 The first webcast/streamed fashion show was the hypercommercial and traditionally theatrical Victoria's Secret Fashion Show in 1999, which was produced and directed by French fashion show designer and producer Alexandre de Batek.

15 Terri Pous, "The Democratization of Fashion: A Brief History," *Time*, 6 February 2013, http://style.time.com/2013/02/06/the-democratization-of-fashion-a-brief -history/.

16 Julianne Pederson, "Meta-Modernism in Fashion and Style Practice: Authorship and the Consumer," in *From Production to Consumption: The Cultural Industry of Fashion*, ed. Marco Pedroni (Oxford: Inter-Disciplinary Press, 2013), 59.

17 Pederson, "Meta-Modernism in Fashion," 59.

18 See Julia Kristeva, "Word, Dialogue, and Novel," in *Desire in Language: A Semiotic Approach to Literature and Art*, ed. Leon S. Roudiez, trans. Thomas Gora, Alice Jardine, and Leon S. Roudiez (New York: Columbia University Press, 1977), 64–91.

19 "Millenials" are people born between approximately 1981 and 1996. "Generation Z" are those born approximately in 1997 and beyond.

20 Richard Dawkins, *The Selfish Gene* (Oxford: Oxford University Press, 2006).

21 William Safire, "What's the Meta?," *New York Times*, 25 December 2005, https:// www.nytimes.com/2005/12/25/magazine/whats-the-meta.html.

22 Efrat Tseëlon, "Authenticity," in *Fashion and Art*, ed. Adam Geczy and Vicki Karaminas (London: Bloomsbury, 2012), 115.

23 Tseëlon, "Authenticity."

24 José Teunissen, "Fashion: More than Cloth and Form," in *The Handbook of Fashion Studies*, ed. Sandy Black, Amy De La Haye, Joanne Entwistle, Agnès Rocamora, Regina A. Root, and Helen Thomas (London: Bloomsbury, 2013), 212.

25 Anneke Smelik, "The Performance of Authenticity," *Address: Journal for Fashion Writing and Criticism* 1, no. 1 (2011): 82.

26 Smelik, "The Performance of Authenticity," 77.

27 Smelik, "The Performance of Authenticity," 77.

28 Smelik, "The Performance of Authenticity," 77.

29 See B. Joseph Pine II and James H. Gilmore, *The Experience Economy* (Boston: Harvard Business Review Press, 2011).

30 Ana Andjelic, "Opinion: The Experience Economy Is Blurring the Lines between Hospitality and Retail," *Glossy*, 17 June 2019, https://www.glossy.co/fashion /opinion-thanks-to-the-experience-economy-hospitality-and-retail-are-closer-than -ever.

31 Elizabeth Moor, "Branded Spaces: The Scope of 'New Marketing,'" *Journal of Consumer Culture* 3, no. 1 (2003): 42–43.

32 https://canary---yellow.com/ now acts as somewhat of a memorial site for the late designer's catalogue of work.

33 Walter Benjamin, "The Work of Art in the Age of Mechanical Reproduction," in *Illuminations*, ed. Hannah Arendt, trans. Harry Zohn (New York: Schocken Books, 1969), 104.

34 Alice Hines, "A Copy of a Copy: Ingenuity in a Swath of Prado Polyester," *Vestoj Journal: On Authenticity*, no. 8 (2017): 53.

35 Hines, "A Copy of a Copy," 53.

36 See Claude Lévi-Strauss, *The Savage Mind* (Chicago: University of Chicago Press, 1966), where he describes the theory of the "bricoleur" who is adept at many tasks and draws from many materials that are close at hand to create; in other words, a DYI creation or work that draws upon disparate things to create something new.

37 See Guy Debord, *Society of the Spectacle* (New York: Zone Books, 1994).

38 Arthur Danto, *After the End of Art: Contemporary Art and the Pale of History* (Princeton, NJ: Princeton University Press, 1997), 47.

39 Arthur Danto, "The End of Art: A Philosophical Defence," *History and Theory* 37, no. 4 (1998): 128.

40 Danto, "The End of Art," 134.

41 Danto, *After the End of Art*, 5.

42 Danto, *After the End of Art*, 5.

43 Seth Abramson, "Ten Basic Principles of Metamodernism," *Huffington Post*, 27 March 2015, https://www.huffingtonpost.com/seth-abramson/ten-key-principles-in-met_b_7143202.html.

44 Abramson, "Ten Basic Principles."

45 Lou Stoppard, *Fashion Together: Fashion's Most Extraordinary Duos on the Art of Collaboration* (New York: Rizzoli, 2017), 13.

46 Eleanor Gibson, "Commes des Garçons Is 'Nothing about Clothes,'" *Dezeen*, 9 May 2019, https://www.dezeen.com/2019/05/09/rei-kawakubo-comme-des-garcons-interview/?li_source=LI&li_medium=rhs_block_2.

47 Gibson, "Commes des Garçons."

Chapter 4   Collaboration and Experimentation between Fashion and Art

1 Caroline Stevenson, "(I Was There) When It All Went Down," in *Vestoj Journal: On Capital*, ed. Anya Aronowsky Cronberg (Naples: Nava Press, 2019), 42.

2 Stevenson, "(I Was There)," 42.

3 Stevenson, "(I Was There)," 42.

4 Efrat Tseëlon, "Authenticity," in *Fashion and Art*, ed. Adam Geczy and Vicki Karaminas (London: Bloomsbury, 2012), 113.

5 See Pierre Bourdieu, *The Field of Cultural Production* (New York: Columbia University Press, 1993).

6 Bourdieu, *The Field of Cultural Production*, 38.

7 Bourdieu, *The Field of Cultural Production*, 35.

8 Valerie Steele, "Fashion," in Geczy and Karaminas, *Fashion and Art*, 23.

9 Robert Radford, "Dangerous Liaisons: Art, Fashion, and Individualism," *Fashion Theory* 2, no. 2 (1998): 154.

10 Radford, "Dangerous Liaisons," 154.

11 Rosalind Krauss, "Sculpture in the Expanded Field," *October* 8 (Spring 1979): 30–44.

12 George Baker, "Photography's Expanded Field," *October* 114 (2005): 121–140; Malene Leerberg, "Design in the Expanded Field: Rethinking Contemporary Design," *Nordes*, no. 3 (June 2009), http://www.nordes.org/opj/index.php/n13/article/view/52.

13 Krauss, "Sculpture in the Expanded Field," 34.

14 Krauss, "Sculpture in the Expanded Field," 38.

15 Annes Hollander, *Seeing through Clothes* (New York: Viking, 1978), xi.

16 Marco Pecorari, "Zones-in-Between: The Creation of New Fashion Praxis," *Art Monthly* 242 (August 2011): 68.

17 Lou Stoppard, *Fashion Together: Fashion's Most Extraordinary Duos on the Art of Collaboration* (New York: Rizzoli, 2017), 7.

18 Nicky Ryan, "Prada and the Art of Patronage," *Fashion Theory* 10, no. 3 (2007): 1–2.

19 See Pierre Bourdieu and Y. Delsaut, "Le Couturier et sa griffe: Contribution à une théorie de la magie," *Actes de la recherche en sciences sociales* 1 (1975): 7–36.

20 Ryan, "Prada and the Art of Patronage," 5.

21 Stoppard, *Fashion Together*, 8.

22 Stoppard, *Fashion Together*, 12.

23 Jessica Bugg, "Fashion at the Interface: Designer-Wearer-Viewer," *Fashion Practice: The Journal of Design, Creative Process & the Fashion Industry* 1, no. 1 (2009): 12.

24 Ena Szkoda, "Exhibition Review: *Art/Fashion*. Guggenheim Museum Soho," *Fashion Theory* 1, no. 3 (1997): 321.

25 Germano Celant, *Looking at Fashion: Catalogue Bienale di Firenze* (Milan: Skira, 1996), 1.

26 Celant, *Looking at Fashion*, 13.

27 Celant, *Looking at Fashion*, 13.

28 Geczy and Karaminas, *Fashion and Art*, 3.

29 Geczy and Karaminas, *Fashion and Art*, 3.

30 Elizabeth Wilson, *The Contradictions of Culture: Cities, Culture, Women* (London: Sage Publications, 2001), 50.

31 Amy M. Spindler, "Fashion as Art. Or Maybe Not," *New York Times*, 15 September 1996, http://www.nytimes.com/1996/09/15/arts/fashion-as-art-or-maybe-not.html.

32 Bourdieu, *The Field of Cultural Production*, 37.

33 See Katherine Gleason, *Alexander McQueen Evolution* (New York: Race Point, 2012).

34 Caroline Evans, *Fashion at the Edge: Spectacle, Modernity and Deathliness* (New Haven, CT: Yale University Press, 2003), 67.

35 Since Bowery's tragic and untimely death from AIDS in 1994, the influence of his interdisciplinary performances and aesthetic have been reimagined and remixed. Fashion practitioners such as the English label Art School and Scottish designer Charles Jeffrey integrate the subversion of gendered bodies into their expanded practices.

36 Barbara Vinken, *Fashion Zeitgeist: Trends and Cycles in the Fashion System* (New York: Berg, 2005).

37 Performance studies as a field of research is much like that of fashion studies insofar as it is interdisciplinary and uses the general study of performance as a lens to study the world. As outlined by Richard Schechner in *Performance Studies: An Introduction* (New York: Routledge, 2019), performance is examined in two categories: artistic and cultural.

38 Robyn Healy, "Immateriality," in *The Handbook of Fashion Studies*, ed. Sandy Black, Amy De La Haye, Joanne Entwistle, Agnès Rocamora, Regina A. Root, and Helen Thomas (London: Bloomsbury, 2013), 326.

Chapter 5 Fashion as a Concept

1 Alex Coles, *Design and Art: Documents on Contemporary Art* (Cambridge, MA: MIT Press, 2007), 122.

2 Coles, *Design and Art*.

3 Arthur C. Danto, "The End of Art: A Philosophical Defence," *History and Theory* 37, no. 4 (1998): 127–143.

4 Arthur C. Danto, *The Philosophical Disenfranchisement of Art* (New York: Columbia University Press, 1986), 110–111.

5 Hazel Clark, "Conceptual Fashion," in *Fashion and Art*, ed. Adam Geczy and Vicki Karaminas (London: Bloomsbury, 2012), 67.

6 Clark, "Conceptual Fashion," 67.

7 See Tate Modern, https://www.tate.org.uk/art/art-terms/d/dada.

8 Mark Lowenthal, translator's introduction to Francis Picabia, *I Am a Beautiful Monster: Poetry, Prose, and Provocation* (Cambridge MA: MIT Press, 2007), 1–25.

9 The work has since been attributed to Dadaist Elsa von Freytag-Loringhoven in Irene Gammel's biography *Baroness Elsa: Gender, Dada, and Everyday Modernity; A Cultural Biography* (Cambridge, MA: MIT Press, 2002).

10 Siri Hustvedt, "A Woman in the Men's Room: When Will the Art World Recognise the Real Artist behind Duchamp's Fountain?," *The Guardian*, 29 March 2019, https://www.theguardian.com/books/2019/mar/29/marcel-duchamp-fountain -women-art-history.

11 Hustvedt, "A Woman in the Men's Room."

12 Clark, "Conceptual Fashion," 68.

13 Clark, "Conceptual Fashion," 68; Adam Geczy and Vicki Karaminas, *Critical Fashion Practice: From Westwood to Beirendonck* (London: Bloomsbury, 2017).

14 Clark, "Conceptual Fashion," 68.

15 Clark, "Conceptual Fashion," 68.

16 Issey Miyake, "The Concepts and Work of Issey Miyake," http://mds.isseymiyake .com/im/en/work/.

17 Miyake, "The Concepts and Work of Issey Miyake."

18 Miyake, "The Concepts and Work of Issey Miyake."

19 Kazuko Koike, *Issey Miyake: East Meets West* (Tokyo: Heibonsha, 1978).

20 Issey Miyake, "Chronology," http://mds.isseymiyake.com/im/en/chronology/.

21 Herbert Muschamp, "Easy to Pack. Harder to Understand," *New York Times*, 27 December 1998, 376.

22 Kif Leswing, "A New Version of Steve Jobs' Iconic Black Turtleneck Costs $270," *Business Insider*, 28 June 2017, https://www.businessinsider.com.au/steve-jobs-iconic -black-turtleneck-by-issey-miyake-costs-270-2017-6.

23 Liz Raiss, "Master Class: Issey Miyake," *Heroine Magazine*, 31 October 2017, https://www.heroine.com/the-editorial/master-class-issey-miyake.

24 Miyake, "The Concepts and Work of Issey Miyake."

25 Miyake, "The Concepts and Work of Issey Miyake."

26 Ted Stansfield, "When Hussein Chalayan Turned Furnishings in to Fashion," *Another Magazine*, 26 January 2016, http://www.anothermag.com/fashion-beauty /8248/when-hussein-chalayan-turned-furnishings-into-fashion.

27 Muschamp, "Easy to Pack," 376.

28 Geczy and Karaminas, *Critical Fashion Practice*.

29 Adam Geczy and Vicki Karaminas, "Time, Cruelty and Destruction in Deconstructivist Fashion: Kawakubo, Margiela and Vetements," *Zone Moda Journal* 10, no. 1 (2020): 75.

30 Clark, "Conceptual Fashion," 72.

31 Clark, "Conceptual Fashion," 72.

32 Clark, "Conceptual Fashion," 74.

33 A. Smelik, "The Performance of Authenticity," *Address: Journal for Fashion Writing and Criticism* 1, no. 1 (2011): 77.

34 Guy Debord, *The Society of the Spectacle* (New York: Zone Books, 1994).

35 Douglas Kellner, "Media Culture and the Triumph of the Spectacle," in *The Spectacle of the Real: From Hollywood to "Reality" TV and Beyond*, ed. Geoff King (Bristol, UK: Intellect, 2005), 19.

36 Caroline Evans, *Fashion at the Edge: Spectacle, Modernity and Deathliness* (New Haven, CT: Yale University Press, 2003), 67.

37 See Caroline Evans, "The Enchanted Spectacle," *Fashion Theory* 5, no. 3 (2001): 271–310.

38 Smelik, "The Performance of Authenticity," 79.

39 Ginger Gregg Duggan, "The Greatest Show on Earth: A Look at Contemporary Fashion Shows and Their Relationship with Performance Art," *Fashion Theory* 5, no. 3 (2001): 243–270.

40 Natalie Khan, "Catwalk Politics," in *Fashion Cultures: Theories, Explanations and Analysis*, ed. Stella Bruzzi and Pamela Church Gibson (New York: Routledge, 2000); Natalie Khan, "Fashion as Mythology," in *Fashion Cultures: Theories, Explanations and Analysis Revisited*, ed. Stella Bruzzi and Pamela Church Gibson (New York: Routledge, 2013).

41 Adam Geczy and Vicki Karaminas, *Fashion's Double: Representations of Fashion in Painting, Photography and Film* (London: Bloomsbury, 2012), 112.

42 Hazel Clark, "SLOW + FASHION—an Oxymoron—or a Promise for the Future . . . ?," *Fashion Theory* 12, no. 4 (2008): 427.

43 Clark, "SLOW + FASHION," 427.

44 Lou Stoppard, "Fashion as Installation," *ADF Papers*, Fashion Paper no. 4 (January 2014): 4.

45 Stoppard, "Fashion as Installation," 4.

46 Jess Cartner-Morley, "The Catwalk, Darling? It's So Last Year," *The Guardian*, 13 October 2003, https://www.theguardian.com/world/2003/oct/13/france.arts; Vanessa Friedman, "Fashion Week, Reinvented," *New York Times*, 9 September 2015, http://www.nytimes.com/2015/09/10/fashion/fashion-week-spring-2016-reinvented .html?_r=0; Vanessa Friedman, "How Smartphones Are Killing Off the Fashion Show," *New York Times*, 11 February 2016, https://www.nytimes.com/2016/02/11 /fashion/new-york-fashion-week-smartphones-killing-off-runway-show.html; Emma Hope Allwood, "Is Fashion Week Becoming Outdated?," *Dazed and Confused*, June 2016, http://www.dazeddigital.com/fashion/article/31244/1/is-fashion-week -becoming-outdated.

47 Adam Geczy and Vicki Karaminas, *Fashion Installation: Body, Space and Performance* (London: Bloomsbury, 2019), 8.

48 Geczy and Karaminas, *Fashion Installation*, 104.

49 Geczy and Karaminas, *Fashion Installation*, 104.

50 Geczy and Karaminas, *Fashion Installation*, 104.

51 Geczy and Karaminas, *Fashion Installation*, 104.

52 Geczy and Karaminas, *Fashion Installation*, 10.

53 Efrat Tseëlon, "Authenticity," in *Fashion and Art*, ed. Adam Geczy and Vicki Karaminas (London: Bloomsbury, 2012), 115.

54 Owen Hopkins, "Dezeen's Guide to Bauhaus Architecture and Design," *Dezeen*, 1 November 2018, https://www.dezeen.com/2018/11/01/bauhaus-100-guide-architec ture-design/.

55 Geczy and Karaminas, *Fashion Installation*, 73; Faye Ran, *A History of Installation Art and the Development of New Art Forms* (New York: Peter Lang, 2009), 66. On Wagner, see Richard Wagner, *The Art-Work of the Future, and Other Works*, trans. W. Ashton Ellis (Lincoln: University of Nebraska Press, 1993).

56 Ran, *A History of Installation Art*, 66.

57 Ran, *A History of Installation Art*, 66.

58 Hopkins, "Dezeen's Guide to Bauhaus."

59 See Walter Benjamin, *The Arcades Project* (Cambridge, MA: Harvard University Press, 2002).

60 Geczy and Karaminas, *Fashion's Double*, 121–123.

61 Caroline Evans, "John Galliano: Modernity and Spectacle," Showstudio, 2 March 2002, http://showstudio.com/project/past_present_couture/essay.

62 Evans, "John Galliano."

63 At the time of this writing, Collette had shut its doors as of December 2017. Christopher Morency, "Top Ten Influential Retailers off Fashion's Beaten Path," *Business of Fashion*, 26 June 2017, https://www.businessoffashion.com/articles /intelligence/10-influential-luxury-retailers-off-of-fashions-beaten-path.

64 Morency, "Top Ten Influential Retailers."

65 Eleanor Gibson, "Virgil Abloh and AMO Design Flexible Flagship Off-White Store in Miami That 'Can Host a Runway Show,'" *Dezeen*, 12 August 2020, https://www .dezeen.com/2020/08/12/off-white-miami-design-district-flagship-virgil-abloh-amo/.

66 Gibson, "Virgil Abloh and AMO."

Chapter 6   Virgil Abloh's Democratic Fashion Practice

1 Edward Enninful quoted in Jonathan Wingfield, "What Is Virgil Abloh?," *System Magazine* 10 (November 2017).

2 Angelo Flaccavento quoted in Wingfield, "What Is Virgil Abloh?"

3 For example, Robin Torres, "Virgil Abloh's Raw Creative Vision," *i-D*, December 2016, https://i-d.vice.com/en_us/article/j5mezb/virgil-ablohs-raw-creative-vision; Jane Keltner De Valle, "Inside the World of Virgil Abloh, Kanye West's Creative Director," *Architectural Digest*, February 2017, https://www.architecturaldigest.com /story/inside-the-world-of-virgil-abloh-kanye-wests-creative-director.

4 Mary Anne Hobbs and Virgil Abloh, BBC radio interview, 2018, https://www.bbc .co.uk/sounds/play/p06tfzb5.

5 Brent Luvaas, *DIY Style: Fashion, Music and Global Digital Cultures* (London: Bloomsbury, 2012); Arjun Appadurai, *Modernity at Large: Cultural Dimensions of Globalization* (Minneapolis: University of Minnesota Press, 1996).

6 Luvaas, *DIY Style*.

7 Luvaas, *DIY Style*, 2.

8 Ted Polhemus, *Street Style: From Sidewalk to Catwalk* (London: Thames and Hudson, 1994), 8.

9 Alessio Ascari and Virgil Abloh, "One of Us," *Kaleidoscope Magazine*, no. 33 (Fall/ Winter 2018/2019): 116–117.

10 Ascari and Abloh, "One of Us," n.p.

11 Christoper Morency, "The Unlikely Success of Virgil Abloh," *Business of Fashion*, 29 September 2016, https://www.businessoffashion.com/articles/intelligence/the -unlikely-success-of-virgil-abloh-off-white.

12 See Thomas Bettridge, "Duchamp Is My Lawyer," *032c*, 22 September 2017, https://032c.com/virgil-abloh-duchamp; Morency, "The Unlikely Success of Virgil Abloh"; Diane Solway, "Virgil Abloh and His Army of Disruptors," *W Magazine*, 20 April 2017, https://www.wmagazine.com/story/virgil-abloh-off-white-kanye-west-raf -simons.

13 Polhemus, *Street Style*, 6.

14 Polhemus, *Street Style*, 7.

15 Polhemus, *Street Style*, 7.

16 Anneke Smelik, "The Performance of Authenticity," *Address: Journal for Fashion Writing and Criticism* 1, no. 1 (2011): 82.

17 Lou Stoppard, "Fashion Is the Messenger," in *Virgil Abloh: Figures of Speech*, ed. Michael Darling (New York: Delmonic/Prestel Books, 2019), 135.

18 King Adz and Wilma Stone, *This Is Not Fashion: Streetwear Past Present and Future* (London: Thames and Hudson, 2018), 23.

19 Adz and Stone, *This Is Not Fashion*, 23.

20 Adz and Stone, *This Is Not Fashion*, 23.

21 Adz and Stone, *This Is Not Fashion*, 24.

22 Stoppard quoted in Darling, *Virgil Abloh*, 136.

23 Adz and Stone, *This Is Not Fashion*, 24, 26.

24 Stoppard quoted in Darling, *Virgil Abloh*, 136.

25 Jake Woolf, "The One Thing Virgil Abloh Is Scared Of," *GQ*, 27 June 2016, https://www.gq.com/story/virgil-abloh-interview-paris-off-white-book.

26 Jamie Lauren Keiles, "Barbara Kruger's Supreme Performance," *New Yorker*, November 2017, https://www.newyorker.com/culture/culture-desk/barbara-krugers-supreme-performance.

27 Virgil Abloh's digital archive, available at https://canary---yellow.com/.

28 Abloh, https://canary---yellow.com/.

29 Maurizio Cattelan, "In Conversation with Virgil Abloh," *Flash Art Magazine* 329, no. 53 (February–March 2020): n.p.

30 Virgil Abloh, "Core Studio Lecture: Virgil Abloh, 'Insert Complicated Title Here,'" Harvard University Graduate School of Design, https://www.gsd.harvard.edu/event/virgil-abloh/ (accessed 26 October 2017).

31 Abloh, "Core Studio Lecture."

32 Bettridge, "Duchamp Is My Lawyer."

33 Adam Geczy and Vicki Karaminas, "Time, Cruelty and Destruction in Deconstructivist Fashion: Kawakubo, Margiela and Vetements," *Zone Moda Journal* 10, no. 1 (2020): 72.

34 Bettridge, "Duchamp Is My Lawyer."

35 See *The Fashion Law*, https://www.thefashionlaw.com/; @Diet Prada on Instagram.

36 Bettridge, "Duchamp Is My Lawyer."

37 "Fashion influencer" refers to the everyday fashion consumer who has created an identity on online social media forums and gained a significant following.

38 Emma Elizabeth Davidson, "Martin Margiela Outlines Pressures of Fashion's Fast Pace in New Letter," *Dazed Digital*, 12 October 2018, http://www.dazeddigital.com/fashion/article/41804/1/maison-martin-margiela-belgian-fashion-awards-acceptance-letter.

39 Vikram Alexei Kansara, "Virgil Abloh: 'I Am Not a Designer,'" *Business of Fashion*, 12 September 2018, https://www.businessoffashion.com/articles/professional/virgil-abloh-i-am-not-a-designer.

40 Solway, "Virgil Abloh."

41 Morency, "The Unlikely Success of Virgil Abloh."

42 See Jean Baudrillard, *Simulations* (New York: Semiotext(e), 1983).

43 Fredric Jameson, *Postmodernism or, the Cultural Logic of Late Capitalism* (London: Verso, 1991), 18.

44 See Seth Abramson, "Ten Basic Principles of Metamodernism," *Huffington Post*, 27 April 2015, https://www.huffingtonpost.com/seth-abramson/ten-key-principles-in -met_b_7143202.html.

45 Alex Coles, *Design and Art: Documents of Contemporary Art* (Cambridge, MA: MIT Press, 2007), 122.

46 Yuniya Kawamura, *Sneakers: Fashion, Gender, and Subculture* (London: Bloomsbury, 2016), 1.

47 Nike Air Jordans were produced for American basketball champion Michael Jordan in 1984 by a team that included tinker Hatfield and were released to the public later that year. They quickly became the best-selling sneaker in Nike's history. They hold great cultural power and cachet due to their ongoing popularity and ability to transcend sociocultural barriers.

48 Cody Delistraty, "Virgil Abloh Is Searching for Virgil Abloh," *Esquire*, January 2017, https://www.esquire.com/style/mens-fashion/a52288/virgil-abloh-profile -interview/.

49 Stuart Hall, "Cultural Identity and Diaspora," in *Contemporary Postcolonial Theory: A Reader*, ed. Padmini Mongia (London: Arnold, 1996), 113.

50 Hall, "Cultural Identity and Diaspora," 113–114.

51 Darling, *Virgil Abloh*, 20.

52 Abloh, "Core Studio Lecture."

53 Abloh, "Core Studio Lecture."

54 Charlie Porter, "How to Build a Hype Brand," *Financial Times*, April 2018, https:// www.ft.com/content/b87a174c-30e0-11e8-b5bf-23cb17fd1498.

55 Chantal Fernandez, "Peak Collaboration? Not for Virgil Abloh," *Business of Fashion*, 14 January 2019, https://www.businessoffashion.com/articles/news-analysis/peak -collaboration-not-for-virgil-abloh.

56 Fernandez, "Peak Collaboration?"

57 Cattelan, "Conversation with Virgil Abloh."

58 Abloh, "Core Studio Lecture."

59 Susanne Madsen, "Virgil Abloh on Getting Political with Jenny Holzer," *Dazed Digital*, June 2017, http://www.dazeddigital.com/fashion/article/36381/1/virgil -abloh-on-getting-political-with-jenny-holzer-pitti-ss18-off-white.

60 Collaboration with fashion designers is not something new for Holzer, who collaborated on an installation with Austrian artist and former fashion designer Helmut Lang at the Florence Biennale in 1996, curated by Ingrid Sischy. This was one of the first moments that collaborations between fashion and art practitioners manifested in this immersive and critical form.

61 Madsen, "Virgil Abloh on Getting Political."

62 Virgil Abloh and Takashi Murakami, "Future History Exhibition," press release, Gagosian Gallery, London, 2018, https://gagosian.com/media/exhibitions/2018 /murakami-abloh-future-history/Gagosian_Murakami_Abloh_Future_History _2018_Press_Release.pdf.

63 Gary Warnett, "Textbook" (n.p.: Nike NYC Studio, 2017), https://www.kixart.lt /media/images/Nuotraukos/nike-x-off-white/textbook.pdf.

64 "Technetronic" refers to something that is shaped or influenced by changes in communication technology.

65 Steven Vogel, *Streetwear* (London: Thames and Hudson, 2007), 7.

66 Kawamura, *Sneakers*, 5.

67 Paul McCobb was a midcentury modern industrial designer, who initially trained in fine arts and had no traditional design education. He is responsible for the

development of the classic American midcentury furniture aesthetic that offered both affordability and style.

68 Virgil Abloh and Rem Koolhas interview, *System Magazine* 10 (November 2017).

69 Eleanor Gibson, "IKEA Offers First Look at Furniture Designed for Millennials by Virgil Abloh," *Dezeen*, 1 May 2018, https://www.dezeen.com/2018/05/01/ikea-virgil-abloh-furniture-millennial/.

70 Alice Rawsthorn, "Power Move," *Wallpaper*, 5 May 2019, https://www.wallpaper.com/design/virgil-abloh-furniture-venice-biennale-2019.

71 Darling, *Virgil Abloh*, 2.

72 Rem Koolhaas quoted in Darling, *Virgil Abloh*, 18.

73 Kimberly Drew, "The Artist as Network," *Kaleidoscope Magazine*, no. 33 (Fall/Winter 2018/2019): 150.

74 Enrique Menendez, "Virgil and Kanye's Rise to Fashion Supremacy," *Hypebeast*, 28 August 2017, https://hypebeast.com/2017/8/virgil-abloh-kanye-west-designer-vs-creator.

Chapter 7 Aitor Throup's Divergent Design

1 Maisie Skidmore, "Aitor Throup—The Anomalous Designer," *It's Nice That*, 5 June 2015, http://www.itsnicethat.com/features/aitor-throup-the-anomalous-designer-we-meet-aitor-thoup-in-his-studio-to-discuss-his-unusual-practice.

2 Skidmore, "Aitor Throup."

3 José Teunissen, "Fashion: More than Cloth and Form," in *The Handbook of Fashion Studies*, ed. Sandy Black, Amy De La Haye, Joanne Entwistle, Agnès Rocamora, Regina A. Root, and Helen Thomas (London: Bloomsbury, 2013), 197.

4 Teunissen, "Fashion," 197.

5 Teunissen, "Fashion," 212.

6 Lara Torres, "Fashion in the Expanded Field: Strategies for Critical Fashion Practice," *Journal of Asia-Pacific Pop Culture* 2, no. 2 (2017): 167.

7 Torres, "Fashion in the Expanded Field," 168.

8 Torres, "Fashion in the Expanded Field," 168.

9 Torres, "Fashion in the Expanded Field," 177.

10 Torres, "Fashion in the Expanded Field," 167.

11 See Hugo Ball, *Dada Manifesto* (1916), trans. Christopher Middleton, in Hugo Ball, *Flight Out of Time: A Dada Diary* (Berkeley: University of California Press, 1996); André Breton, *First Manifesto of Surrealism* (1924), in *Art in Theory 1900–1990: An Anthology of Changing Ideas*, ed. Charles Harrison and Paul Wood (Oxford: Blackwell, 1992).

12 Vivienne Westwood, *Manifesto: Active Resistance to Propaganda* (London: Serpentine Gallery, 2008).

13 Adam Geczy and Vicki Karaminas, *Critical Fashion Practice: From Westwood to Beirendonck* (London: Bloomsbury, 2017), 9.

14 Geczy and Karaminas, *Critical Fashion Practice*, 9.

15 Karen de Perthuis, "Breaking the Idea of Clothes: Rei Kawakubo's Fashion Manifesto," *Fashion Theory* 24, no. 5 (2020): 662; Hans Ulrich Obrist, "Rei Kawakubo's Quiet Revolution Just Got Louder," *System Magazine* 2 (2013), http://system-magazine.com/issue2/rei-kawakubo/.

16 Marco Pecorari, "Zones-in-Between: The Creation of New Fashion Praxis," *Art Monthly*, no. 242 (August 2011): 68.

17 Aitor Throup, *New Object Research Manifesto* (London: AT Studio, 2012), n.p.

18 Throup, *New Object Research Manifesto* (2012), n.p.

19 Throup, *New Object Research Manifesto* (2012), n.p.
20 Throup, *New Object Research Manifesto* (2012), n.p.
21 Aitor Throup, *New Object Research Manifesto* (London: AT Studio, 2016), n.p.
22 Throup, *New Object Research Manifesto* (2016), n.p.
23 Throup, *New Object Research Manifesto* (2016), n.p.
24 Aitor Throup, *A Portrait of Noomi Rapace*, Nowness, 29 September 2014, https://www.nowness.com/story/noomi-rapace-by-aitor-throup.
25 Geczy and Karaminas, *Critical Fashion Practice*, 80.
26 Geczy and Karaminas, *Critical Fashion Practice*, 80.
27 Geczy and Karaminas, *Critical Fashion Practice*, 79–80.
28 Throup, *New Object Research Manifesto* (2016), n.p.
29 Skidmore, "Aitor Throup."
30 Skidmore, "Aitor Throup."
31 Suzanne Zhang, "Aitor Throup: Innovation in Its Pure Form," *Rooms Magazine* (May 2014), n.p.
32 Marcus Boon and Gabriel Levine, eds., *Practice: Documents of Contemporary Art* (Cambridge, MA: MIT Press, 2018), 13.
33 Boon and Levine, *Practice*, 13.
34 Boon and Levine, *Practice*, 14.
35 Boon and Levine, *Practice*, 15.
36 Boon and Levine, *Practice*, 14.
37 Malene Leerberg, "Design in the Expanded Field: Rethinking Contemporary Design," *Nordes*, no. 3 (June 2009), 1, http://www.nordes.org/opj/index.php/n13/article/view/52.
38 Leerberg, "Design in the Expanded Field," 1.
39 Leerberg, "Design in the Expanded Field," 1.
40 Paul Heavener, "Aitor Throup's Homecoming," *Hypebeast*, 23 April 2020, https://hypebeast.com/2020/4/aitor-throup-streetwear-dsa-interview.
41 Throup, *New Object Research Manifesto* (2012), n.p.
42 Skidmore, "Aitor Throup."
43 Jo Turney, *Fashion Crimes: Dressing for Deviance* (London: Bloomsbury, 2019), 1.
44 Turney, *Fashion Crimes*, 1.
45 Throup, *New Object Research Manifesto* (2012), n.p.
46 Throup, *New Object Research Manifesto* (2012), n.p.
47 Throup, *New Object Research Manifesto* (2012), n.p.
48 Xerxes Cook, "Adventures in Denim with Aitor Throup," *SSENSE*, 17 May 2017, https://www.ssense.com/en-us/interview/aitor-throup-adventures-in-denim.
49 Throup, *New Object Research Manifesto*, 2012.
50 Ruby Boddington, "Aitor Throup Designs Modular, Layered Costumes for Wayne McGregor's Autobiography," *It's Nice That*, October 2017, https://www.itsnicethat.com/news/aitor-throup-wayne-mcgregor-autobiography-fashion-051017.
51 *Encyclopaedia Britannica Online*, s.v. "Leonardo da Vinci," https://www.britannica.com/biography/Leonardo-da-Vinci/Anatomical-studies-and-drawings (accessed 26 August 2020).
52 *Encyclopaedia Britannica Online*, s.v. "Leonardo da Vinci."
53 Cook, "Adventures in Denim."
54 Vanessa Hsieh, "Aitor Throup Discusses G-Star Raw and the Future of Fashion," *Dazed Digital*, 17 January 2017, http://www.dazeddigital.com/fashion/article/34402/1/aitor-throup-discusses-g-star-raw-and-the-future-of-fashion.
55 Elizabeth Wilson, *Adorned in Dreams: Fashion and Modernity* (London: I. B. Tauris, 2007), 1.

56 Wilson, *Adorned in Dreams*, 1.

57 Geczy and Karaminas, *Critical Fashion Practice*, 78.

58 Geczy and Karaminas, *Critical Fashion Practice*, 78.

59 Adam Geczy and Vicki Karaminas, *Fashion Installation: Body, Space and Performance* (London: Bloomsbury, 2019), 77.

60 Geczy and Karaminas, *Fashion Installation*, 11.

61 Lou Stoppard, "Fashion as Installation," *ADF Papers*, Fashion Paper no. 4 (January 2014): 5.

62 Geczy and Karaminas, *Fashion Installation*, 104.

63 Geczy and Karaminas, *Fashion Installation*, 104.

64 Aitor Throup, *The Funeral of New Orleans Part One*, http://showstudio.com/project/the_funeral_of_new_orleans_part_one (accessed 3 November 2016).

65 Stoppard, "Fashion as Installation," 5.

66 Stoppard, "Fashion as Installation," 5.

67 Stoppard, "Fashion as Installation," 5.

68 Tim Blanks, "Decrypting the Manifesto of Aitor Throup," *Business of Fashion*, 15 June 2016, https://www.businessoffashion.com/articles/fashion-show-review/decrypting-the-manifesto-of-aitor-throup.

69 Blanks, "Decrypting the Manifesto."

70 Blanks, "Decrypting the Manifesto."

71 Stoppard, "Fashion as Installation," 4.

72 Throup, *New Object Research Manifesto* (2012), n.p.

73 Blanks, "Decrypting the Manifesto."

74 Blanks, "Decrypting the Manifesto."

75 Cook, "Adventures in Denim."

76 Skidmore, "Aitor Throup."

77 C. P. Company, "20th Anniversary of the 1000m Goggle Jacket," https://www.cpcompany.co.uk/blogs/archive/62330885-20th-anniversary-of-the-1000m-goggle-jacket-by-aitor-throup-2009 (accessed 28 August 2020).

78 C. P. Company, "20th Anniversary."

79 Leonie Cooper, "Aitor Throup on His Curtain Raising Moment," *Dazed*, July 2014, http://www.dazeddigital.com/artsandculture/article/20636/1/aitor-throup-on-his-curtain-raising-moment.

80 Alice Morby, "Aitor Throup Designs 'Clothes not Costumes' for Wayne McGregor's Latest Production," *Dezeen*, 6 October 2017, https://www.dezeen.com/2017/10/06/aitor-throup-designs-clothes-not-costumes-wayne-mcgregor-ballet-autobiography/.

81 Morby, "Aitor Throup Designs."

82 Morby, "Aitor Throup Designs."

83 Geczy and Karaminas, *Critical Fashion Practice*, 84.

84 Geczy and Karaminas, *Critical Fashion Practice*, 86.

85 Jian DeLeon, "Aitor Throup Talks Practical Design," *High Snobiety*, 28 June 2017, http://www.highsnobiety.com/2017/06/27/g-star-raw-research-aitor-throup-interview/.

Chapter 8   Iris van Herpen's New Couture

1 See "Manus × Machina: Fashion in an Age of Technology," Metropolitan Museum of Art, Exhibition Galleries, 2016, https://www.metmuseum.org/exhibitions/listings/2016/manus-x-machina/exhibition-galleries.

2 Vikram Alexei Kansara, "Iris van Herpen's Science Fashion," *Business of Fashion*, 6 July 2015, https://www.businessoffashion.com/articles/long-view/iris-van-herpens -technology-science-fashion.

3 Kansara, "Iris van Herpen's Science Fashion."

4 Kansara, "Iris van Herpen's Science Fashion."

5 See "The House of Iris van Herpen," Iris van Herpen website, http://www.irisvan herpen.com/about.

6 Kathleen Beckett, "Iris Van Herpen and 'A Different Way of Thinking,'" *New York Times*, 1 December 2014, https://www.nytimes.com/2014/12/02/fashion/iris-van -herpen-and-a-different-way-of-thinking.html.

7 Beckett, "Iris Van Herpen."

8 Arianne Koek, "Retrospective: Iris Van Herpen," *System Magazine* 10 (2017): 2.

9 Koek, "Retrospective," 2.

10 Koek, "Retrospective," 2.

11 Kin Woo, "'The Woodstock of Fashion': Remembering Thierry Mugler's Most Legendary Show," *New York Times*, 1 March 2019, https://www.nytimes.com/2019 /03/01/t-magazine/thierry-mugler-1995-show.html.

12 Sarah Mower, "Alexander McQueen FW 2006 Runway Review," *Vogue*, 3 March 2006, https://www.vogue.com/fashion-shows/fall-2006-ready-to-wear/alexander -mcqueen.

13 Sandy Black, "Science, Technology, and New Fashion," in *The Handbook of Fashion Studies*, ed. Sandy Black, Amy De La Haye, Joanne Entwistle, Agnès Rocamora, Regina A. Root, and Helen Thomas (London: Bloomsbury, 2013), 429.

14 Black, "Science, Technology, and New Fashion," 429.

15 Black, "Science, Technology, and New Fashion," 429.

16 See Anneke Smelik, "New Materialism: A Framework for Fashion in the Age of Technological Innovation," *International Journal of Fashion Studies* 5, no. 1 (2018): 33–54.

17 Charmaine Li, "Iris Van Herpen: The Unknownness of Everything," *Mono Kultur*, Summer 2019, 23.

18 Hannah Rose Mendoza, "3D Printed Dress from Iris van Herpen Pushes Boundaries of Fashion," *3D Print*, 30 January 2018, https://3dprint.com/201774/3d-printed-dress -iris-van-herpen/.

19 See Mediated Matter, "Overview," MIT Media Lab, 5 March 2019, https://www .media.mit.edu/groups/mediated-matter/overview/.

20 Nello Barile and Satomi Sugiyama, "Wearing Data: From McLuhan's 'Extended Skin' to the Integration between Wearable Technologies and a New Algorithmic Sensibility," *Fashion Theory* 24, no. 2 (2020): 215–216.

21 See Iris van Herpen, "*Voltage*," press release, 2013, https://www.irisvanherpen.com /haute-couture/voltage.

22 Van Herpen, "*Voltage*."

23 Lisa Immordino Vreeland, "Art of Style: Iris Van Herpen," *M2M*, https://m2m.tv /watch/iris-van-herpen, accessed 16 February 2018.

24 Marco Pecorari, "Zones-in-Between: The Creation of New Fashion Praxis," *Art Monthly*, no. 242 (August 2011): 67.

25 Annamari Vänskä, "How to Do Humans with Fashion: Towards a Posthuman Critique of Fashion," *International Journal of Fashion Studies* 5, no. 1 (2018): 15.

26 Barile and Sugiyama, "Wearing Data," 215.

27 Marshell McLuhan, *Understanding Media: The Extensions of Man* (Cambridge, MA: MIT Press, 1994), 3.

28 Nicole Phelps, "Iris van Herpen: Fall 2019 Couture Review," *Vogue Runway*, 2 July 2019, https://www.vogue.com/fashion-shows/fall-2019-couture/iris-van -herpen.

29 Smelik, "New Materialism," 38.

30 Smelik, "New Materialism," 34.

31 Smelik, "New Materialism," 34.

32 Smelik, "New Materialism," 34.

33 Georgina Evans, "Posthumanism in Fashion," Showstudio, 18 June 2018, https:// www.showstudio.com/projects/queer/essay_posthumanism_in_fashion.

34 Donna Haraway, "A Cyborg Manifesto: Science, Technology, and Socialist- Feminism in the Late Twentieth Century," in *Simians, Cyborgs and Women: The Reinvention of Nature* (New York: Routledge, 1991), 149.

35 Haraway, "A Cyborg Manifesto," 150.

36 Haraway, "A Cyborg Manifesto," 150.

37 Haraway, "A Cyborg Manifesto," 150.

38 Iris van Herpen, "*Shift Souls*," press release, 2019, https://www.irisvanherpen.com /haute-couture/shift-souls.

39 Van Herpen, "*Shift Souls*."

40 Van Herpen, "*Shift Souls*."

41 Van Herpen, "*Shift Souls*."

42 Iris Van Herpen, "*Aeriform*," press release, 2017, http://www.irisvanherpen.com /about.

43 Van Herpen, "*Aeriform*."

44 Adam Geczy and Vicki Karaminas, *Fashion Installation: Body, Space and Performance* (London: Bloomsbury, 2019), 89.

45 Van Herpen, "*Aeriform*."

46 Van Herpen, "*Aeriform*."

47 Rebecca Mead, "Iris Van Herpen's High-Tech Couture," *New Yorker*, 25 September 2017, https://www.newyorker.com/magazine/2017/09/25/iris-van-herpens-hi -tech-couture.

48 Mead, "Iris Van Herpen's High-Tech Couture."

49 Elizabeth Wilson, "Fashion and the Postmodern Body," in *Chic Thrills: A Fashion Reader*, ed. J. Ash and E. Wilson (London: Pandora, 1992), 4.

50 Wilson, "Fashion and the Postmodern Body," 4.

51 See Alice Payne, "Fashion Futuring in the Anthropocene: Sustainable Fashion as 'Taming' and 'Rewilding,'" *Fashion Theory* 23, no. 1 (2019): 5–23.

52 Payne, "Fashion Futuring," 6.

53 Payne, "Fashion Futuring," 6.

54 Payne, "Fashion Futuring," 6.

55 Payne, "Fashion Futuring," 6–7.

56 Wilson, "Fashion and the Postmodern," 4–5.

57 Aileen Ribeiro, "Utopian Dress," in *Chic Thrills: A Fashion Reader*, ed. J. Ash and E. Wilson (London: Pandora, 1992), 233.

58 Ribeiro, "Utopian Dress," 234.

59 Richard Noble, *Utopias: Documents of Contemporary Art* (Cambridge, MA: MIT Press, 2009), 12.

60 Noble, *Utopias*, 12.

61 See Jean Baudrillard, *Simulations* (New York: Semiotext(e), 1983).

62 See Caroline Evans, *Fashion at the Edge: Spectacle, Modernity and Deathliness* (New Haven, CT: Yale University Press, 2003).

63 Iris van Herpen, *Hybrid Holism*," press release, 2012, https://www.irisvanherpen
.com/haute-couture/hybrid-holism.

64 Lou Stoppard, *Fashion Together: Fashion's Most Extraordinary Duos on the Art of
Collaboration* (New York: Rizzoli, 2017), 272.

65 Vreeland, "Art of Style."

66 Li, "The Unknownness of Everything."

67 Li, "The Unknownness of Everything."

68 Laird Borrelli-Persson, "10 Questions for Iris van Herpen as She Prepares to Celebrate
10 Years of Fashion Innovation at Couture," *Vogue*, 30 June 2017, https://www.vogue
.com/article/iris-van-herpen-haute-couture-anniversary-interview.

69 Showstudio, "About" page, https://showstudio.com/about (accessed 14 June 2019).

70 Natalie Khan, "Cutting the Fashion Body: Why the Fashion Image Is No Longer
Still," *Fashion Theory* 16, no. 2 (2012): 236.

71 Vreeland, "Art of Style."

72 For images of the *Splash!* project, see Showstudio, "Splash!," http://showstudio.com
/project/splash.

73 Stoppard, "Fashion as Installation," 7.

74 Stoppard, "Fashion as Installation," 7.

75 Vreeland, "Art of Style."

76 Vreeland, "Art of Style."

77 Timotheus Vermeulen and Robin van den Akker, "Utopia, Sort Of: A Case Study in
Metamodernism," *Studia Neophilologica* 87, no. 1 (2015): 57.

78 Vermeulen and van den Akker, "Utopia, Sort Of," 57.

Chapter 9   Eckhaus Latta's Community-Led Brand

1 Alec Leach, "Eckhaus Latta Are Embracing Their Outsider Status," *Indie Magazine*,
10 September 2019, https://indie-mag.com/2019/09/eckhaus-latta/.

2 Josie Thaddeus-Johns, "Eckhaus Latta: There Is No Target Group," *Sleek Magazine*,
20 July 2015, https://www.sleek-mag.com/article/eckhaus-latta-there-is-no-target-group/.

3 See Judith Butler, *Gender Trouble: Feminism and the Subversion of Identity* (New
York: Routledge, 1990).

4 Alexandra Weiss, "Five Reasons to Go See Eckhaus Latta's Extremely Meta
Exhibition," *Dazed Digital*, 6 August 2018, http://www.dazeddigital.com/fashion
/article/40915/1/eckhaus-latta-new-exhibition-possessed-the-whitney-pop-up-meta.

5 Laird Borrelli-Persson, "An Oral History of New York's Most Avant-Garde (and
Underrated) Creators, Threeasfour," *Vogue World*, 3 September 2019, https://www
.vogue.com/vogueworld/article/20-years-on-fashions-fringes-an-oral-history-of
-threeasfour-new-yorks-most-avant-garde-and-underrated-creators.

6 Ted Polhemus, "Fashion-v-Anti-Fashion," *The Anthropology of Dress and Fashion*, ed.
Brent Luvaas and Joanne B. Eicher (London: Bloomsbury, 2019), 42.

7 These oral histories were documented in an online editorial in 2019 by US *Vogue*,
offering anecdotal vignettes from friends and collaborators of the time.

8 Borrelli-Persson, "An Oral History."

9 Borrelli-Persson, "An Oral History."

10 Borrelli-Persson, "An Oral History."

11 Caroline Evans, "The Ontology of the Fashion Model," *AA Files* 63 (2011): 58–59.

12 Adam Geczy, *The Artificial Body in Fashion and Art* (London: Bloomsbury, 2017), 94.

13 "Articles of Interest: A Fantasy of Fashion," *99% Invisible* (podcast), 13 May 2020,
https://99percentinvisible.org/episode/a-fantasy-of-fashion-articles-of-interest-7/.

14 Malte Fabien Rauch, "Camouflaged with a Visual Language," *Diaphanes Magazine*, 23 August 2019, https://www.diaphanes.com/titel/where-the-negative-holds-court -6064.

15 Rauch, "Where the Negative Holds."

16 Guy Debord, *The Society of the Spectacle* (New York: Zone Books, 1994), 193.

17 Anastasiia Fedorova, "Making Movies with Eckhaus Latta and Alexa Karolinski," *i-D*, 8 February 2017, https://i-d.vice.com/en_uk/article/d3pzkq/making-movies -with-eckhaus-latta-and-alexa-karolinski.

18 Steff Yotka, "Eckhaus Latta's New Store Is an Oasis in New York's Retail Scene," *Vogue*, 27 November 2018, https://www.vogue.com/article/eckhaus-latta-new-york -store.

19 Joanne Entwistle, "Fashion and the Fleshy Body: Dress as Embodied Practice," *Fashion Theory* 4, no. 3 (2000).

20 Adam Geczy and Vicki Karaminas, *Critical Fashion Practice: From Westwood to Beirendonck* (London: Bloomsbury, 2017).

21 See Butler, *Gender Trouble*.

22 See Butler, *Gender Trouble*.

23 Butler, "Critically Queer," *GLQ: A Journal of Lesbian and Gay Studies* 1, no. 1 (1993): 18.

24 Joanne Entwistle, *The Fashioned Body* (London: Sage Publications, 2000), 142.

25 See Kimberlé Crenshaw, "Demarginalizing the Intersection of Race and Sex: A Black Feminist Critique of Antidiscrimination Doctrine, Feminist Theory and Antiracist Politics," *University of Chicago Legal Forum* 1, no. 8 (1989): 139–167.

26 "Cis-gender" is a term for people whose gender identity matches their sex assigned at birth.

27 Entwistle, *The Fashioned Body*, 121.

28 Vanessa Friedman, "Virginia Woolf Is Trending," *New York Times*, 22 January 2020, https://www.nytimes.com/2020/01/22/style/givenchy-margiela-armani-couture-paris .html.

29 Entwistle, *The Fashioned Body*, 63.

30 Cathaleen Chen, "Why Genderless Fashion Is the Future," *Business of Fashion*, 22 November 2019, https://www.businessoffashion.com/articles/news-analysis/voices -talk-alok-v-menon-gender-clothes-fashion.

31 Chen, "Why Genderless Fashion."

32 Chen, "Why Genderless Fashion."

33 Jake Hall, "Design and Disruption of the Human Body," Showstudio, 19 May 2018, https://www.showstudio.com/projects/queer/essay_design_and_disruption_of_the _human_body.

34 Entwistle, *The Fashioned Body*, 141.

35 Entwistle, *The Fashioned Body*, 141.

36 Alexa Karolinski, *Coco*, 2017, https://vimeo.com/211689869; Stephanie Eckhardt, "Eckhaus Latta Tackles Actual Reality TV in New Video," *W Magazine*, 25 April 2017, https://www.wmagazine.com/story/eckhaus-latta-new-video-reality-tv-juliana -huxtable/.

37 Eckhardt, "Eckhaus Latta."

38 Vanessa Hseih, "Eckhaus Latta's New Campaign Features IRL Couples Having Sex," 30 March 2017, https://www.dazeddigital.com/fashion/article/35344/1/eckhaus -lattas-new-campaign-sees-real-couples-having-sex.

39 Pamela Church-Gibson and Vicki Karaminas, "Letter from the Editors," *Fashion Theory* 18, no. 2 (2014): 118.

40 Church-Gibson and Karaminas, "Letter from the Editors."

41 Ross Simonini, "Eckhaus Latta," *Art in America* 37 (April 2016).

42 Holland Cotter, "ART REVIEW; Fluffing Up Warhol: Where Art and Fashion Intersect," *New York Times*, 7 November 1997, https://www.nytimes.com/1997/11/07/arts/art-review-fluffing-up-warhol-where-art-and-fashion-intersect.html.

43 Cathy Horyn, "A Museum Show Where You Can Wear the Art Home: The Whitney's Eckhaus Latta Installation Doubles as a Clothing Store," *The Cut*, 2018, https://www.thecut.com/2018/08/the-whitney-museums-eckhaus-latta-possessed-reviewed.html.

44 See Whitney Museum of American Art, "Eckhaus Latta: Possessed," Whitney Museum of American Art, "Exhibitions," https://whitney.org/exhibitions/eckhaus-latta.

45 Horyn, "A Museum Show."

46 Steff Yotka, "The Making of Eckhaus Latta's Shoppable Whitney Museum Exhibition," *Vogue*, 3 August 2018, https://www.vogue.com/article/eckhaus-latta-whitney-museum-possessed.

47 Gill Perry and Paul Wood, *Themes in Contemporary Art* (New Haven, CT: Yale University Press, 2004), 185.

48 Yotka, "The Making of Eckhaus."

49 Alex Rakestraw, "How Camper Went from Mall Brand to Gosha Rubchinskiy Collaborator," *Highsnobiety*, 30 May 2018, https://www.highsnobiety.com/p/camper-interview-gosha-rubchinskiy/.

50 Ted Stansfield, "Hari Nef Stars in Camper × Eckhaus Latta's Campaign," *Dazed Digital*, 9 November 2016, https://www.dazeddigital.com/fashion/article/33648/1/hari-nef-stars-in-eckhaus-lattas-new-campaign-film.

51 Rakestraw, "How Camper Went."

52 Fedorova, "Making Movies."

53 Fedorova, "Making Movies."

54 Nick Rees-Roberts, *Fashion Film: Art and Advertising in the Digital Age* (London: Bloomsbury, 2019), 5.

55 Rees-Roberts, *Fashion Film*, 5.

56 Rees-Roberts, *Fashion Film*, 6.

57 Alexa Karolinski, "Uniform Exercises," Nowness, 29 July 2012, https://www.nowness.com/series/age-appropiate/uniform-exercises.

58 Marketa Uhlirova, "100 Years of the Fashion Film: Frameworks and Histories," *Fashion Theory* 17, no. 2 (2015): 139.

59 Alexa Karolinski, *Dinner*, 2013, https://vimeo.com/61838623.

60 See Timotheus Vermeulen and Robin van den Akker, *Metamodern: Historicity, Affect, and Depth after Postmodernism* (London: Rowman and Littlefield, 2017).

61 Alexa Karolinski, *Smile*, 2016, https://vimeo.com/153393224.

62 Hilary Moss, "Eckhaus Latta's Latest Photo Shoot Breaks the Fourth Wall," *New York Times*, 1 February 2016, https://www.nytimes.com/2016/02/01/t-magazine/fashion/eckhaus-latta-smile-hammer-museum.html.

63 Fedorova, "Making Movies."

64 Fedorova, "Making Movies."

65 Elizabeth Moor, "Branded Spaces: The Scope of 'New Marketing,'" *Journal of Consumer Culture* 3, no. 1 (2003): 39.

66 *A Magazine Curated By*, homepage, https://amagazinecuratedby.com/history/ (accessed 31 January 2020).

67 Alice Hines, "A Copy of a Copy: Ingenuity in a Swath of Prado Polyester," *Vestoj Journal: On Authenticity*, no. 8 (2017): 53.

68 Ane Lynge-Jorlén, *Niche Fashion Magazines: Changing the Face of Fashion* (London: I. B. Tauris, 2017), 5.

69 Lynge-Jorlén, *Niche Fashion Magazines*, 5.

70 Lynge-Jorlén, *Niche Fashion Magazines*, 6.

71 *A Magazine Curated By: Eckhaus Latta*, 2017, https://amagazinecuratedby.com/collection/eckhaus-latta/.

Conclusion

1 See Pierre Bourdieu, *The Field of Cultural Production* (New York: Columbia University Press, 1993).

2 Adam Geczy and Vicki Karaminas, *Fashion Installation: Body, Space and Performance* (London: Bloomsbury, 2019).

3 Timotheus Vermeulen and Robin van den Akker, "Notes on Metamodernism," *Journal of Aesthetics & Culture* 2, no. 1 (2010): 56–77; Julianne Pederson, "Meta-Modernism in Fashion and Style Practice: Authorship and the Consumer," in *From Production to Consumption: The Cultural Industry of Fashion*, edited by Marco Pedroni (Oxford: Inter-Disciplinary Press, 2013), 59–75; Marcia A. Morgado, "Fashion Phenomena and the Post-postmodern Condition," *Fashion, Style & Popular Culture* 1, no. 3 (2014): 313–339.

4 Elizabeth Wilson, *The Contradictions of Culture: Cities, Culture, Women* (London: Sage Publications, 2001), 50.

5 Tiziana Cardini, "A Conversation with Critic and Curator Maria Luisa Frisa," *Vogue*, 13 April 2020, https://www.vogue.com/article/maria-luisa-frisa-coronavirus-conversation.

6 Caroline Roux, "Elizabeth Peyton: The Exceptional Portrait," *The Gentlewoman*, Autumn–Winter 2013, https://thegentlewoman.co.uk/library/elizabeth-peyton.

7 Roux, "Elizabeth Peyton."

Bibliography

Published Sources

Abloh, Virgil. *The Incidents: "Insert Complicated Title Here."* Berlin and Cambridge, MA: Sternberg Press and Harvard University Graduate School of Design, 2017.

Abloh, Virgil, and Takashi Murakami. "Future History Exhibition." Press release, Gagosian Gallery, London, 2018. https://gagosian.com/media/exhibitions/2018/murakami-abloh-future-history/Gagosian_Murakami_Abloh_Future_History_2018_Press_Release.pdf.

Abnett, Kate. "Fashion's Fourth Industrial Revolution." *Business of Fashion*, 16 August 2016. https://www.businessoffashion.com/community/voices/discussions/what-does-the-fourth-industrial-revolution-mean-for-fashion/fashions-fourth-industrial-revolution-2.

Abnett, Kate. "The Store of the Future." *Business of Fashion*, 10 July 2016. https://www.businessoffashion.com/community/voices/discussions/what-will-the-store-of-the-future-look-like/the-store-of-the-future.

Abraham, Tamara. "Let's Reimagine 'Fashion Month.'" *Business of Fashion*, 20 February 2017. https://www.businessoffashion.com/community/voices/discussions/how-to-fix-fashion-week/reimagining-fashion-month.

Abramson, Seth. "Five More Basic Principles of Metamodernism." *Huffington Post*, 14 May 2015. https://www.huffingtonpost.com/seth-abramson/five-more-basic-principle_b_7269446.html.

Abramson, Seth. "METAMERICANA: What 'Into the Woods' Has to Do with David Foster Wallace." *Indiewire*, 28 April 2015. https://www.indiewire.com/2015/04/metamericana-what-into-the-woods-has-to-do-with-david-foster-wallace-132947/.

Abramson, Seth. "Ten Basic Principles of Metamodernism." *Huffington Post*, 27 April 2015. https://www.huffingtonpost.com/seth-abramson/ten-key-principles-in-met_b_7143202.html.

Adams, Tim. "Francis Fukuyama: 'Trump Instinctively Picks Racial Themes to Drive People on the Left Crazy.'" *Guardian Online*, 16 September 2018. https://www.theguardian.com/books/2018/sep/16/francis-fukuyama-interview-trump-picks-racial-themes-to-drive-people-on-the-left-crazy.

Adorno, Theodor W., and Christoph Doswald. *Double-Face: The Story about Fashion and Art from Mohammed to Warhol.* Exhibition catalogue. Zurich: JRP Ringier, 2006.

Adz, Kin, and Wilma Stone. *This Is Not Fashion: Streetwear Past Present and Future.* London: Thames and Hudson, 2018.

Agins, Teri. *The End of Fashion: The Mass Marketing of the Clothing Business.* New York: William Morrow, 1999.

Ahmed, Osmud. "Lumps and Bumps at Comme des Garçons S/S97." *Another Magazine,* 5 January 2016. http://www.anothermag.com/fashion-beauty/8174/lumps-and-bumps-at-comme-des-garcons-s-s97.

Ahmed, Osmud. "Meet London's Next Genration of Polymath Creatives." *Business of Fashion,* 17 February 2017. https://www.businessoffashion.com/articles/intelligence/meet-londons-next-generation-of-polymath-creatives.

Aleksander, Irina. "Sweatpants Forever." *New York Times,* 6 August 2020. https://www.nytimes.com/interactive/2020/08/06/magazine/fashion-sweatpants.html.

Allen, Mike. *The Sage Encyclopedia of Communication Research Methods.* Los Angeles: Sage Reference, 2017.

Allwood, Emma Hope. "Is Fashion Week Becoming Outdated?" *Dazed and Confused,* June 2016. http://www.dazeddigital.com/fashion/article/31244/1/is-fashion-week-becoming-outdated.

Amed, Imran, Achim Berg, Leonie Brantberg, and Saskia Hedrich. "The State of Fashion 2017." McKinsey, December 2016. https://www.mckinsey.com/industries/retail/our-insights/the-state-of-fashion.

Anand, Keshav. "Aitor Throup: Artist, Designer, Creative Director." *Something Curated,* 17 October 2017. http://somethingcurated.com/2017/10/17/interview-aitor-throup-artist-designer-creative-director/.

Andjelic, Ana. "Opinion: The Experience Economy Is Blurring the Lines between Hospitality and Retail." *Glossy,* 17 June 2019. https://www.glossy.co/fashion/opinion-thanks-to-the-experience-economy-hospitality-and-retail-are-closer-than-ever.

Appadurai, Arjun. *Modernity at Large: Cultural Dimensions of Globalization.* Minneapolis: University of Minnesota Press, 1996.

Archer, Michael. *Art since 1960.* London: Thames and Hudson, 2015.

Arlen, Michael. "The Living Room War." *New Yorker,* 15 October 1966.

Arnold, Rebecca. *Fashion, Desire & Anxiety: Image and Morality in the 20th Century.* London: I. B. Tauris, 2001.

Arnold, Sara K. "An Alternative to Consumerism Does Exist: The Performance Economy." *Business of Fashion,* 17 August 2017. https://www.businessoffashion.com/articles/opinion/an-alternative-to-consumerism-does-exist-the-performance-economy.

"Articles of Interest: A Fantasy of Fashion." *99% Invisible* (podcast), 13 May 2020. https://99percentinvisible.org/episode/a-fantasy-of-fashion-articles-of-interest-7/.

Ascari, Alessio, and Virgil Abloh. "One of Us." *Kaleidoscope Magazine,* no. 33 (Fall/Winter 2018/2019): 116–117.

Ash, Juliet, and Elizabeth Wilson. *Chic Thrills: A Fashion Reader.* London: Pandora, 1992.

Bäckström, Åsa. "Skateboarding beyond the Limits of Gender? Strategic Interventions in Sweden." *Leisure Studies* 37, no. 4 (2018): 424–439.

Baker, George. "Photography's Expanded Field." *October* 114 (2005): 121–140.

Ball, Hugo. *Dada Manifesto* (1916), trans. Christopher Middleton. In Hugo Ball, *Flight Out of Time: A Dada Diary.* Berkeley: University of California Press, 1996.

Bambrook, Jonathan, and Edward Booth-Clibborn. *Fashion and Art Collusion: Britain Creates*. London: Abrams, 2012.

Bannister, Laura. "A Conversation with Aitor Throup: The Designer behind New Object Research and Creative Consultant to a New-Era G-Star RAW." *Museum Magazine*, 8 September 2016. http://museum-magazine.com/2016/09/on-burnley -amsterdam-and-logo-culture/.

Barile, Nello, and Satomi Sugiyama. "Wearing Data: From McLuhan's 'Extended Skin' to the Integration between Wearable Technologies and a New Algorithmic Sensibility." *Fashion Theory* 24, no. 2 (2020): 211–227.

Barnard, Malcolm. *Fashion as Communication*. London: Routledge, 2002.

Barry, Ben, and Andrew Reilly. *Crossing Gender Boundaries: Fashion to Create, Disrupt and Transcend*. Bristol, UK: Intellect, 2020.

Baudelaire, Charles. *The Painter of Modern Life and Other Essays*. London: Phaidon, 1970.

Baudrillard, Jean. *Simulations*. New York: Semiotext(e), 1983.

Beckett, Kathleen. "Iris Van Herpen and 'A Different Way of Thinking.'" *New York Times*, 1 December 2014. https://www.nytimes.com/2014/12/02/fashion/iris-van -herpen-and-a-different-way-of-thinking.html.

Benjamin, Walter. *The Arcades Project*. Cambridge, MA: Harvard University Press, 2002.

Benjamin, Walter. "The Work of Art in the Age of Mechanical Reproduction." In *Illuminations*, edited by Hannah Arendt, translated by Harry Zohn, 211–244. London: Fontana Press, 1992.

Bettridge, Thomas. "Duchamp Is My Lawyer." *032c*, 22 September 2017. https://032c .com/virgil-abloh-duchamp.

Bettridge, Thomas. "Friend-Crushing with Eckhaus Latta." *SSENSE*, 1 November 2018. https://www.ssense.com/en-us/editorial/fashion/friend-crushing-with-eckhaus -latta.

Bettridge, Thomas. "Group Chat: The Oral Hisotry of Virgil Abloh." *GQ*, 4 March 2019. https://www.gq.com/story/virgil-abloh-cover-story-spring-2019.

Bishop, Claire. *Installation Art: A Critical History*. London: Tate Publishing, 2005.

Black, Sandy. "Science, Technology, and New Fashion." In *The Handbook of Fashion Studies*, edited by Sandy Black, Amy De La Haye, Joanne Entwistle, Agnès Rocamora, Regina A. Root, and Helen Thomas. London: Bloomsbury, 2013.

Black, Sandy, Amy De La Haye, Joanne Entwistle, Agnes Rocamora, Regina A. Root, and Helen Thomas, eds. *The Handbook of Fashion Studies*. London: Bloomsbury, 2013.

Blanks, Tim. "Decrypting the Manifesto of Aitor Throup." *Business of Fashion*, 15 June 2016. https://www.businessoffashion.com/articles/fashion-show-review/decrypting -the-manifesto-of-aitor-throup.

Blanks, Tim. "Inside JW Anderson's 'Disobedient Bodies.'" *Business of Fashion*, 20 March 2017. https://www.businessoffashion.com/articles/intelligence/jw-anderson-disobedi ent-bodies-the-hepworth-wakefield.

Blanks, Tim. "JW Anderson Experiments with 'Workshops' Uniting Culture and Commerce." *Business of Fashion*, 20 January 2016. https://www.businessoffashion .com/articles/bof-exclusive/bof-exclusive-jw-anderson-experiments-with-workshops -uniting-culture-and-commerce.

Bobb, Brooke. "Virgil Abloh on His New Chicago Exhibition and Why He's an Archi tect First." *Vogue*, 11 June 2019. https://www.vogue.com/article/virgil-abloh-figures -of-speech-chicago-museum-of-contemporary-art.

Boddington, Ruby. "Aitor Throup Designs Modular, Layered Costumes for Wayne McGregor's Autobiography." *It's Nice That*, October 2017. https://www.itsnicethat .com/news/aitor-throup-wayne-mcgregor-autobiography-fashion-051017.

Bolton, Andrew. *Alexander McQueen: Savage Beauty*. New York and New Haven, CT: Metropolitan Museum of Art and Yale University Press, 2011.

Bolton, Andrew. *Manus × Machina: Fashion in an Age of Technology*. New York: Metropolitan Museum of Art, 2016.

Boon, Marcus, and Gabriel Levine, eds. *Practice: Documents of Contemporary Art*. Cambridge, MA: MIT Press, 2018.

Borrelli-Persson, Laird. "Aitor Throup Enters 2020 with Two New Projects 15 Years in the Making (and They Were Totally Worth the Wait)." *Vogue*, 15 January 2020. https://www.vogue.com/article/aitor-throup-on-the-dsa-and-his-soon-to-be-released -conceptual-menswear-line.

Borrelli-Persson, Laird. "An Oral History of New York's Most Avant-Garde (and Underrated) Creators, Threeasfour." *Vogue World*, 3 September 2019. https://www .vogue.com/vogueworld/article/20-years-on-fashions-fringes-an-oral-history-of -threeasfour-new-yorks-most-avant-garde-and-underrated-creators.

Borrelli-Persson, Laird. "10 Questions for Iris van Herpen as She Prepares to Celebrate 10 Years of Fashion Innovation at Couture." *Vogue*, 30 June 2017. https://www.vogue .com/article/iris-van-herpen-haute-couture-anniversary-interview.

Bourdieu, Pierre. *Distinction: A Cultural Critique of the Judgement of Taste*. Cambridge, MA: Harvard University Press, 1984.

Bourdieu, Pierre. *The Field of Cultural Production*. New York: Columbia University Press, 1993.

Bourdieu, Pierre, and Y. Delsaut. "Le Couturier et sa griffe: Contribution à une théorie de la magie." *Actes de la recherche en sciences sociales* 1 (1975): 7–36.

Bourriaud, Nicolas. *The Radicant*. New York: Lukas & Sternberg, 2009.

Brand, Jan, and José Teunissen. *Fashion and Imagination: About Clothes and Art*. Arnhem, Netherlands: ArtEZ Press, 2009.

Breton, André. *First Manifesto of Surrealism* (1924). In *Art in Theory 1900–1990: An Anthology of Changing Ideas*, edited by Charles Harrison and Paul Wood. Oxford: Blackwell, 1992.

Breward, Christopher. "Between the Museum and the Academy: Fashion Research and Its Constituencies." *Fashion Theory* 12, no. 1 (2015): 83–93.

Breward, Christopher. *The Culture of Fashion: A New History of Fashionable Dress*. Manchester: Manchester University Press, 1995.

Breward, Christopher. "Cultures, Identities, Histories: Fashioning a Cultural Approach to Dress." *Fashion Theory* 2, no. 4 (1998): 301–313.

Bugg, Jessica. "Fashion at the Interface: Designer-Wearer-Viewer." *Fashion Practice: The Journal of Design, Creative Process & the Fashion Industry* 1, no. 1 (2009): 9–31.

Butler, Judith. "Critically Queer." *GLQ: A Journal of Lesbian and Gay Studies* 1, no. 1 (1993): 17–32.

Butler, Judith. *Gender Trouble: Feminism and the Subversion of Identity*. New York: Routledge, 1990.

C. P. Company. "20th Anniversary of the 1000m Goggle Jacket." https://www.cpcom pany.co.uk/blogs/archive/62330885-20th-anniversary-of-the-1000m-goggle-jacket-by -aitor-throup-2009 (accessed 28 August 2020).

Calefato, Patrizia. *The Clothed Body*. Oxford: Berg, 2004.

Calefato, Patrizia. "Fashionscapes." In *The End of Fashion: Clothing and Dress in the Age of Globalization*, edited by Adam Geczy and Vicki Karaminas. London: Bloomsbury, 2019.

Calefato, Patrizia. *Luxury: Fashion Lifestyle and Excess*. London: Bloomsbury, 2014.

Caramanica, Jon. "Can Virgil Abloh Fit in a Museum?" *New York Times*, 22 August 2019. https://www.nytimes.com/2019/08/22/arts/design/virgil-abloh-mca-chicago.html.

Cardini, Tiziana. "A Conversation with Critic and Curator Maria Luisa Frisa." *Vogue*, 13 April 2020. https://www.vogue.com/article/maria-luisa-frisa-coronavirus-conversation.

Cartner-Morley, Jess. "The Catwalk, Darling? It's So Last Year." *The Guardian*, 13 October 2003. https://www.theguardian.com/world/2003/oct/13/france.arts.

Cattelan, Maurizio. "In Conversation with Virgil Abloh." *Flash Art Magazine* 329, no. 53 (February–March 2020): n.p.

Celant, Germano. *Looking at Fashion: Catalogue Bienale di Firenze*. Milan: Skira, 1996.

Chen, Cathaleen. "Why Genderless Fashion Is the Future." *Business of Fashion*, 22 November 2019. https://www.businessoffashion.com/articles/news-analysis/voices-talk-alok-v-menon-gender-clothes-fashion.

Christensen, Michael. "Off-White's Virgil Abloh on the Future of Fashion." *GQ*, December 2017. https://www.gq.com.au/style/news/offwhites-virgil-abloh-on-the-future-of-fashion-youth-culture-is-still-the-engine/news-story/245b64d91c70ef10ae7e3946dc2adf7e.

Church-Gibson, Pamela. *Fashion and Celebrity Culture*. Oxford: Berg, 2012.

Church-Gibson, Pamela, and Vicki Karaminas. "Letter from the Editors." *Fashion Theory* 18, no. 2 (2014): 117–122.

Clark, Hazel. "Conceptual Fashion." In *Fashion and Art*, edited by Adam Geczy and Vicki Karaminas, 67–76. London: Bloomsbury, 2012.

Clark, Hazel. "SLOW + FASHION—an Oxymoron—or a Promise for the Future . . . ?" *Fashion Theory* 12, no. 4 (2008): 427–446.

Clark, Hazel, and Annamari Vänskä. *Fashion Curating: Critical Practice in the Museum and Beyond*. London: Bloomsbury Academic, 2018.

Clark, Judith. *Spectres: When Fashion Turns Back*. London: V&A Publications, 2004.

Clark, Judith, Amy De La Haye, and Jeffrey Horsley. *Exhibiting Fashion: Before and after 1971*. New Haven, CT: Yale University Press, 2014.

Clark, T. J. *Farewell to an Idea: Episodes from a History of Modernism*. New Haven, CT: Yale University Press, 2001.

Cohen-Cruz, Jan, and Mady Schutzman. *Dialogues of Theatre and Cultural Politics*. London: Routledge, 2006.

Coles, Alex. *Design and Art: Documents of Contemporary Art*. Cambridge, MA: MIT Press, 2007.

Colman, David. "Who Wore It Better? Art or Commerce?" *New York Times*, 1 August 2018. https://www.nytimes.com/2018/08/01/style/eckhaus-latta-whitney.html.

Conlon, Scarlett. "Aitor Throup on Making Clothes Matter." *British Vogue*, 23 June 2017. http://www.vogue.co.uk/article/how-aitor-throup-is-fusing-fashion-with-art.

Cook, Xerxes. "Adventures in Denim with Aitor Throup." *SSENSE*, 17 May 2017. https://www.ssense.com/en-us/interview/aitor-throup-adventures-in-denim.

Cooper, Leonie. "Aitor Throup on His Curtain Raising Moment." *Dazed*, July 2014. http://www.dazeddigital.com/artsandculture/article/20636/1/aitor-throup-on-his-curtain-raising-moment.

Cotter, Holland. "ART REVIEW; Fluffing Up Warhol: Where Art and Fashion Intersect." *New York Times*, 7 November 1997. https://www.nytimes.com/1997/11/07/arts/art-review-fluffing-up-warhol-where-art-and-fashion-intersect.html.

Craik, Jennifer. *Fashion: The Key Concepts*. Oxford: Berg, 2009.

Crenshaw, Kimberlé. "Demarginalizing the Intersection of Race and Sex: A Black Feminist Critique of Antidiscrimination Doctrine, Feminist Theory and Antiracist Politics." *University of Chicago Legal Forum* 1, no. 8 (1989): 139–167.

Crewe, Louise. *The Geographies of Fashion: Consumption, Space and Value*. London: Bloomsbury, 2017.

Cronberg, Anja Aronowsky. "Can Fashion Ever Be Democratic?" *Vestoj*, 2016. http:// vestoj.com/can-fashion-ever-be-democratic/.

Cronberg, Anja Aronowsky, ed. *Vestoj Journal: "On Authenticity."* Milan: Nava Press, 2017.

Cronberg, Anja Aronowsky, ed. *Vestoj Journal: On Capital*. Milan: Nava Press, 2019.

Dalton, Rosie. "How Fast Fashion Killed Creativity." *Catalogue*, 5 January 2017. https://www.cataloguemagazine.com.au/feature/how-fast-fashion-killed-creativity.

Danto, Arthur Coleman. *After the End of Art: Contemporary Art and the Pale of History*. Princeton, NJ: Princeton University Press, 1997.

Danto, Arthur Coleman. "The End of Art: A Philosophical Defence." *History and Theory* 37, no. 4 (1998): 127–143.

Danto, Arthur Coleman. *The Philosophical Disenfranchisement of Art*. New York: Columbia University Press, 1986.

Darling, Michael. *Virgil Abloh: Figures of Speech*. New York: Delmonic/Prestel Books, 2019.

Davidson, Emma Elizabeth. "Martin Margiela Outlines Pressures of Fashion's Fast Pace in New Letter." *Dazed Digital*, 12 October 2018. http://www.dazeddigital.com /fashion/article/41804/1/maison-martin-margiela-belgian-fashion-awards-accep tance-letter.

Dawkins, Richard. *The Selfish Gene*. Oxford: Oxford University Press, 2006.

Debord, Guy. *The Society of the Spectacle*. New York: Zone Books, 1994.

De la Haye, Amy. "Vogue and the V&A Vitrine." *Fashion Theory* 10, no. 1 (2006): 127–152.

DeLeon, Jian. "Aitor Throup Talks Practical Design." *High Snobiety*, 28 June 2017. http://www.highsnobiety.com/2017/06/27/g-star-raw-research-aitor-throup -interview/.

Deleuze, Gilles, and Félix Guattari. *A Thousand Plateaus: Captitalism and Schizophrenia*. Translated by Brian Massumi. London: Continuum, 2004.

Delistraty, Cody. "Virgil Abloh Is Searching for Virgil Abloh." *Esquire*, January 2017. https://www.esquire.com/style/mens-fashion/a52288/virgil-abloh-profile-interview/.

de Perthuis, Karen. "Breaking the Idea of Clothes: Rei Kawakubo's Fashion Manifesto." *Fashion Theory* 24, no. 5 (2020): 659–677.

Dhillon, Kam. "The Very Best #TFWGucci Memes." *Highsnobiety*, 12 April 2017. https://www.highsnobiety.com/2017/04/12/gucci-memes-instagram/.

Drew, Kimberly. "The Artist as Network." *Kaleidoscope Magazine*, no. 33 (Fall/Winter 2018/2019): 150.

Duggan, Ginger Gregg. "The Greatest Show on Earth: A Look at Contemporary Fashion Shows and Their Relationship with Performance Art." *Fashion Theory* 5, no. 3 (2001): 243–270.

Dumitrescu, Alexandra E. "Towards a Metamodern Literature." Doctoral thesis, University of Otago, 2014.

Dumitrescu, Alexandra E. "What Is Metamodernism and Why Bother? Meditations on Metamodernism as a Period Term and as a Mode." *Electronic Book Review*, 4 December 2016. https://electronicbookreview.com/essay/what-is-metamodernism

-and-why-bother-meditations-on-metamodernism-as-a-period-term-and-as-a
-mode/.

Duncan, Fiona. "User Experience: Eckhaus Latta's Los Angeles Store." *SSENSE*,
5 December 2017. https://www.ssense.com/en-us/editorial/fashion/user-experience
-eckhaus-lattas-los-angeles-store.

Eckhardt, Stephanie. "Eckhaus LAtta Tackles Actual Reality TV in New Video." *W
Magazine*, 25 April 2017. https://www.wmagazine.com/story/eckhaus-latta-new
-video-reality-tv-juliana-huxtable/.

Eckhardt, Stephanie. "How Models Ended up Having Actual Sex in Eckhaus Latta's
Spring 2017 Campaign." *W Magazine*, 30 March 2017. https://www.wmagazine.com
/story/eckhaus-latta-spring-2017-campaign-heji-shin-models-actual-sex.

Edelkoort, Lidewij. *Anti_Fashion: A Manifesto for the Next Decade*. New York: Trend
Union, 2015.

Edquist, Harriet, and Laurene Vaughan. *Design Collective: An Approach to Practice*.
Newcastle upon Tyne: Cambridge Scholars, 2012.

Eicher, Joanne B., and Brent Luvaas. *The Anthropology of Dress and Fashion: A Reader*.
London: Bloomsbury, 2019.

Encyclopaedia Britannica Online. S.v. "Leonardo da Vinci." https://www.britannica.com
/biography/Leonardo-da-Vinci/Anatomical-studies-and-drawings (accessed 26
August 2020).

Entwistle, Joanne. *The Aesthetic Economy of Fashion: Markets and Values in Clothing
and Modelling*. Oxford: Berg, 2009.

Entwistle, Joanne. "Fashion and the Fleshy Body: Dress as Embodied Practice." *Fashion
Theory* 4, no. 3 (2000): 323–347.

Entwistle, Joanne. *The Fashioned Body*. London: Sage, 2000.

Entwistle, Joanne, and Agnes Rocamora. "The Field of Fashion Materialized: A Study
of London Fashion Week." *Sociology* 40, no. 4 (2006): 735–751.

Entwistle, Joanne, and Elizabeth Wilson. *Body Dressing*. Oxford: Berg, 2001.

Eror, Aleks. "Why Demna Gvasalia Is the First Designer to Really Understand Internet
Culture." *Highsnobiety*, 1 August 2017. https://www.highsnobiety.com/2017/07/31
/demna-gvasalia-vetements-irony/.

Essop, Anas. "Iris van Herpen 3D Printed 'Face Jewellery' Expresses Hybridity at Paris
Fashion Week 2019." *3D Printing Industry*, 28 January 2019. https://3dprinting
industry.com/news/iris-van-herpen-3d-printed-face-jewellery-expresses-hybridity-at
-paris-fashion-week-2019-147926/.

Evans, Caroline. "The Enchanted Spectacle." *Fashion Theory* 5, no. 3 (2001): 271–310.

Evans, Caroline. *Fashion at the Edge: Spectacle, Modernity and Deathliness*. New Haven,
CT: Yale University Press, 2003.

Evans, Caroline. "John Galliano: Modernity and Spectacle." Showstudio, March 2002.
http://showstudio.com/project/past_present_couture/essay.

Evans, Caroline. *The Mechanical Smile: Modernism and the First Fashion Shows in
France and America 1900–1929*. New Haven, CT: Yale University Press, 2013.

Evans, Caroline "The Ontology of the Fashion Model." *AA Files* 63 (2011): 56–59.

Evans, Caroline. "Posthumanism in Fashion." Showstudio, 18 June 2018. https://www
.showstudio.com/projects/queer/essay_posthumanism_in_fashion.

Evans, Caroline, Suzy Menkes, and Bradley Quinn. *Hussein Chalayan*. Groninger: NAi
Publishers, 2005.

Fairs, Marcus. "Li Edelkoort Introduces Hybrid Design to Parsons 'to Loosen Things
Up.'" *Dezeen*, 6 July 2015. https://www.dezeen.com/2015/07/06/li-edelkoort-new
-hybrid-design-studies-department-parsons-school-design-new-york/.

Fairs, Marcus. "Products and Buildings Are the Same Says Heatherwick, as Designers Turn to Architecture." *Dezeen*, 1 July 2015. https://www.dezeen.com/2015/07/01 /products-and-buildings-the-same-thomas-heatherwick-designers-turn-to -architecture/.

Fedorova, Anastasiia. "Making Movies with Eckhaus Latta and Alexa Karolinski." *i-D*, 8 February 2017. https://i-d.vice.com/en_uk/article/d3pzkq/making-movies-with -eckhaus-latta-and-alexa-karolinski.

Fernandez, Chantal. "Eckhaus Latta, beyond the Fringe." *Business of Fashion*, 9 February 2018. https://www.businessoffashion.com/articles/news-analysis/eckhaus-latta -beyond-the-fringe.

Fernandez, Chantal. "Peak Collaboration? Not for Virgil Abloh." *Business of Fashion*, 14 January 2019. https://www.businessoffashion.com/articles/news-analysis/peak -collaboration-not-for-virgil-abloh.

Fernandez, Chantal. "Turning Physical Stores into Living Advertorial." *Business of Fashion*, 21 December 2017. https://www.businessoffashion.com/articles/profes sional/turning-physical-stores-into-living-advertorials.

Fisher, Fiona, Trevor Keeble, Patricia Lara-Betancourt, and Brenda Martin. *Performance, Fashion and the Modern Interior: From the Victorians to Today*. New York: Berg, 2011.

Flood, Alison. "'Post-Truth' Named Word of the Year by Oxford Dictionaries." *The Guardian*, 15 November 2016. https://www.theguardian.com/books/2016/nov/15 /post-truth-named-word-of-the-year-by-oxford-dictionaries.

Foster, Peter, Roger Gomm, and Martyn Hammersley. *Case Study Method: Key Issues, Key Texts*. London: Sage Publications, 2000.

Frankel, Susannah. "Art of the Unwearable: Can Fashion Designer Hussein Chalayan Conquer the Art World?" *The Independent*, September 2010. http://www.indepen dent.co.uk/life-style/fashion/features/art-of-the-unwearable-can-fashion-designer -hussein-chalayan-conquer-the-art-world-2067712.html.

Frankel, Susannah. *Visionaries: Interviews with Fashion Designers*. London: V&A Publications, 2001.

Fried, Michael. *Art and Objecthood*. Chicago: University of Chicago Press, 1998.

Friedman, Vanessa. "Fashion Week, Reinvented." *New York Times*, 9 September 2015. http://www.nytimes.com/2015/09/10/fashion/fashion-week-spring-2016-reinvented .html?_r=0.

Friedman, Vanessa. "How Smartphones Are Killing Off the Fashion Show." *New York Times*, 11 February 2016. https://www.nytimes.com/2016/02/11/fashion/new-york -fashion-week-smartphones-killing-off-runway-show.html.

Friedman, Vanessa. "Libraries, Gardens, Museums. Oh, and a Clothing Store." *New York Times*, 19 November 2018. https://www.nytimes.com/2018/11/19/fashion /shopping-malls-asia.html.

Friedman, Vanessa. "Virginia Woolf Is Trending." *New York Times*, 22 January 2020. https://www.nytimes.com/2020/01/22/style/givenchy-margiela-armani-couture -paris.html.

Fukuyama, Francis. "The End of History?" *The National Interest* 16 (Summer 1989): 3–18.

Fury, Alexander. "Death Becomes Her: Gucci, and Fashion's Immortality Immorality." *Another*, 31 May 2018. http://www.anothermag.com/fashion-beauty/10897/death -becomes-her-gucci-and-fashions-immortality-immorality.

Gammel, Irene. *Baroness Elsa: Gender, Dada, and Everyday Modernity; A Cultural Biography*. Cambridge, MA: MIT Press, 2002.

Geczy, Adam. *The Artificial Body in Fashion and Art*. London: Bloomsbury, 2017.

Geczy, Adam. *What Is Installation? An Anthology of Writings on Australian Installation Art*. Sydney: Power Publications, 2006.

Geczy, Adam, and Vicki Karaminas. *Critical Fashion Practice: From Westwood to Beirendonck*. London: Bloomsbury, 2017.

Geczy, Adam, and Vicki Karaminas, eds. *The End of Fashion: Clothing and Dress in the Age of Globalization*. London: Bloomsbury, 2019.

Geczy, Adam, and Vicki Karaminas, eds. *Fashion and Art*. London: Bloomsbury, 2012.

Geczy, Adam, and Vicki Karaminas. *Fashion Installation: Body, Space and Performance*. London: Bloomsbury, 2019.

Geczy, Adam, and Vicki Karaminas. *Fashion's Double: Representations of Fashion in Painting, Photography and Film*. London: Bloomsbury Academic, 2016.

Geczy, Adam, and Vicki Karaminas. "Lady Gaga: *American Horror Story*, Montrosity and the Grotesque." *Fashion Theory* 21, no. 6 (2017): 709–731.

Geczy, Adam, and Vicki Karaminas. "Time, Cruelty and Destruction in Deconstructivist Fashion: Kawakubo, Margiela and Vetements." *Zone Moda Journal* 10, no. 1 (2020): 65–77.

Geczy, Adam, and Vicki Karaminas. "What Is Critical Fashion." Unpublished, 2019.

Gibson, Eleanor. "Commes des Garçons Is 'Nothing about Clothes.'" *Dezeen*, 9 May 2019. https://www.dezeen.com/2019/05/09/rei-kawakubo-comme-des-garcons-interview/?li_source=LI&li_medium=rhs_block_2.

Gibson, Eleanor. "IKEA Offers First Look at Furniture Designed for Millennials by Virgil Abloh." *Dezeen*, 1 May 2018. https://www.dezeen.com/2018/05/01/ikea-virgil-abloh-furniture-millennial/.

Gibson, Eleanor. "Virgil Abloh and AMO Design Flexible Flagship Off-White Store in Miami that 'Can Host a Runway Show.'" *Dezeen*, 12 August 2020. https://www.dezeen.com/2020/08/12/off-white-miami-design-district-flagship-virgil-abloh-amo/.

Gill, Alison. "Jacques Derrida: Fashion under Erasure." In *Thinking through Fashion: An Introduction*, edited by Agnes Rocamora and Anneke Smelik. London: I. B. Tauris, 2016.

Gilmore, James, and Joseph Pine. *Authenticity: What Consumers Really Want*. Boston: Harvard Business School Press, 2007.

Gindt, Dirk. "Performative Processes: Björk's Creative Collaborations with the World of Fashion." *Fashion Theory* 15, no. 4 (2011): 425–449.

Gleason, Katherine. *Alexander McQueen Evolution*. New York: Race Point, 2012.

Goldberg, Rosa Lee. *Performance Art: From Futurism to the Present*. London: Thames and Hudson, 2011.

Granata, Francesca. *Experimental Fashion: Performance Art, Carnival and the Grotesque Body*. London: I. B. Tauris, 2017.

Granata, Francesca. "Fashion Studies In-Between: A Methodological Case Study and an Inquiry into the State of Fashion Studies." *Fashion Theory* 16. no. 1 (2012): 67–82.

Grau, Donatien. "An Interview with Marina Abramovic." *Another*, 13 December 2010. http://origin.anothermag.com/fashion-beauty/680/marina-abramovic.

Gregg Duggan, Ginger. "The Greatest Show on Earth: A Look at Contemporary Fashion Shows and Their Relationship to Performance Art." *Fashion Theory* 5, no. 3, (2001): 243–270.

Gregotti, Vittorio. *Inside Architecture*. Cambridge, MA: MIT Press, 1996.

Hall, Jake. "Design and Disruption of the Human Body." Showstudio, 19 May 2018. https://www.showstudio.com/projects/queer/essay_design_and_disruption_of_the_human_body.

Hall, Stuart. "Cultural Identity and Diaspora." In *Contemporary Postcolonial Theory: A Reader*, edited by Padmini Mongia, 110–121. London: Arnold, 1996.

Hannah, Dorita, and Olav Harslof. *Performance Design*. Copenhagen: Museum Tusculanum Press, 2008.

Haraway, Donna. "A Cyborg Manifesto: Science, Technology, and Socialist-Feminism in the Late Twentieth Century." In *Simians, Cyborgs and Women: The Reinvention of Nature*, 149–181. New York: Routledge, 1991.

Hawkins, Jennifer Morey. "Textual Analysis." In *The Sage Encyclopedia of Communication Research Methods*, 1755. Los Angeles: Sage Reference, 2017.

Healy, Claire-Marie. "In an Age of Fast Fashion, Molly Goddard Takes It Slow." *Dazed and Confused*, February 2016. http://www.dazeddigital.com/fashion/article/30007/1/in-an-age-of-fast-fashion-molly-goddard-takes-it-slow.

Healy, Robyn. "Immateriality." In *The Handbook of Fashion Studies*, edited by Sandy Black, Amy De La Haye, Joanne Entwistle, Agnès Rocamora, Regina A. Root, and Helen Thomas. London: Bloomsbury, 2013.

Heavener, Paul. "Aitor Throup's Homecoming." *Hypebeast*, 23 April 2020. https://hypebeast.com/2020/4/aitor-throup-streetwear-dsa-interview.

Hewson, Claire, Carl Vogel, and Dianna Laurent. *Internet Research Methods*. Los Angeles: Sage Publications, 2016.

Hine, Samuel. "Meet Kerwin Frost, Your Favourite Influencer's Favourite Influencer." *GQ*, 11 April 2019. https://www.gq.com/story/kerwin-frost-profile-2019.

Hines, Alice. "A Copy of a Copy: Ingenuity in a Swath of Prado Polyester." *Vestoj Journal: On Authenticity*, no. 8 (2017): 47–56.

Hobbs, Mary Anne, and Virgil Abloh. BBC radio interview. https://www.bbc.co.uk/sounds/play/p06tfzb5. Accessed 5 December 2018.

Holgate, Mark. "'Body Beautiful' Will Celebrate Diversity at the National Museum of Scotland in 2019." *Vogue*, 17 November 2018. https://www.vogue.com/article/body-beautiful-2019-national-museum-of-scotland.

Hollander, Anne. *Seeing through Clothes*. New York: Viking, 1978.

Hollander, Anne. *Sex and Suits: The Evolution of Modern Dress*. New York: Knopf, 1994.

Hopkins, Owen. "Dezeen's Guise to Bauhaus Architecture and Design." *Dezeen*, 1 November 2018. https://www.dezeen.com/2018/11/01/bauhaus-100-guide-architecture-design/.

Horsely, Jeffrey. "A Fashion 'Museographie': The Delineation of Innovative Presentation Modes at ModeMuseum Antwerp." *Fashion Theory* 19, no. 1 (2015): 43–66.

Horyn, Cathy. "A Museum Show Where You Can Wear the Art Home: The Whitney's Eckhaus Latta Installation Doubles as a Clothing Store." *The Cut*, 2018. https://www.thecut.com/2018/08/the-whitney-museums-eckhaus-latta-possessed-reviewed.html.

"The House of Iris van Herpen." Iris van Herpen website. http://www.irisvanherpen.com/about.

Howarth, Dan. "Aitor Throup Shows New Object Research Fashion Collection on Life-Size Puppets." *Dezeen*, 13 June 2016. https://www.dezeen.com/2016/06/13/aitor-throup-new-object-research-project-menswear-fashion-collection-london-life-sized-puppets/.

Hsieh, Vanessa. "Aitor Throup Discusses G-Star Raw and the Future of Fashion." *Dazed Digital*, 17 January 2017. http://www.dazeddigital.com/fashion/article/34402/1/aitor-throup-discusses-g-star-raw-and-the-future-of-fashion.

Hsieh, Vanessa. "Eckhaus Latta's New Campaign Features IRL Couples Having Sex." *Dazed Digital*, 30 March 2017. https://www.dazeddigital.com/fashion/article/35344/1/eckhaus-lattas-new-campaign-sees-real-couples-having-sex.

Hunt, James. "Letter from the Editor." *Journal of Design Strategies* 5, no. 1 (2012): 5–10.

Hustvedt, Siri. "A Woman in the Men's Room: When Will the Art World Recognise the Real Artist behind Duchamp's Fountain?" *The Guardian*, 29 March 2019. https://www.theguardian.com/books/2019/mar/29/marcel-duchamp-fountain -women-art-history.

Hutcheon, Linda. *The Politics of Postmodernism*. London: Routledge, 2003.

Hyland, Veronique. "Designers Misread the Mood at New York Fashion Week." *New York*, 17 February 2017. http://nymag.com/thecut/2017/02/nyfw-fall-2017-cognitive -dissonance.html?mid=facebook_thecutblog.

Hyman, Dan. "Virgil Abloh Has Designs on High Culture." *New York Times*, 23 May 2019. https://www.nytimes.com/2019/05/23/arts/design/virgil-abloh.html?search ResultPosition=2.

Inns, Tom. *Designing for the 21st Century: Interdisciplinary Questions and Insights*. Aldershot, UK: Gower, 2010.

Jameson, Fredric. *Archaeologies of the Future: The Desire Called Utopia and Other Science Fictions*. London: Verso, 2007.

Jameson, Fredric. *The Cultural Turn: Selected Writings on the Postmodern, 1983–1998*. London: Verso, 1998.

Jameson, Fredric. *Postmodernism or, the Cultural Logic of Late Capitalism*. London: Verso, 1991.

Jenkins, Henry. *Convergence Culture: Where Old and New Media Collide*. New York: New York University Press, 2006.

Jenss, Heike. *Fashion Studies: Research Methods, Sites, and Practices*. London: Bloomsbury Academic, 2016.

Jiang, Edwin. "Virtual Reality: Growth Engine for Fashion?" *Business of Fashion*, 28 February 2017. https://www.businessoffashion.com/articles/fashion-tech/virtual -reality-growth-engine-for-fashion?trk_component=PinnedArticles&trk_placement =MainColumn&trk_design=2ColumnWithLargeCards&trk_page=HomePage&trk _source=Pinned.

Johnson, Grant. "Citing the Sun: Marc Jacobs, Olafur Eliasson, and the Fashion Show." *Fashion Theory*, 19, no. 3 (2015): 315–330.

Joselit, David. *After Art*. Princeton, NJ: Princeton University Press, 2013.

Joy, Annamma, John F. Sherry Jr., Alladi Venkatesh, Jeff Wang, and Ricky Chan. "Fast Fashion, Sustainability, and the Ethical Appeal of Luxury Brands." *Fashion Theory* 16, no. 3 (2012): 273–295.

Kaiser, Susan B., Richard H. Nagasawa, and Sandra S. Hutton. "Fashion, Postmodernity and Personal Appearance: A Symbolic Interactionist Formulation." *Symbolic Interaction* 14, no. 2 (1991): 165–185.

Kansara, Vikram Alexei. "Iris van Herpen's Science Fiction." *Business of Fashion*, 6 July 2015. https://www.businessoffashion.com/articles/long-view/iris-van-herpens-tech nology-science-fashion.

Kansara, Vikram Alexei. "Virgil Abloh: 'I Am Not a Designer.'" *Business of Fashion*, 12 September 2018. https://www.businessoffashion.com/articles/professional/virgil -abloh-i-am-not-a-designer.

Karaminas, Vicki. "Image: Fashionscapes—Notes towards an Understanding of Media Technologies and Their Impact on Contemporary Fashion Imagery." In *Fashion and Art*, edited by Adam Geczy and Vicki Karaminas. London: Bloomsbury, 2012.

Kawamura, Yuniya. *Doing Research in Fashion and Dress: An Introduction to Qualitative Methods*. Oxford: Berg, 2011.

Kawamura, Yuniya. *Fashion-ology: An Introduction to Fashion Studies*. London: Bloomsbury, 2018.

Kawamura, Yuniya. *Sneakers: Fashion, Gender, and Subculture*. London: Bloomsbury, 2016.

Keiles, Jamie Lauren. "Barbara Kruger's Supreme Performance." *New Yorker*, November 2017. https://www.newyorker.com/culture/culture-desk/barbara-krugers-supreme-performance.

Kellner, Douglas. "Media Culture and the Triumph of the Spectacle." In *The Spectacle of the Real: From Hollywood to "Reality" TV and Beyond*, edited by Geoff King. Bristol, UK: Intellect, 2005.

Kellner, Douglas. *The Spectacle of the Real: From Hollywood to "Reality" TV and Beyond*. Bristol, UK: Intellect, 2005.

Keltner De Valle, Jane. "Inside the World of Virgil Abloh, Kanye West's Creative Director." *Architectural Digest*, February 2017. https://www.architecturaldigest.com/story/inside-the-world-of-virgil-abloh-kanye-wests-creative-director.

Khan, Natalie. "Catwalk Politics." In *Fashion Cultures: Theories, Explanations and Analysis*, edited by Stella Bruzzi and Pamela Church Gibson. New York: Routledge, 2000.

Khan, Natalie. "Cutting the Fashion Body: Why the Fashion Image Is No Longer Still." *Fashion Theory* 16, no. 2 (2012): 235–249.

Khan, Natalie. "Fashion as Mythology." In *Fashion Cultures: Theories, Explanations and Analysis Revisited*, edited by Stella Bruzzi and Pamela Church Gibson. New York: Routledge, 2013.

Kirby, Alan. *Digimodernism: How New Technologies Dismantle the Postmodern and Reconfigure Our Culture*. New York: Continuum, 2009.

Knudsen, Stephen. "Beyond Postmodernism: Putting a Face on Metamodernism without the Easy Clichés." *Artpulse Magazine*. http://artpulsemagazine.com/beyond-postmodernism-putting-a-face-on-metamodernism-without-the-easy-cliches (accessed 13 August 2019).

Koek, Arianne. "Retrospective: Iris Van Herpen." *System Magazine* 10 (2017): 286–299.

Koike, Kazuko, ed. *Issey Miyake: East Meets West*. Tokyo: Heibonsha, 1978.

Krauss, Rosalind. "Notes on the Index: Seventies Art in America." *October* 3 (Spring 1977): 68–81.

Krauss, Rosalind. "Sculpture in the Expanded Field." *October* 8 (Spring 1979): 30–44.

Kristeva, Julia. "Word, Dialogue, and Novel." In *Desire in Language: A Semiotic Approach to Literature and Art*, edited by Leon S. Roudiez, translated by Thomas Gora, Alice Jardine, and Leon S. Roudiez, 64–91. New York: Columbia University Press, 1977.

Kristiansen, Erik, and Olav Harslof. *Engaging Spaces: Sites of Performance, Interaction and Reflection*. Copenhagen: Museum Tusculanum Press, 2015.

Leach, Alec. "Eckhaus Latta Are Embracing Their Outsider Status." *Indie Magazine*, 10 September 2019. https://indie-mag.com/2019/09/eckhaus-latta/.

Leavy, Patricia, and Sharlene Nagy Hesse-Biber. *Handbook of Emergent Methods*. New York: Guilford Press, 2008.

Leerberg, Malene. "Design in the Expanded Field: Rethinking Contemporary Design." *Nordes*, no. 3 (June 2009). http://www.nordes.org/opj/index.php/n13/article/view/52.

Leswing, Kif. "A New Version of Steve Jobs' Iconic Black Turtleneck Costs $270." *Business Insider*, 28 June 2017. https://www.businessinsider.com.au/steve-jobs-iconic-black-turtleneck-by-issey-miyake-costs-270-2017-6.

Lévi-Strauss, Claude. *The Savage Mind.* Chicago: University of Chicago Press, 1966.

Li, Charmaine. "Iris Van Herpen: The Unknownness of Everything." *Mono Kultur,* Summer 2019.

Linde, Matthew. "Fashion Is Not a Revelation: An Appeal for Critical Curation." *Flash Art,* 16 June 2017. http://www.flashartonline.com/2017/06/fashion-is-not-a-revelation-an-appeal-for-critical-curation/.

Linde, Matthew. "The New Spirit of New York Fashion Week." *Flash Art,* 29 September 2017. https://flash---art.com/2017/09/the-new-spirit-of-new-york-fashion-week/.

Linds, Warren. "METAXIS Metaxis: Dancing (in) the In-Between." In *Dialogues of Theatre and Cultural Politics,* edited by Jan Cohen-Cruz and Mady Schutzman. London: Routledge, 2006.

Lipovetsky, Gilles. *The Empire of Fashion: Dressing Modern Democracy.* Translated by Catherine Porter. Princeton, NJ: Princeton University Press, 2004.

Lipovetsky, Gilles. *Hypermodern Times: Themes for the 21st Century.* New York: Wiley, 2005.

Lowenthal, Mark. Translator's introduction to Francis Picabia, *I Am a Beautiful Monster: Poetry, Prose, and Provocation,* 1–25. Cambridge, MA: MIT Press, 2007.

Luvaas, Brent. *DIY Style: Fashion, Music and Global Digital Cultures.* London: Bloomsbury, 2012.

Lynge-Jorlén, Ane. *Niche Fashion Magazines: Changing the Face of Fashion.* London: I. B. Tauris, 2017.

Lyotard, Jean-François. *The Postmodern Condition: A Report on Knowledge.* Minneapolis: University of Minnesota Press, 1984.

Mackrell, Alice. *Art and Fashion: The Impact of Art on Fashion and Fashion on Art.* London: Batsford, 2005.

Mackrell, Judith. "The Dancer Wears Prada: How Couture Went from Catwalk to Ballet and Beyond." *The Guardian,* 16 January 2018. https://www.theguardian.com/stage/2018/jan/16/dancer-prada-couture-catwalk-ballet-alexander-mcqueen?CMP=share_btn_link.

Madsen, Anders Christian. "Brave New World: Rick Owens and the New Era of His Brand." *i-D,* 19 October 2016. https://i-d.vice.com/en_gb/article/brave-new-world-rick-owens-and-the-new-era-of-his-brand.

Madsen, Susanne. "Virgil Abloh on Getting Political with Jenny Holzer." *Dazed Digital,* June 2017. http://www.dazeddigital.com/fashion/article/36381/1/virgil-abloh-on-getting-political-with-jenny-holzer-pitti-ss18-off-white.

"Manus × Machina: Fashion in an Age of Technology." Metropolitan Museum of Art, Exhibition Galleries, 2016. https://www.metmuseum.org/exhibitions/listings/2016/manus-x-machina/exhibition-galleries.

Martin, Richard. "A Note: Art & Fashion, Viktor & Rolf." *Fashion Theory* 3, no. 1 (1999): 109–120.

Mayo Davies, Dean. "Ain't Nobody Fucking with Rick Owen's Clique." *Dazed Digital,* February 2014. http://www.dazeddigital.com/fashion/article/17371/1/ain-t-nobody-fucking-with-rick-owens-clique.

McLuhan, Marshall. *The Gutenberg Galaxy: The Making of Typographic Man.* Toronto: University of Toronto Press, 1962.

McLuhan, Marshall. *Understanding Media: The Extensions of Man.* Cambridge, MA: MIT Press, 1994.

McNeil, Peter. "Georg Simmel: The Philosophical Monet." In *Thinking through Fashion,* edited by Agnes Rocamora and Anneke Smelik. London: I. B Tauris.

McNeil, Peter. "'We're Not in the Fashion Business': Fashion in the Museum and the Academy." *Fashion Theory* 12, no. 1 (2008): 65–81.

Mead, Rebecca. "Iris van Herpen's Hi-Tech Couture." *New Yorker*, 25 September 2017. https://www.newyorker.com/magazine/2017/09/25/iris-van-herpens-hi-tech -couture.

Mediated Matter. "Overview." MIT Media Lab, 5 March 2019. https://www.media.mit .edu/groups/mediated-matter/overview/.

Mellery-Pratt, Robin. "Hope Trumps Fear at the London Men's Shows." *Business of Fashion*, 10 January 2017. https://www.businessoffashion.com/articles/fashion-show -review/hope-trumps-fear-at-the-london-mens-shows.

Mendoza, Hannah Rose. "3D Printed Dress from Iris van Herpen Pushes Boundaries of Fashion." *3D Print*, 30 January 2018. https://3dprint.com/201774/3d-printed-dress -iris-van-herpen/.

Menendez, Enrique. "Virgil and Kanye's Rise to Fashion Supremacy." *Hypebeast*, 28 August 2017. https://hypebeast.com/2017/8/virgil-abloh-kanye-west-designer-vs -creator.

Menkes, Suzy. "Museum Integrity versus Designer Flash." *International Herald Tribune*, 25 February 2007.

Millar, Sandra. "Fashion as Art; Is Fashion Art?" *Fashion Theory* 11, no. 1 (2007): 25–40.

Millet, Yves. "Atopia and Aesthetics: A Modal Perspective." *Contemporary Aesthetics* 11 (2013): 1–12.

Moor, Elizabeth. "Branded Spaces: The Scope of 'New Marketing.'" *Journal of Consumer Culture* 3, no. 1 (2003): 39–60.

Morby, Alice. "Aitor Throup Designs 'Clothes not Costumes' for Wayne McGregor's Latest Production." *Dezeen*, 6 October 2017. https://www.dezeen.com/2017/10/06 /aitor-throup-designs-clothes-not-costumes-wayne-mcgregor-ballet-autobiography/.

Morency, Christopher. "Top Ten Influential Retailers off Fashion's Beaten Path." *Business of Fashion*, 26 June 2017. https://www.businessoffashion.com/articles /intelligence/10-influential-luxury-retailers-off-of-fashions-beaten-path.

Morency, Christopher. "The Unlikely Success of Virgil Abloh." *Business of Fashion*, 29 September 2016. https://www.businessoffashion.com/articles/intelligence/the -unlikely-success-of-virgil-abloh-off-white.

Morgado, Marcia A. "Coming to Terms with *Postmodern*: Theories and Concepts of Contemporary Culture and Their Implications for Apparel Scholars." *Clothing and Textiles Research Journal* 14, no. 1 (1996): 41–53.

Morgado, Marcia A. "Fashion Phenomena and the Post-postmodern Condition." *Fashion, Style & Popular Culture* 1, no. 3 (2014): 313–339.

Morris, Catherine, and Dara Meyers-Kingsley. "Off the Wall: The Development of Roberts Kushner's Fashion and Performance Art, 1970–1976." *Fashion Theory* 5, no. 3 (2001): 311–330.

Moss, Hilary. "Eckhaus Latta's Latest Photo Shoot Breaks the Fourth Wall." *New York Times*, 1 February 2016. https://www.nytimes.com/2016/02/01/t-magazine/fashion /eckhaus-latta-smile-hammer-museum.html?_r=0.

Mower, Sarah. "Alexander McQueen FW 2006 Runway Review." *Vogue*, 3 March 2006. https://www.vogue.com/fashion-shows/fall-2006-ready-to-wear/alexander-mcqueen.

Müller, Florence. *Art and Fashion*. London: Thames and Hudson, 2000.

Muschamp, Herbert. "Easy to Pack. Harder to Understand." *New York Times*, 27 December 1998.

Newall-Hanson, Alice. "The Graduates." *T Magazine*, 13 April 2020. https://www .nytimes.com/interactive/2020/04/13/t-magazine/royal-academy-antwerp.html.

Noble, Richard. *Utopias: Documents of Contemporary Art*. Cambridge, MA: MIT Press, 2009.

Nollert, Angelika. *Performative Installation*. Cologne: Snoeck, 2003.

Obrist, Hans Ulrich. "Rei Kawakubo's Quiet Revolution Just Got Louder." *System Magazine* 2 (2013). http://system-magazine.com/issue2/rei-kawakubo/.

O'Neill, Alistair. "Exhibition Review: Malign Muses: When Fashion Turns Back and Spectres: When Fashion Turns Back." *Fashion Theory* 12, no. 2 (2008): 253–260.

Papalas, Marylaura. "Avant-garde Cuts: Schiaparelli and the Construction of a Surrealist Femininity." *Fashion Theory* 20, no. 5 (2016): 503–522.

Payne, Alice. "Fashion Futuring in the Anthropocene: Sustainable Fashion as 'Taming' and 'Rewilding.'" *Fashion Theory* 23, no. 1 (2019): 5–23.

Pecorari, Marco. "Zones-in-Between: The Creation of New Fashion Praxis." *Art Monthly*, no. 242 (August 2011): 67–70.

Pederson, Julianne. "Meta-Modernism in Fashion and Style Practice: Authorship and the Consumer." In *From Production to Consumption: The Cultural Industry of Fashion*, edited by Marco Pedroni, 59–75. Oxford: Inter-Disciplinary Press, 2013.

Pedroni, Marco, ed. *From Production to Consumption: The Cultural Industry of Fashion*. Oxford: Inter-Disciplinary Press, 2013.

Perry, Gill, and Paul Wood. *Themes in Contemporary Art*. New Haven, CT: Yale University Press, 2004.

Petty, Felix. "How Virgil Abloh's Louis Vuitton Changed Everything about Fashion." *i-D*, 27 June 2018. https://i-d.vice.com/en_uk/article/zm8dxe/virgil-abloh-louis -vuitton-changed-everything-fashion?utm_source=stylizedembed_i-d.vice.com& utm_campaign=kzxpzv&site=i-d.

Phelps, Nicole. "Iris van Herpen: Fall 2019 Couture Review." *Vogue Runway*, 2 July 2019. https://www.vogue.com/fashion-shows/fall-2019-couture/iris-van-herpen.

Phillips, Kaitlin. "The Enigma of Bernadette Corporation, the Anonymous 90s Art and Fashion Collective." 4 January 2019. https://www.ssense.com/en-us/editorial/art /the-enigma-of-bernadette-corporation-the-anonymous-90s-art-and-fashion -collective.

Pine, B. Joseph, II, and James H. Gilmore. *The Experience Economy*. Boston: Harvard Business Review Press, 2011.

Pine, B. Joseph, II, and James H. Gilmore. "Stage Experiences or Go Extinct." *Business of Fashion*, 13 July 2016. https://www.businessoffashion.com/community/voices /discussions/what-will-the-store-of-the-future-look-like/op-ed-stage-experiences-or -go-extinct.

Plato. *Symposium*. c. 385–370 B.C.

Poletti, Federico. *The Fashion Set: The Art of the Fashion Show*. Dublin: Roads Publishing, 2016.

Polhemus, Ted. "Fashion-v-Anti-Fashion." In *The Anthropology of Dress and Fashion*, edited by Brent Luvaas and Joanne B. Eicher, 38–42. London: Bloomsbury, 2019.

Polhemus, Ted. *Street Style: From Sidewalk to Catwalk*. London: Thames and Hudson, 1994.

Porter, Charlie. "How to Build a Hype Brand." *Financial Times*, April 2018. https:// www.ft.com/content/b87a174c-30e0-11e8-b5bf-23cb17fd1498.

Potvin, Jon. *The Places and Spaces of Fashion*. New York: Routledge, 2008.

Pous, Terri. "The Democratization of Fashion: A Brief History." *Time*, 6 February 2013. http://style.time.com/2013/02/06/the-democratization-of-fashion-a-brief-history/.

Radford, Robert. "Dangerous Liaisons: Art, Fashion, and Individualism." *Fashion Theory* 2, no. 2 (1998): 151–163.

Radner, Hilary. "The Ghost of Cultures Past: Fashion, Hollywood and the End of Everything." *Film, Fashion & Consumption* 3, no. 2 (2014): 83–91.

Raiss, Liz. "Master Class: Issey Miyake." *Heroine Magazine*, 31 October 2017. https://www.heroine.com/the-editorial/master-class-issey-miyake.

Rakestraw, Alex. "How Camper Went from Mall Brand to Gosha Rubchinskiy Collaborator." *Highsnobiety*, 30 May 2018. https://www.highsnobiety.com/p/camper-interview-gosha-rubchinskiy/.

Ran, Faye. *A History of Installation Art and the Development of New Art Forms*. New York: Peter Lang, 2009.

Rauch, Malte Fabien. "Camouflaged with a Visual Language," *Diaphanes Magazine*, 23 August 2019. https://www.diaphanes.com/titel/where-the-negative-holds-court-6064.

Rawsthorn, Alice. "Power Move." *Wallpaper*, 5 May 2019. https://www.wallpaper.com/design/virgil-abloh-furniture-venice-biennale-2019.

Rebentisch, Juliane. *Aesthetics of Installation Art*. Berlin: Sternberg Press, 2012.

Rees-Roberts, Nick. *Fashion Film: Art and Advertising in the Digital Age*. London: Bloomsbury, 2019.

Rees-Roberts, Nick. "Raf Simons and Interdisciplinary Fashion: From Post-Punk to Neo-Modern." *Fashion Theory* 19, no. 1 (2015): 9–42.

Ribeiro, Aileen. "Utopian Dress." In *Chic Thrills: A Fashion Reader*, edited by Juliet Ash and Elizabeth Wilson, 225–238. London: Pandora, 1992.

Riegels Melchoir, Marie, and Birgitta Svensson. *Fashion and Museums: Theory and Practice*. London: Bloomsbury Academic, 2014.

Roberts, David. *The Total Work of Art in European Modernism*. Ithaca, NY: Cornell University Press, 2011.

Rocamora, Agnès. "High Fashion and Pop Fashion: The Symbolic Production of Fashion in *Le Monde* and *The Guardian*." *Fashion Theory* 5, no. 2 (2001): 123–142.

Rocamora, Agnès. "Mediatization and Digital Media in the Field of Fashion." *Fashion Theory* 21, no. 5 (2017): 505–522.

Rocamora, Agnes. "Pierre Bourdieu: The Field of Fashion." In *Thinking through Fashion: A Guide to Key Theorists*, edited by Agnès Rocamora and Anneke Smelik. London: I. B. Tauris, 2016.

Rocamora, Agnès, and Anneke Smelik, eds. *Thinking through Fashion: A Guide to Key Theorists*. London: I. B. Tauris, 2016.

Rosenthal, Mark. *Understanding Installation Art: From Duchamp to Holzer*. New York: Prestal, 2003.

Roux, Caroline. "Elizabeth Peyton: The Exceptional Portrait." *The Gentlewoman*, Autumn–Winter 2013. https://thegentlewoman.co.uk/library/elizabeth-peyton.

Rudrum, David, and Nicholas Stavris. *Supplanting the Postmodern: An Anthology of Writings on the Arts and Culture of the Early 21st Century*. London: Bloomsbury, 2015.

Rush, Michael. "A Note: Performance Art Lives." *Fashion Theory* 5, no. 3 (2001): 331–341.

Ryan, Nicky. "Prada and the Art of Patronage." *Fashion Theory* 10, no. 3 (2007): 1–18.

Safire, William. "What's the Meta?" *New York Times*, 25 December 2005. https://www.nytimes.com/2005/12/25/magazine/whats-the-meta.html.

Sargent, Antwaun, and Lou Stoppard. "How Fashion Tripped over the Hip-Hop Economy." *Financial Times*, 28 February 2019. https://www.ft.com/content/8ecf1b40-3760-11e9-9988-28303f70fcff.

Satran, Rory. "Eckhaus Latta's Brilliant Parody of a September Issue Revels in Magazine Culture." *i-D*, 31 October 2017. https://i-d.vice.com/en_us/article/wxenq9/meet-the-latest-generation-of-new-york-creatives.

Schechner, Richard. *Performance Studies: An Introduction*. New York: Routledge, 2019.

Shackleton, Holly. "Step inside Rick Owens' World." *i-D*, 15 September 2008. http://i-d
.vice.com/en_gb/read/interviews/4661/rick-owens-world.

Shinkle, Eugenie. "The Feminine Awkward: Graceless Bodies and the Performance of
Femininity in Fashion Photographs." *Fashion Theory* 21, no. 2 (2017): 201–217.

Showstudio. "About." https://showstudio.com/about (accessed 14 June 2019).

Showstudio. "Splash!" http://showstudio.com/project/splash (accessed 14 June 2019).

Shumate, Michal Lynn. "Fashion in the Expanded Field." *Dress: The Journal of the
Costume Society of America* 40, no. 1 (2014): 67–78.

Simmel, Georg. "Fashion." *International Quarterly* 10, no. 1 (October 1904): 130–155.

Simon, Marie. *Fashion in Art: The Second Empire and Impressionism*. London: Zwem-
mer, 1995.

Simonini, Ross. "Eckhaus Latta." *Art in America* 37 (April 2016).

Singer, Olivia. "Eckhaus Latta and the Fertility of Artifice." *Another Magazine*, 15
February 2016. http://www.anothermag.com/fashion-beauty/8374/eckhaus-latta
-and-the-fertility-of-artifice.

Skidmore, Maisie. "Aitor Throup—The Anomalous Designer." *It's Nice That*, 5
June 2015. http://www.itsnicethat.com/features/aitor-throup-the-anomalous
-designer-we-meet-aitor-thoup-in-his-studio-to-discuss-his-unusual-practice.

Smelik, Anneke. *Delft Blue to Denim Blue: Contemporary Dutch Fashion*. London:
I. B. Tauris, 2017.

Smelik, Anneke. "New Materialism: A Framework for Fashion in the Age of Technological Innovation." *International Journal of Fashion Studies* 5, no. 1 (2018): 33–54.

Smelik, Anneke. "The Performance of Authenticity." *Address: Journal for Fashion
Writing and Criticism* 1, no. 1 (2011): 76–82.

Snowden, Heather. "From Firsts to Fenty: A Timeline of Rihanna's Fashion Career."
Highsnobiety, 25 June 2019. https://www.highsnobiety.com/p/rihanna-fashion
-timeline/.

Solway, Diane. "The Story behind Virgil Abloh and Jenny Holzer's Potent, Political
Off-White Show at Pitti Uomo." *W Magazine*, June 2017. https://www.wmagazine
.com/story/virgil-abloh-jenny-holzer-off-white-spring-2018-mens-pitti-uomo.

Solway, Diane. "Virgil Abloh and His Army of Disruptors." *W Magazine*, 20 April 2017.
https://www.wmagazine.com/story/virgil-abloh-off-white-kanye-west-raf-simons.

Southan, Abigail. "Eckhaus Latta Is Reinventing New York Fashion." *The Last Magazine*, 4 April 2018. https://thelast-magazine.com/eckhaus-latta-fashion-designer
-interview/.

Spindler, Amy M. "Fashion as Art. Or Maybe Not." *New York Times*, 15 September
1996. http://www.nytimes.com/1996/09/15/arts/fashion-as-art-or-maybe-not
.html.

Stake, Richard E. *Multiple Case Study Analysis*. New York: Guilford Press, 2006.

Stansfield, Ted. "Hari Nef Stars in Camper × Eckhaus Latta's Campaign." *Dazed
Digital*, 9 November 2016. https://www.dazeddigital.com/fashion/article/33648/1
/hari-nef-stars-in-eckhaus-lattas-new-campaign-film.

Stansfield, Ted. "When Hussein Chalayan Turned Furnishings in to Fashion." *Another
Magazine*, 26 January 2016. http://www.anothermag.com/fashion-beauty/8248
/when-hussein-chalayan-turned-furnishings-into-fashion.

Steele, Valerie. "Fashion." In *Fashion and Art*, edited by Adam Geczy and Vicki
Karaminas, 1–28. London: Bloomsbury, 2012.

Steele, Valerie. "A Museum of Fashion Is More than a Clothes-Bag." *Fashion Theory* 2,
no. 4 (1998): 327–335.

Steele, Valerie. "Museum Quality: The Rise of the Fashion Exhibition." *Fashion Theory* 12, no. 1 (2008): 7–30.

Steele, Valerie. *A Queer History of Fashion: From the Closet to the Catwalk*. New York: FIT, 2013.

Steele, Valerie. *Women of Fashion: Twentieth Century Designers*. New York: Rizzoli International, 1991.

Stephens, Doug. "Why Retail Is Getting 'Experience' Wrong." *Business of Fashion*, 1 March 2017. https://www.businessoffashion.com/articles/opinion/op-ed-why-retail -is-getting-experience-wrong.

Stern, Radu. *Against Fashion: Clothing as Art, 1850–1930*. Cambridge MA: MIT Press, 2004.

Stevensen, N. J. "The Fashion Retrospective." *Fashion Theory* 12, no. 2 (2008): 219–235.

Stevenson, Caroline. "(I Was There) When It All Went Down." In *Vestoj Journal: On Capital*, edited by Anya Aronowsky Cronberg, 41–48. Naples: Nava Press, 2019.

St Felix, Doreen. "Virgil Abloh, Menswear's Biggest Star." *New Yorker*, 18 March 2019. https://www.newyorker.com/magazine/2019/03/18/virgil-abloh-menswears-biggest -star.

Stierstorfer, Klaus. *Beyond Postmodernism*. Berlin: Walter de Gruyter GmbH, 2003.

Stoppard, Lou. "Fashion as Installation." *ADF Papers*, Fashion Paper no. 4 (January 2014): 2–8.

Stoppard, Lou. "Fashion Is the Messenger." In *Virgil Abloh: Figures of Speech*, edited by Michael Darling. New York: Delmonic/Prestel Books, 2019.

Stoppard, Lou. *Fashion Together: Fashion's Most Extraordinary Duos on the Art of Collaboration*. New York: Rizzoli, 2017.

Szkoda, Ena. "Exhibition Review: *Art/Fashion*. Guggenheim Museum Soho." *Fashion Theory* 1, no. 3 (1997): 321–327.

Taylor, Trey. "Eckhaus Latta Redefined the Erogenous Zone." *Interview Magazine*, 13 September 2017. https://www.interviewmagazine.com/fashion/eckhaus-latta -redefined-erogenous-zone.

Teunissen, José. "Fashion: More than Cloth and Form." In *The Handbook of Fashion Studies*, edited by Sandy Black, Amy De La Haye, Joanne Entwistle, Agnès Rocamora, Regina A. Root, and Helen Thomas. London: Bloomsbury, 2013.

Thaddeus-Johns, Josie. "Eckhaus Latta: There Is No Target Group." *Sleek Magazine*, 20 July 2015. https://www.sleek-mag.com/article/eckhaus-latta-there-is-no-target-group/.

Thorpe, Harriet. "Virgil Abloh's Cheat Codes Courtesy of Harvard Graduate School of Design." *Wallpaper*, 19 June 2018. https://www.wallpaper.com/architecture/virgil -abloh-the-incidents-book-harvard-gsd-sternberg-press.

Throup, Aitor. "Aitor Throup: New Object Research S/S17." *Style Zeitgeist*, 13 June 2016. https://www.sz-mag.com/news/2016/06/aitor-throup-new-object-research-ss17/.

Throup, Aitor. *The Funeral of New Orleans Part One*. http://showstudio.com/project /the_funeral_of_new_orleans_part_one (accessed 3 November 2016).

Throup, Aitor. *New Object Research Manifesto*. London: AT Studio, 2012.

Throup, Aitor. *New Object Research Manifesto*. London: AT Studio, 2016.

Tinti, Mary. *Installation Art*. Oxford: Oxford University Press, 2011.

Torres, Lara. "Fashion in the Expanded Field: Strategies for Critical Fashion Practice." *Journal of Asia-Pacific Pop Culture* 2, no. 2 (2017): 167–183.

Torres, Robin. "Virgil Abloh's Raw Creative Vision." *i-D*, December 2016. https://i-d .vice.com/en_us/article/j5mezb/virgil-ablohs-raw-creative-vision.

Townsend, Chris. *Rapture: Art's Seduction by Fashion since 1970*. London: Thames and Hudson, 2002.

Troy, Nancy. *Couture Culture: A Study in Modern Art and Fashion*. Cambridge, MA: MIT Press, 2003.

Tseëlon, Efrat. "Authenticity." In *Fashion and Art*, edited by Adam Geczy and Vicki Karaminas, 111–122. London: Bloomsbury, 2012.

Tseëlon, Efrat. "Fashion Research and Its Discontents." *Fashion Theory* 5, no. 4 (2001): 435–451.

Tseëlon, Efrat. "Outlining a Fashion Studies Project." In *Critical Studies in Fashion and Beauty Volume One*, edited by Efrat Tseëlon, Ana Marta Gonzalez, and Susan Kaiser, 3–53. Bristol, UK: Intellect, 2010.

Tseëlon, Efrat, Ana Marta Gonzalez, and Susan Kaiser, eds. *Critical Studies in Fashion and Beauty Volume One*. Bristol, UK: Intellect, 2012.

Turney, Jo. *Fashion Crimes: Dressing for Deviance*. London: Bloomsbury, 2019.

Ugelvig, Jeppe. "Notes on Metamodernism—A Critique." *1 Granary*, 30 June 2015. http://1granary.com/central-saint-martins-fashion/metamodernism/.

Uhlirova, Marketa. "100 Years of the Fashion Film: Frameworks and Histories." *Fashion Theory* 17, no. 2 (2015): 137–157.

Van den Akker, Robin, and Timotheus Vermeulen. "Periodising the 2000s, or, the Emergence of Metamodernism." In *Metamodernism: Historicity, Affect, and Depth after Postmodernism*, edited by Robin van den Akker, Alison Gibbons, and Timotheus Vermeulen. London: Rowman and Littlefield, 2017.

Van der Wouw, Debbie. "In the Future, Fashion Designers Will No Longer Need Pencil and Paper." *i-D*, 28 May 2018. https://i-d.vice.com/nl/article/mbk7an/in-de-toekomst-hebben-modeontwerpers-geen-potlood-en-papier-meer-nodig.

Van Herpen, Iris. "*Aeriform*." Press release, 2017. http://www.irisvanherpen.com/about.

Van Herpen, Iris. "*Hybrid Holism*." Press release, 2012. https://www.irisvanherpen.com/haute-couture/hybrid-holism.

Van Herpen, Iris. "*Shift Souls*." Press release, 2019. https://www.irisvanherpen.com/haute-couture/shift-souls.

Van Herpen, Iris. "*Voltage*." Press release, 2013. https://www.irisvanherpen.com/haute-couture/voltage.

Van Meter, Jonathan. "'My Job Is to Be a Spirit Leader': Behind the Scenes with Virgil Abloh." *Vogue*, 15 May 2019. https://www.vogue.com/article/virgil-abloh-interview-off-white-louis-vuitton.

Vänskä, Annamari. "How to Do Humans with Fashion: Towards a Posthuman Critique of Fashion." *International Journal of Fashion Studies* 5, no. 1 (2018): 15–31.

Veblen, Thorstein. *The Theory of the Leisure Class: An Economic Study of Institutions*. London: Taylor and Francis, 2017.

Vermeulen, Timotheus, and Robin van den Akker. *Metamodern: Historicity, Affect, and Depth after Postmodernism*. London: Rowman and Littlefield, 2017.

Vermeulen, Timotheus, and Robin van den Akker. "Notes on Metamodernism." *Journal of Aesthetics & Culture* 2, no. 1 (2010): 56–77.

Vermeulen, Timotheus, and Robin van den Akker. "Utopia, Sort Of: A Case Study in Metamodernism." *Studia Neophilologica* 87, no. 1 (2015): 55–67.

Victorine, Jacob. "Why Supreme's (Mis)appropriation of Barbara Kruger's Art Matters More than Ever." Heroine, November 2017. https://www.heroine.com/the-editorial/supreme-barbara-kruger.

Vinken, Barbara. *Fashion Zeitgeist: Trends and Cycles in the Fashion System*. New York: Berg, 2005.

Vinken, Barbara. "Transvesty-Travesty: Fashion and Gender." *Fashion Theory* 3, no. 1 (1999): 33–49.

Vogel, Steven. *Streetwear*. London: Thames and Hudson, 2007.

Wagner, Richard. *The Art-Work of the Future, and Other Works*. Translated by W. Ashton Ellis. Lincoln: University of Nebraska Press, 1993.

Warnett, Gary. "Textbook." N.p.: Nike NYC Studio, 2017. https://www.kixart.lt /media/images/Nuotraukos/nike-x-off-whrite/textbook.pdf.

Weinstock, Tish. "Take a Front Row Seat at the Most Controversial and Spectacular Catwalk Shows of All Time." *i-D*, 18 January 2017. https://i-d.vice.com/en_gb /article/take-a-front-row-seat-at-the-most-controversial-and-spectacular-catwalk -shows-of-all-time.

Weiss, Alexandra. "Five Reasons to Go See Eckhaus Latta's Extremely Meta Exhibition." *Dazed Digital*, 6 August 2018. http://www.dazeddigital.com/fashion/article /40915/1/eckhaus-latta-new-exhibition-possessed-the-whitney-pop-up-meta.

Westwood, Vivienne. *Manifesto: Active Resistance to Propaganda*. London: Serpentine Gallery, 2008.

Whitney Museum of American Art. "Eckhaus Latta: Possessed." Whitney Museum of American Art, "Exhibitions." https://whitney.org/exhibitions/eckhaus-latta.

Wilcox, Claire, ed. *Radical Fashion*. London: V&A Publications, 2001.

Wilson, Elizabeth. *Adorned in Dreams: Fashion and Modernity*. London: I. B. Tauris, 2007.

Wilson, Elizabeth. *The Contradictions of Culture: Cities, Culture, Women*. London: Sage Publications, 2001.

Wilson, Elizabeth. "Fashion and Memory." *Vestoj Journal*, 29 August 2014. http://vestoj .com/fashion-and-memory/.

Wilson, Elizabeth. "Fashion and the Postmodern Body." In *Chic Thrills: A Fashion Reader*, edited by J. Ash and E. Wilson, 3–16. London: Pandora, 1992.

Wingfield, Jonathan. "What Is Virgil Abloh?" *System Magazine* 10 (November 2017).

Wolf, Ella Lu. "The Brand as Product—How Eckhaus Latta, Vetements and Ssense Are Redefining Fashion Marketing in the Experience Economy." 2016, unpublished. https://www.academia.edu/26491674/THE_BRAND_AS_PRODUCT_HOW _ECKHAUS_LATTA_VETEMENTS_AND_SSENSE_ARE_REDEFINING _FASHION_MARKETING_IN_THE_EXPERIENCE_ECONOMY.

Wollen, Peter. *Addressing the Century, 100 Years of Art and Fashion*. London: Hayward Gallery, 1999.

Wollen, Peter. "The Concept of Fashion in the Arcades Project." *Boundary 2* 30, no. 1 (2003): 131–142.

Woo, Kin. "'The Woodstock of Fashion': Remembering Thierry Mugler's Most Legendary Show." *New York Times*, 1 March 2019. https://www.nytimes.com/2019 /03/01/t-magazine/thierry-mugler-1995-show.html.

Woolf, Jake. "The One Thing Virgil Abloh Is Scared Of." *GQ*, 27 June 2016. https:// www.gq.com/story/virgil-abloh-interview-paris-off-white-book.

Yin, Robert K. *Case Study Research: Design and Methods*. Los Angeles: Sage, 2014.

Yotka, Steff. "Eckhaus Latta's New Store Is an Oasis in New York's Retail Scene." *Vogue*, 27 November 2018. https://www.vogue.com/article/eckhaus-latta-new-york-store.

Yotka, Steff. "The Making of Eckhaus Latta's Shoppable Whitney Museum Exhibition." *Vogue*, 3 August 2018. https://www.vogue.com/article/eckhaus-latta-whitney-museum -possessed.

Zavarzadeh, Mas'ud. "The Apocalyptic Fact and the Eclipse of Fiction in Recent American Prose Narratives." *Journal of American Studies* 9, no. 1 (1975): 69–83.

Zerbo, Julie. "Is Fashion Really about the Clothes and Not about the Hype?" *The Fashion Law*, April 2018. http://www.thefashionlaw.com/home/is-fashion-really -about-the-clothes-and-not-about-the-hype.

Zhang, Suzanne. "Aitor Throup: Innovation in Its Pure Form." *Rooms Magazine*, May 2014.
Žižek, Slavoj. *Living in the End Times*. London: Verso, 2010.

Videos/Film

Abloh, Virgil. "Core Studio Lecture: Virgil Abloh, 'Insert Complicated Title Here.'" Harvard University Graduate School of Design, 27 October 2017. https://www.gsd.harvard.edu/event/virgil-abloh/.
Görtz, Daniel P. "Metamodern Values Explained." *Ted Talks × Berlin*, 5 September 2019. https://www.youtube.com/watch?v=5USomyB3mZQ.
Karolinski, Alexa. *Coco*. 2017. https://vimeo.com/211689869.
Karolinski, Alexa. *Dinner*. 2013. https://vimeo.com/61838623.
Karolinski, Alexa. *Smile*. 2016. https://vimeo.com/153393224.
Karolinski, Alexa. "Uniform Exercises." Nowness, 29 July 2012. https://www.nowness.com/series/age-appropiate/uniform-exercises.
Prince-Fraser, Taylor. "A-COLD-WALL*: Brand or Art Project?" Live Panel Discussion—Autumn/Winter 2020." Showstudio, 14 January 2020. https://www.youtube.com/watch?v=vLwvkl5IFTk.
Showstudio. "Fashion Week Discussions." https://www.youtube.com/playlist?list=PLaDs4bekfOXRH1JdvPJBuZaJhaNgPCX4d (accessed 6 December 2018).
Throup, Aitor. *A Portrait of Noomi Rapace*. Nowness, 29 September 2014. https://www.nowness.com/story/noomi-rapace-by-aitor-throup.
Vreeland, Lisa Immordino. "Art of Style: Iris Van Herpen." *M2M*, https://m2m.tv/watch/iris-van-herpen (accessed 16 February 2018).

Websites

Abloh, Virgil. https://canary---yellow.com/.
The Fashion Law. https://www.thefashionlaw.com/.
A Magazine Curated By. Homepage. https://amagazinecuratedby.com/history/.
Miyake, Issey. "The Concepts and Work of Issey Miyake." http://mds.isseymiyake.com/im/en/work/.
Miyake, Issey. "Selected Chronology." http://mds.isseymiyake.com/im/en/chronology/.

Index

About the Author

VANESSA GERRIE is a researcher and lecturer at the College of Creative Arts at Massey University Wellington, Aotearoa New Zealand. Her scholarship focuses on art history and theory, visual culture, and media studies, with an emphasis on fashion practices and how they intersect with critical theory.